Wayne G. Broehl, Jr., is Benjamin Ames Kimball Professor of the Science of Administration at the Amos Tuck School of Business Administration, Dartmouth College. He is the author of *Trucks, Trouble and Triumph* (1954), *Precision Valley* (1959), *The Molly Maguires* (1964), and *International Basic Economy Corporation* (1968).

The Village Entrepreneur

THE VILLAGE ENTREPRENEUR

Change Agents in India's Rural Development

Wayne G. Broehl, Jr.

Harvard University Press
Cambridge, Massachusetts
and London, England
1978

Printed in the United States of America

Library of Congress Cataloging in Publication Data
  Broehl, Wayne G.
    The village entrepreneur.

    Includes bibliographical references and index.
    1. Businessmen—India.   2. Rural development—
India.   3. Agriculture—Economic aspects—India.
I. Title.
HC435.2.B78   338'.04'0954   77-18880
ISBN 0-674-93915-8

Preface

In the early 1960s I was given the opportunity by the National Planning Association to explore a unique entrepreneurial venture—the efforts of Nelson Rockefeller to bring responsible private-enterprise capitalism to the less developed world. The vehicle for his work was a private corporation owned in part by the Rockefeller family, in part by the public, and called the International Basic Economy Corporation (IBEC). Since its founding in 1947 IBEC has created and then managed new businesses in thirty-four countries, most of them less developed countries in Latin America, Africa, and Asia. The firm's objective has been to upgrade the basic economies of these countries— by lowering food prices, building sound housing, mobilizing savings, fostering industrialization—and in the process maximizing long-run profits within a framework of social responsibility. By doing this well, IBEC was able to serve as a catalyst—a change agent—in encouraging others, especially nationals, to set up similar efforts and thereby bring about a multiplier development effect.

Subsequent analysis (for my book, *International Basic Economy Corporation*) of the more than two hundred individual companies begun by this organization—supermarkets, milk companies, low-cost housing projects, mutual funds, hybrid seed businesses, poultry breeding operations—allowed me a remarkable "extensive" view of the entrepreneur. My previous studies of entrepreneurship in the United States—one involving high technology (*Precision Valley*, a book about three machine tool companies), a second on service and distribution (*Trucks, Trouble, and Triumph,* about a large interstate trucking company)—now could be balanced against analyses of literally hundreds of entrepreneurs all through the world of the less developed countries (LDCs). Specifically, my interests in innovation that already spanned three decades were deepened in the process of seeing just how a high-technology innovation from the United States could be adapted to the environmental constraints of a less developed country.

Entrepreneurial theory had long intrigued me; I wanted to understand better the underlying reasons why only certain people are able to carry an innovation through to fruition and thus become change agents in their particular milieus. My IBEC research took me to India in 1965, to study poultry operations near Poona; that first of many visits led to the present study. With the Indian village entrepreneur as model, I have added to my theoretical insights through an "intensive" view of entrepreneurship in one particular place: among agro-industry entrepreneurs and other village businessmen in South India. The vehicle for accomplishing this study has been a large-scale collaborative program, the Entrepreneurial Research Project (ERP), financed by the Ford Foundation and the Government of India (first through the Ministry of Education and later by the Indian Council on Social Science Research). Five colleagues from India, all faculty members in Indian management institutes, joined with me in this endeavor, although each of us carried on separate studies.

This book, which covers only my own research, presents a set of conceptual tools. The village represents any village in a less developed country. Of course, villages vary in size, composition, and ethos in each of about a hundred less developed countries. Village India itself is so complex and varied that one must be cautious in generalizing about its peoples and cultures. Still, the lessons of the thousands of years of history in India's villages and of today's traumatic problems of unemployment, poverty, illness, and tensions through much of rural India have profound implications on rural development as it is practiced throughout the less developed world. India's experience in rural development should have considerable relevance to other parts of Asia, as well as to countries in Africa and Latin America.

I make an explicit value assumption in this book: that change is the sine qua non of development. This change necessarily will be both economic and social and is likely to include political change as well. There are very strong believers in tradition in many villages, in India as elsewhere, who will categorically reject this value premise. I believe that only with change can come the development so desperately needed in the poorer countries of the world. To consider how these ideas can be carried through to reality, I focus from the beginning on the entrepreneur.

Contents

The Village Entrepreneur

1

An Entrepreneurial
System Model

"Entrepreneur" is a highly respected word in the developed world; it conjures up visions of active, purposeful men and women accomplishing a wide variety of significant deeds. The entrepreneur is an important change agent in every society. Yet he is one of the most enigmatic characters in the drama of economic development, particularly in the less developed world. Although it is his purposive activity that bridges the gap between plan and reality, the precise way that this change agent-entrepreneur acts is often unclear.

A better understanding of entrepreneurship in the less developed countries could have a particularly high return for mankind. Entrepreneurship is clearly not a uniformly distributed quality, yet the appearance of the entrepreneur is considered by most analysts to be nonrandom. If we could identify the origins of the quality of entrepreneurship, we might be able to develop educational methods to upgrade the entrepreneurial skills and achievement of potential change agents. The goal of this book is to study village entrepreneurship in India, and to extrapolate to the larger stage of rural economic development in the less developed countries.

It will be helpful for our study of entrepreneurship to view both its nature and its locus. We center first on the psychological attributes of successful entrepreneurs and ask why it is that particular individuals are achievement oriented or prepared to take risks. Then, turning to the organization and management of operating economic units, we frame entrepreneurship in a dynamic, system-based set of interdependencies, scattered over a wide range of business functions, to bring out the effects of entrepreneurship within the structure of the business itself.

The entrepreneur also performs a central mediating role between the larger society and a single operating unit. Alterations or changes in entrepreneurial action generate a process that is likely to mediate changes for *both* the economic unit and its environment and accumulate to produce system-wide effects and feedback responses.

1

These features of nature and locus pose special problems in the less developed countries. There it is often difficult to differentiate between functions of the economy and those of other social institutions. A complex pattern of integration between rural entrepreneurs and their counterparts in the metropolitan, industrial economy is generally the rule. Foreign capital usually plays a significant part. Corporate organization structures form a heterogeneous pattern of widely varying levels of sophistication, in which both the making and the implementation of decisions are often so fragmented that it is impossible to identify the individual as entrepreneur. Further, although the family is often still dominant in entrepreneurial activities, the state may perform economic functions and play a major entrepreneurial role. We must scrutinize each situation of entrepreneurship to determine the precise locus of entrepreneurial functions within it and the locus of entrepreneurial responses generated by it.

I propose to represent this universe in a model, one that can provide guidelines for the asking of relevant questions and indicate hypotheses for further investigation and testing. The explanatory model I have formulated (presented schematically in Figure 1) is built on the seminal work done by earlier writers, but includes additional variables I believe are relevant.[1] By analyzing the entrepreneur's actions in a certain context, we can focus on his observable behavior, rather than on some mysterious charisma or the mere perception of opportunities. Primary interest is in the entrepreneurial breakthrough, conceived both in operational and in sequential terms—in short, a system approach that emphasizes an interdisciplinary view.

Influences on the Entrepreneur

The entrepreneur may be either an individual or a group; both are equally significant in less developed countries. As one looks around the less developed world, no ideal milieu for entrepreneurship dominates—for at any given moment the entrepreneur is playing many highly different roles. He belongs to a family, a religious sect, a political party, a kinship group, a caste, and so on. These are value determinants and constraints, fashioned by his own particular world.

We must not assume, incidentally, that the world of the entrepreneur will be synonymous with the nation-state in which he lives; more likely he will see his world in much more complex terms—some dictated by values coming from the government itself, some from political segments within it, others from the social and religious roles he plays. Some less developed countries (LDCs) are strongly nationalistic, with the stage for working out political ideologies that of a nation-state. (The corporatist legacy from Italy adopted in Argentina over the past three decades is a good example.) Conversely, a large

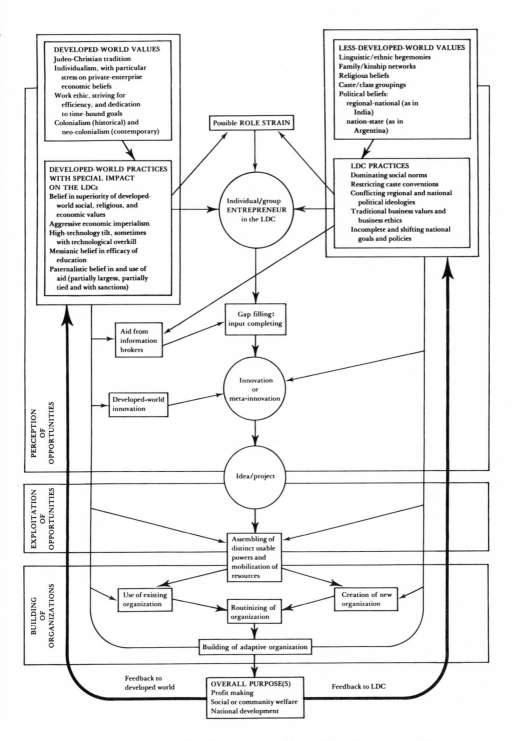

FIGURE 1   A model of entrepreneurship in the less developed world.

number of LDCs are characterized politically by complex regional groupings, sometimes derived from linguistic or ethnic bonds, sometimes from spatial and other geographic bounds. In such a structure there tend to be conflicting regional and national political ideologies that result in incomplete and shifting national goals and policies. This is the sort of situation that has led to the Byzantine complexities of India's state, religious, and ethnic interactions. Business values and business ethics tend to be tradition bound and subject more to values from these other spheres than to maximization concepts out of Western microeconomics. In playing his diverse roles, then, the LDC entrepreneur moves back and forth from one value orientation to another, often in a contradictory way, constantly attempting to accommodate his role effectiveness to pressures on him from divergent value orientations.

The Special Dimensions of Rural Entrepreneurship

Most less developed countries have a pattern of internal dualism, with two sharply differentiated sectors: one limited mainly to peasant agriculture, small industry, and the various trading activities associated with them, the other made up of developed industries — plantations, transport and trading activities, petroleum and mining endeavors, and manufacturing. In other words, the "developed-less developed" syndrome is almost universally found *within* the less developed country, typically along rural-urban lines. The Western market economy, with its central focus on price and market exchange and its thoroughgoing dedication to the principle of optimization, is likely not to map too well onto this rural economy, which tends to be characterized by inflexible or sluggish prices or exchange ratios, inelastic (sometimes absolutely inelastic) supply, and inelastic (again sometimes absolutely inelastic) demand. Barter in kind is common; gift trading is complex, usually based on status and influenced by kinship, magic, superstition, etiquette, and a host of other subtle nonmarket relationships. In rural areas, for example, only part of the labor time of the cultivators is actually spent in agricultural efforts; a significant amount is expended in construction, transportation, and service activities to satisfy needs for clothing, shelter, entertainment, and ceremony. The patterns of exchange of work or goods are often established by long-standing customs, interclass dependencies, and religious or ritualistic beliefs. Complicated patterns of substitutability evolve between noncash transactions and the cash markets and lead the peasant economy still further away from the classic profit-maximization model.[2]

There is room within this system for a panoply of trade, barter, and exchange that makes most villagers no less materialistic in their striving than any Western Adam Smith. The mutual exchange of services among cultivators and artisans in the village becomes so regularized over the centuries that it evolves into an intricate, precise set of relationships, carried on every day in the village and especially accented at such long-standing institutions as weekly fairs, markets, and religious festivals. "Behind the mud walls of an Indian village," comments Milton Singer, "one will not find as much conspicuous consumption as in the towns and cities, but even in the humble village one finds love for fine cloth, bangles and precious gems. And what is perhaps more important, the desire for land and cattle and oxcarts, a good match and education for his children, a job for a relative, are for the villager real desires and express in these local terms his ambition to improve his position."[3]

Peasants in these rural societies do tend to share what George Foster has called the "principle of the limited good."[4] Their behavior suggests that they view their social, economic, and physical environments in such a way that all the desired things of life—land, wealth, health, friendship, love, manliness, honor, respect and status, power and influence, security and safety—exist in finite quantity and are *always* in short supply. If these limited goods cannot be expanded, then it appears to the peasant that the system is closed. An individual or a family can improve its position only at the expense of others.

This has two consequences. First, the strong communal solidarity exhibited within the extended family so common in peasant cultures results in a subordination of individual needs and desires to the prescribed allocative determinations of "the elders," however they are defined in the particular society. Typically the definition is by consanguinity, but sometimes it is cast more broadly to a clan or a tribal basis (see, for example, my earlier study of eighteenth- and nineteenth-century Irish secret societies, *The Molly Maguires*).[5]

The second manifestation is external: as an individual deals with another individual or an organization outside his own extended family, he envisions this interchange as a zero-sum game, one in which he must practice rugged individualism in a perpetual, unrelenting struggle with all others for possession or control over what the individual considers to be his share of scarce resources. Mistrust and skepticism, traits noted widely among peasant societies, begin to dominate.

Typically, the role of the "businessman" is denigrated. Loss minimization becomes the dominant concern, rather than profit maximization. People are wary of risk taking, become content to provide for their subsistence needs rather than take a chance on an investment that might produce higher profit but also might involve the potential loss of the limited capital. Businessmen may indeed make high profits, but frequently these will be generated by speculation based on scarcity and black-market prices. Neither buyer nor seller has a developed notion of a fair or a good price; rather, both operate under hopes and expectations of windfall buying or selling. The businessman waits in anticipation of a scarcity. The gyrations of the market itself may generate this scarcity, or perhaps the government artificially brings it about by inept price regulation or other manipulation of the market. Often the businessman can accentuate this scarcity by hoarding. Thus all of the businessman's acumen is directed toward gaining the confidence of buyers by "reasonable" transactions in order to take advantage of the same buyers at a later point by black-market tactics.

The peasant, keenly aware of oppression or deprivation, constructs his own adaptive mechanisms and designs for living.[6] Traditional society is three tiered: first, the peasantry and other folk leading simple lives; second, the elite class or classes; and third, the trader-financiers. These three groups operate in a well-defined and authoritarian system of hierarchy, under a stable, agreed set of relationships. The society as a totality exhibits strong patterns of impotence and rage in the face of uncontrollable forces (weather, disease, or macroeconomic vicissitudes) and relies heavily on religion and even magic. The peasantry has a strong dependence on the elite, and the elite finds protection in its own economic dominance and ability to levy on the peasant. In two of the groups, the peasantry and the elite, there is a latent desire to dominate, to take aggressions out on others. The peasantry thus tilts always toward authoritarianism. There is a basic lack of creativity, a mistrust of outsiders, a dislike of strange or new ways. The elite's patterns of role differentiation very often include dislike of manual labor and emphasis on property, such as land, cattle, and jewelry.

These elaborate chains of "support-obligation" are particularly well illustrated in India. Giving, for example, typically implies a gift, a giver, and a receiver; this automatically brings the notion of exchange into play. "Wealth can be used to gather debtors, and by extension their followers," notes an observer in Konduru, a South Indian village. "Generosity in sponsoring entertainment and public activities attracts yet others. Political offices can be exploited for personal gain or the advancement of kinsmen and allies. Political associations may provide useful friends or may rob a foe of needed support."[7] Soon a complex set of intertwined dependency relationships ensues. David C. McClelland notes some of the underlying psychological implications of this: "Giving as a kind of repeated exchange is at the center of a natural and moral universe. One attains merit by this process—or we might even say 'system'— of giving; the basic concept of law of *Karma* stresses this action and reaction, this permanent record of merit. Self-sacrifice is the most meritorious form of giving, but this turns out to be a zero-sum game—I can only give away what others receive, I must accumulate in order to give, and the giving will exhaust me." (Thus the concern mentioned by some analysts that any loss of semen, laboriously formed, seriously depletes a man's power.)[8]

Often this pattern of competition, apparently headed for a zero-sum conclusion, is settled by one partner's meekly agreeing (that is, renouncing his competitive power position). In the process, though, bitter psychological fruits are borne, leading to oft-disputatious arguments and legal cases. Renunciation may be performed ritualistically, where one particular person or group requests help out of an expressed pattern of weakness. By openly admitting this weakness, the person or group can avoid the competition; the result is what has been called the Bapu or dependence syndrome. Even children's stories, studied in detail by McClelland, reveal this counterpoise of competitiveness and renunciation, which often engenders feelings of rage and hostility.

Brahmanical Hinduism itself is inextricably linked with animistic belief and superstition in a mosaic of religion and fantasy that is baffling in its profusion. Ritual Hindu law is mixed with witchcraft, sorcery, ghost affliction, and astrology in subtle, complex ways that give conflicting and often opposing messages to village people. One writer averred that the wife of the late prime minister Lal Bahadur Shastri would not move to a larger house from their smaller one because her astrologer had said that her present address was lucky; thus all the business of state had to be conducted from the smaller place. "Even scientists working for the Ford Foundation have been known to postpone a trip because a last-minute horoscope proved unfavorable," this same writer maintained.[9] Superstitions are legion, and virtually everything that can be imagined is invested with good or bad luck.

These nonrational beliefs, at the core of people's values, exert profound influences on daily life in the villages. There are auspicious times for various activities, ritualistic ways of carrying them out. For example, in business dealings the practice of consulting one's horoscope for favorable signs is widespread, even among sophisticated urban business people. The fatalistic nature of these kinds of decision-making tools inevitably leads to a gambling mentality in many relationships. The notion of a probabilistically based discounted risk would be sharply at variance with much village thinking. This is not to say that villagers do not have a keen sense of risk taking in their various agricultural and business dealings. Yet many of these decisions are infiltrated with superstition-based hunches and guesses, and villagers tend to swing widely from risk aversion to high-risk gambling and back to risk aversion. The result is often a pervasive mistrust, combined with a fatalism laced with elements of rage at the implacability of the fates. This mistrust and rage readily spills over to hatred and suspicion among participants in a business arrangement.

One cannot discuss social values in rural India without injecting the profound influence of the caste system. Perhaps no other single manifestation so epitomizes historical, traditional India.[10] Although "untouchability" was explicitly outlawed in the Constitution of 1950 and its practice in any form made an offense in 1955, the realities of caste distinction are as potent and virulent today as ever. Great progress has been made in bringing the untouchables—the "harijans" or the "children of God," to use the names given by Gandhi—into the mainstream of Indian life by special concessions on university admissions, government jobs, and the like. Still, when it comes to inter-family social relations, marriages, the realities of government and private-industry job placements, business contracts, and the whole gamut of inter-personal relationships that involve quid pro quos, the realities of caste continue to play a dominant role.

A facet of particular impact to this study is the *jajmani* system, for it estab-lishes an additional dependency syndrome that bears directly on questions of competition, innovation, and modernization. William H. Wiser was the first to articulate the explicit economic parameters of *jajmani*, with the occupa-tional division of labor and the distribution of services providing a "system" or network of role relationships.[11] Pauline Kolenda gives a succinct definition:

> The *jajmani* system is a system of distribution in Indian villages whereby high-caste landowning families called *jajmans* are provided services and products by various lower castes such as carpenters, potters, blacksmiths, water carriers, sweepers, and laundrymen. Pure ritual services may be provided by Brahman priests and various sectarian castes and almost all serving castes have ceremonial and ritual duties at their *jajman's* births, marriages, funerals, and at some of the religious festivals. Important in the latter duties is the lower castes' capacity to absorb pollution by handling clothing and other things defiled by birth or death pollution, gathering up banquet dishes after the feasts, and administering various bodily attentions to a new mother, bride or groom . . . The landowning *jajmans* pay the serving castes in kind, with grain, clothing, sugar, fodder, and animal products like butter and milk. Payment may amount to a little of every-thing produced on the land, in the pastures, and in the kitchen. Sometimes land is granted to servants, especially as charity to Brahman priests . . . The middle and lower castes either subscribe to each other's services in return for compensa-tions and payments, or exchange services with one another.[12]

The psychological effect of this economic interdependence is that the divi-sive effects of competition are reduced and in many cases completely elimi-nated. Each household is economically dependent on other households from specialist *jatis* (castes) and ritually dependent on households from each of the major jatis in the area. "In effect," as Allen Beals put it, "the myth that makes multi-jati villages possible is the myth that the survival and proper functioning of any one jati is dependent on the survival and proper function-ing of every other."[13]

Given these traditional patterns, what *are* the potentials for entrepreneur-ship in rural areas of the LDCs? To begin with, there is often a supply prob-lem. Those rural people with the strongest intellects either obtain what edu-cation is available in the rural areas and then migrate to the cities, or go to the cities for the education itself. In either case it is difficult to get many of them back, and the human capital of the rural areas dwindles by its own brain drain. Often the more modern, innovating attitudes are found to be correlated with better education (though not always), and some of the progressiveness of the rural areas is channeled off.

Yet there are so many people who do remain in the rural areas that there is a perennial and often worsening problem of underemployment and unemployment. Birth rates tend to be high and exacerbate problems of land tenure and other ownership patterns, such as village businesses. Thus very large numbers of agricultural and village-industry laborers have no ownership stake in the enterprises in which they work. Problems of infrastructure complicate the situation. Ineffectual transportation systems are common, with poor roads, inefficient rail service (often with no interchangeability of equipment), and serious shortages of transport equipment. Availability of agricultural services, irrigation, or field and processing equipment is often not sufficiently reliable for input decisions to be made with confidence. Finance, especially credit, is less available than in the cities; in India, for example, the difficulties of trying to persuade the banks to serve the rural areas finally resulted in a decision by the central government in 1969 to nationalize fourteen of the largest banks.

Still, the people who do remain have valuable strengths—balanced, practical skill sets, intuitive knowledge and instincts—that make the rural population potentially more change oriented than many have assumed. Often there is a greater social unity among villagers than among city people. Agriculturists can see the fruits of their labors as physical products from the farms; workers in village industries see at least the first stages of vertical integration, where their products are processed within the village from nearby raw materials and finally sent away to the city. It seems legitimate to hypothesize that there is an identifiably different pattern of rural entrepreneurship—and that entrepreneurs are indeed present.

Neither the rural nor the urban sectors of these less developed countries can operate in a vacuum; inevitably, strong value influences flow in from the developed world (with a much smaller number of influences operating in the reverse direction). Such potent value determinants as the Judeo-Christian tradition, belief in the efficacy of individualism (particularly private-enterprise economic beliefs), the related work ethic, the striving for efficiency and thoroughgoing dedication to time-bound goals, all are exported to the LDCs in one form or another. This frequently is evidenced through patterns of colonialism—straightforwardly in the past, more subtly in the present. The developed-world leaders of thought tend to exhibit strong beliefs in the superiority of developed-world social, religious, and economic values. The result is often aggressive varieties of economic imperialism, a high-technology tilt (sometimes getting out of hand and resulting in technological overkill) and often-messianic beliefs in the efficacy of education. Many countries of the developed world have also faced up to their privileged positions, and extensive aid has come from the developed world to less developed countries, generally under a paternalistic rubric, a combination of largess and aid sometimes linked with economic, political, or social sanctions.

Little wonder, then, that this cacophony of value determinants can easily produce "role strains" in the entrepreneur's self-image. As the would-be entrepreneur steps from the certainty and the constraints of his traditional world into a milieu of modernity characterized by a complex set of change forces indigenous to his own country, with the addition of often-subtle value conflicts from the developed world, the environment for the entrepreneurial act can quickly become threatening and personally upsetting. The cross-national business world is a fast-paced one, with change and adaptation a necessary way of life. Whether or not the village entrepreneur actually participates in it directly through engaging in international trade, he now becomes influenced by this stepped-up pace, which is contrary to his traditional way of life. Faced with conflicting "solutions" to problems, the entrepreneur may allow his cultural background to dominate his business decision making, often with less-than-effective results. Alternatively, he may become indecisive, mixing traditional and modern in a way he can little understand or articulate to himself or others. He may opt to break completely away from the tradition of his own culture and adopt the new values in their entirety. This is often unsatisfactory too, for it allows little ground for rapprochement later with his own culture.

Schumpeter's Innovator

We should now be more precise about the term "innovation." Today many analysts seem to confuse true entrepreneurship with other closely related endeavors. Some perspective can be gained by returning to one of the seminal thinkers in this field, Joseph A. Schumpeter,[14] whose concepts have renewed relevance for study of comparative entrepreneurship.

Schumpeter starts with that necessary abstraction of the pure model, "equilibrium." Into this equilibrium an entrepreneur intrudes. Central to his intrusion is a critically important Schumpeterian concept, the introduction of a "new production function," the Schumpeterian way of describing an innovation. This term is not used in its narrow sense, but includes one or more of the following:

(a) The introduction of a new good with which consumers are not yet familiar, or a new quality of good.

(b) The development of a new method of production, one not yet tested by experience; this does not have to be a new discovery—it can also be "a new way of handling a commodity commercially."

(c) The opening of a new market—new to a given country, regardless of whether it has existed before in other locations.

(d) The acquisition of a new source of supply of raw materials or intermediate manufactured goods (again which may have existed previously in another location).

(e) "The carrying out of the new organization of an industry, like the creation of a monopoly position (for example, through justification) or the breaking up of a monopoly position" (Schumpeter's own wording).

These new production functions are brought about by the purposeful action of an entrepreneur. This entrepreneur belongs to a distinct class: he possesses more than ordinary ability to visualize possibilities in these unproved commodities, organizations, methods, markets. The first entrepreneur in a given field must overcome all sorts of obstacles, and he succeeds in smoothing the way for others, producing a wave of business activity that runs its course and finally exhausts the opportunities for gain.

It is hard to distinguish who such entrepreneurs are, not because of lack of precision about their special contribution, but by virtue of the difficulty of finding the persons who actually engage in entrepreneurial activity. No one is an entrepreneur all the time, and no one can be only an entrepreneur. It follows from the nature of the function that it must always be combined with other activities, and that it leads to other activities.

Entrepreneurship is not the process of invention. Although a highly creative function, it does not rest solely on original creativity. An invention sometimes does not lead to innovation (and vice versa). Both economically and sociologically, the two are completely different conceptual functions.

The entrepreneur may be, but need not be, the one who furnishes the capital. Therefore financial risk bearing is not a part of the entrepreneurial function. The capitalist bears the risk, the entrepreneur brings about the changed production function. Probably there is no single distinction more confusing today than that between entrepreneurship and risk taking. The entrepreneur clearly takes great personal risk in the process of introducing often traumatic and upsetting new production functions. He may also put his own money into the new project and thereby become a financial risk taker. The first type of risk taking is directly involved in entrepreneurship; the second may or may not be present.

In sum, the Schumpeterian entrepreneur is a special kind of creative person—creative in bringing about growth through the process of making changes in production functions. It is this special quality of change, innovation, that sets the entrepreneur apart.

Meta-Innovation

Sometimes an innovation in the less developed world becomes an innovation in worldwide terms. The wheat and rice miracle seeds may legitimately be placed in this category; although the two research institutes responsible for the appearance of these seeds were largely financed and staffed from the developed world, the new varieties were actually evolved in Mexico (wheat) and the Philippines (rice). Yet one is hard pressed to think of equally significant innovations in industrial management. Innovators in this area have come from the less developed world, it is true, but their innovations have taken place within the confines of the developed world.

It requires a subtle analytical effort to identify innovation in a rural setting in the less developed countries. On first look there appears to be little if any true innovation being carried through; indeed, there seems to be no entrepreneur. However, a closer look reveals a special form of innovation characteristic of just this kind of situation. This is the innovative effort involved in fitting a developed-world concept (itself probably an innovation at an earlier stage) to the special constraints, difficulties, and opportunities of the less developed world.

We shall term this a "meta-innovation." The prefix "meta," according to Webster, can mean not only "occurring later than or in succession to," but can connote "more highly organized or specialized." Our definition suggests both. Not many analysts of entrepreneurship in the LDCs share this view. For instance, James J. Berna, in his study of entrepreneurship in South India, called his respondents "humbler entrepreneurs," as distinguished from the "Schumpeterian innovators" of the developed world. This interpretation seems to me to overlook a crucially important distinction, namely that an innovator operating on a "small" scale does not necessarily make the process "humbler" or easier than that same application in the developed world. Writers in the literature of innovation have made some useful distinctions among original innovation, transferred innovation, and adaptive innovation. Common to these definitions is the notion that there is a unique act that can be considered an original or true innovation, that is, the shifting of a production function, as Schumpeter would say. This innovation is then transferred in basic outline to other situations, in the process being modified, changed, and adapted to differing environments.

A widely used current term for such adaptation is "technology transfer."[15] The dominant pattern is one of transferred innovation, of sharing within the developed world itself, but there is also great interest in the process of technology transfer to the less developed world. Methods, materials, and other ingredients may be varied along the way, yet the process remains one of replication, in essence mirroring the original innovation. Some analysts use the term "imitation" here; in fact, there is a body of literature that suggests circumstances under which imitation is more attractive than innovation, and that defines which firms are the leaders and which the followers. In some developed countries there is irritation about what appears sometimes to be a mimicry syndrome, which these critics feel brings about a dependency relationship between the high-technology original innovators and their followers.[16]

The third type, adaptive innovation, is often used synonymously with imitation in a manner that clouds the important distinction between transfer and adaptation. Adaptation is intrinsically different from both the original innovation and its transferred variants. It is not just a lower-technology, less complex variation on the original innovation, but an important link back to the innovation process. The linchpin for this link is the meta-innovation. The sheer process of attempting this presumed imitation in environments markedly different from the original is itself an original, an innovative act. Given the information lacks, the gaps in understanding and knowledge, and the weaknesses in infrastructure, the entrepreneur in the less developed country often makes a giant leap across a gap in a discontinuous path in carrying through what ostensibly is a simple adaptation. It is this discontinuous nature, what one writer calls the "innovation boundary," that changes the act from a simple process of modifying or adapting to a process of original innovation. It may even be a more complicated task than the original innovation —what may be "market filling" in a developed-world situation may be "market creating" in the less developed world.[17] Schumpeter often used the term "imitators" for those who spread a new innovation through the economy in a secondary wave, but the secondary wave may well be primary as it hits the less developed country's shores.

Often one hears this same distinction drawn in analyzing how innovations permeate rural areas, with many writers implying again a pattern of imitative, secondary, and market-filling acts. One writer, making a distinction between household (H) innovations and entrepreneurial (E) innovations, continues:

> The former can be treated as continuous wave phenomena, since many adopters are involved and adoption fuses outwards from the centre of innovation, though the strength of the wave declines with distance. E-innovations, on the other hand, may not be adopted at all in small towns and rural areas, and even in larger towns the incidence of adoption may be small. They tend to jump about in a very discontinuous though not necessarily unpredictable manner, and a short-circuiting of distance through the urban hierarchy is a much more appropriate description than the notion of an innovation wave . . . First adoption of an E-innovation in a town of close to threshold size will pre-empt further adoptions there. Of course, in larger towns and cities there will tend to be further adoptions. It follows that E-innovations are largely urban innovations.[18]

This is a reasonable explanation of the diffusion of innovations, but it contains some faulty logic in implying that innovations are not occurring in rural areas. On the contrary, there are many, taking the form of meta-innovations.

Risk taking that moves from the developed world to the less developed world therefore has a special quality. There is a time lag in a great many happenings between these two worlds: What is "old hat" in the developed world may well be startlingly new in the other. If we think of the risk-taking process for a given innovation as having a time-dimension continuum, we can premise that the first innovators in the developed world have the highest incidence of risk. Those who adapt the particular innovation along the time line clearly have less. Then when the innovation is carried to the less developed country, there is a discontinuity in the time line. The incidence of risk moves back up to a level perhaps even higher than the first application in the developed world, as the first new entrepreneur in the less developed world begins to apply the innovation within the confines of a new and less certain situation.

Information Needs and How They Are Met

If there is any single dominant feature of LDC meta-innovations, it is that they are initially ill defined. There are important gaps in the flow of the necessary information that must precede the act of innovation. Some data are simply not yet available in the particular economy. Often the information needs are subtly political in nature rather than straightforwardly economic. In the politicized entrepreneurial environments of many less developed countries, business advantage is often sought (and realized) through political institutions no less than in market interactions. Gaining requisite information is more difficult in the less developed world, for LDCs, in the words of economist Harvey Leibenstein, are "obstructed, incomplete and 'relatively dark' economic systems."[19]

Leibenstein suggests that all over the world the seeking of maximization (however it may be defined) is a less-than-perfect process, that there is an "X-efficiency" short of optimization that is almost always the norm. This is particularly so, he suggests, in the less developed world. The production function turns out to be plural, a set of points along a range of possible efficiencies, rather than a point of optimum allocative efficiency:

> One can visualize a production function as a set of "recipes." Each recipe indicates most of the essential elements that enter into the production of the output, but like a real recipe, or a real blueprint, it does not truly indicate all of them. A given recipe may be carried out slowly or quickly or with careful or sloppy workmanship . . . After all, different cooks will turn out meals of different quality on the basis of the same recipe.[20]

Individuals and groups (firms) generally do not work as hard or as efficiently as they are capable of in searching for new information and techniques, nor is their effort maintained at a constant level. Thus there is a considerable degree of slack that implies the existence of an entrepreneurial opportunity—that of gap filling and input completing. Leibenstein suggests that entrepreneurship should be defined in a new way, that it is necessary to isolate "routine" entrepreneurship—those activities involved in administering a well-established, growing concern in which the parts of the production function in use are well known and one that operates in clearly defined markets—from "new-type" entrepreneurship. In the latter there are great gaps of knowledge about the production function, for which the entrepreneur in some way must compensate.

Most often there is a minimum quantum of information necessary to get a particular project off the drawing board. Frequently the gap in information prevents the reaching of this threshold. In the less developed world, says Leibenstein, the special entrepreneur is the one who performs most or all of these functions:

> Searches for and discovers new economic information;
> Translates this new information into new markets, techniques, and goods;
> Seeks and discovers economic opportunity;
> Evaluates economic opportunities;
> Marshals the financial resources necessary for the enterprise;
> Makes time-binding arrangements;
> Takes ultimate responsibility for management;
> Provides for and is responsible for the motivational system within the firm;
> Provides leadership for the work group;
> Is the ultimate uncertainty or risk bearer.

It is the information dimension implicit in this list, the gap-filling and the input-completing capacities, that requires the unique characteristics of the entrepreneur. These are the truly scarce talents. One finds a few entrepreneurs in less developed countries who connect different markets, who are capable of making up for market deficiencies, who can create or expand business organizations. These special entrepreneurs are the key individuals in the less developed world.

Israel M. Kirzner, in his excellent book on entrepreneurship, has noted that it is the alertness to information, rather than its possession alone, that is the essential entrepreneurial element. "Ultimately, then," Kirzner writes, "the kind of 'knowledge' required for entrepreneurship is knowing where to look for knowledge, rather than knowledge of substantive market information . . . Entrepreneurial knowledge may be described as the 'highest order of knowledge,' the *ultimate* knowledge needed to harness available information already possessed (capable of becoming discovered)."[21] The means by which the entrepreneur is able to fill these gaps and complete the various kinds of inputs is dependent in part upon the quantum of information he is able to accumulate. There is a certain critical mass of data that is necessary in the hands of the most astute gap filler/input completer in order to have the innovation be initially discerned. Leibenstein elsewhere develops at length his thesis that there needs to be a "critical minimum effort" to bring about sustaining development in the less developed countries.[22] Part of this critical minimum effort must inevitably be a critical minimum of information.

Beyond this there is a further dimension, linked to Kirzner's concept of alertness. Many years ago sociologist Vilfredo Pareto noted man's basic "instinct for combination."[23] It is the ability to link together individual pieces of information—to carry through the active process of combination—that distinguishes the new-type entrepreneur.

In a society where family linkages and kinship affiliations play an important part in the founding of a business enterprise, and where there is a dearth of technical know-how, the entrepreneur may develop a network of "information brokers" who supply necessary information and who may even help to formulate the innovative idea or project. Such a situation helps explain why large, extended family connections often give the vested oligarchy so much power. Sometimes the information brokers may formalize their activity by becoming professional suppliers of ideas or projects (on a regular fee basis) for future entrepreneurs. A substantial portion of information brokerage may come from outside the country—supplied on a formal or informal basis by developed-world individuals and firms. Sometimes the fee is a straightforward consulting contract; or varying patterns of ownership, licensing, and other tie-in arrangements may be used. This advice from outside the country is, incidentally, not always appropriate—the unperceived subtleties and complexities of traditional society often lead the developed-world armchair analyst to make serious errors, and indigenous solutions then may be wiser.

Interaction between the entrepreneur and the various information brokers is important, and astute use of brokers can markedly increase the information reach of the entrepreneur. But, as Kirzner points out, "information costs are the costs of transportation from ignorance to omniscience, and seldom can a trader afford to take the entire trip."[24] Inevitably some gaps will remain and some inputs not be fully completed.

How the Entrepreneur Operates

Within this frame of diversity the less-developed-world entrepreneur perceives certain potential innovational opportunities. His hope is that these opportunities will come to fruition. Yet only when the innovation becomes viable, when it can be framed in a realistic, accomplishable manner, does it become an idea/project. Ideas must be there, to be sure, but they must also be developed into projects that lend themselves to exploitation. The moment opportunities are perceived, the entrepreneur must start thinking about alternative strategies for action and tentatively select the most feasible and satisfying course. Judgment, intuition, and flexibility are essential to his future breakthrough. He may well be the first person in the less developed country who recognizes the special situation in which it has become possible to innovate. When — and only when — he frames this as an idea/project does he terminate the process of perception of opportunities and set the stage for a possible exploitation of these opportunities.

Once the idea/project is formulated, the entrepreneur has to bring together a finite combination of distinct usable powers. This discrimination is important for his overall strategy. Only a limited number of coalitions are possible, given the particulars of this idea/project. The success of the entrepreneur lies in seeing his own feasible set of power coalitions more clearly than others and taking the lead in linking them — under his own aegis. The success of an idea/project is of course dependent on the availability of economic opportunities within the given society, but the realization of an idea/project depends on a politically feasible set of coalitions. It is the artistry in assembling such distinct powers around the idea/project that may explain the differential response; that is, given the same economic opportunities, why some succeed and others do not.

Soon the organization, newly created or already existing, must be routinized — that is, established within a dynamic equilibrium to fulfill its objectives. This routinized, equilibrated, organized activity will then interact with its environment through relevant adaptations.

Casualties can occur for any of a number of reasons. For example, for each stage of the process we can posit a different leadership style. A brilliant entrepreneur who makes the first breakthrough may become so frozen in his initial successful modes of functioning that he may be unable to handle the emergent problems of a routinized or adaptive organization; thus he himself will prove a failure. Moreover, in a developing economy the environment is particularly volatile, and the entrepreneur-manager must be especially aware and responsive to the changing milieu. This crucial adaptive behavior is itself generally innovative, for it succeeds in keeping the initial thrust, preserving the tenuous equilibrium, and absorbing the new technology. Thus the entrepreneur is inevitably an agent of change.

An Interactive System

We have drawn a linear model that indicates the stages of development — the entrepreneur's rugged path to achievement. The model aids explanation of the entrepreneurial success or failure brought about by this filtration process and also clarifies the process of differential response—why certain people fail where others succeed, even though the economic opportunities are the same for all. To repeat, entrepreneurship does not stop with accomplishment of the initial breakthrough. Longer-term success lies in creating an organization, without which purposeful activity cannot be carried on or sustained for any length of time. We are interested in the entire ongoing process of entrepreneurship, for the internal dynamism of an organization becomes as important as the initial manipulation of the environment.

The feedback process, as indicated in Figure 1, is an essential part of the model. The move from a newly created organization to a routinized or adaptive one precipitates new environmental problems, which in turn lead to a fresh perception and exploitation of opportunities and require the assembling of different powers to achieve fresh breakthroughs. If feedback is absent, new challenges are met only through old initial responses, a dangerous situation in most cases.

We have come full circle to the particular impact of the social structure and the value system on the society. The entrepreneur as an agent of change affects the social milieu as well as being affected by it: the process is mutually reinforcing. The following chapters will emphasize how an individual or group makes a breakthrough in the entrepreneurial role even though ostensibly constrained by the milieu. Equally demanding of attention is the change generated in the environment as a consequence of the adaptive response of the organization. The interactive system necessarily comprehends both.

2

India's Agriculture and
Agro-Industries

The primary business of most villages and small towns in India is agriculture. The agriculturalist himself — the cultivator — naturally plays a central role, and his innovative (perhaps also entrepreneurial) behavior or his lack thereof is a central determinant of rural productivity. His attitudinal and behavioral patterns will be of much interest to us in this book.

Happenings around the agriculturalist must also concern us. Underlying our actor-centered stage are critical infrastructures that dictate the environment in which the distribution goes on — in particular, the policy systems that affect the incentives and options open to the various participants in the agricultural scene. These have often led to disturbing shortfalls in supply and imbalances in distribution, and we must fit our description of individual entrepreneurship to this institutional frame.

Closer to the agriculturalist we can see important advances in agricultural technology, especially the new miracle food grains, which have promised greatly increased productivity, potential self-sufficiency, and efficient distribution of food throughout the world. This "Green Revolution," to adopt the somewhat inflated euphemism now used almost universally, depends upon efficient mechanisms for input, output, and distribution — the agribusinesses — for the takeoff in agriculture itself. The term agribusiness is not used here in its usual sense of large-scale, often corporate, agricultural services. I shall develop a model for village India much less complex, on a much smaller scale. But I do believe that innovativeness in agribusiness (called "agro-industry" in India) is a key dimension of the system problems of agriculture as a whole. Seed companies hybridize new strains and varieties. Water resources and irrigation projects are developed. Fertilizers, both chemical and organic, are marketed to increase soil productivity, as are pesticides for crop protection. New equipment becomes available for greater mechanization. Better methods take the produce from the farm, efficiently process it, and make it readily available to the consumer. Thus, increased productivity of the cultivator demands greater efficiency on the part of the agro-industry entrepreneur.

This interactive, system-linked relationship will be the focus of our study of rural entrepreneurship throughout the remainder of this book.

India's Food Crisis of the 1950s

It has become almost a profession in certain circles to be a prophet of doom about India. Constantly recurring crises unfortunately have made this easy. A great many have been in the food arena, with some of the world's most tragic famines occurring within India's borders. The climate is monsoon-tropical, with the coming of the monsoons each year the pivot upon which the whole of Indian life swings. According to the United States Department of Agriculture, one year in five in India is dry, and one year in ten brings a severe drought. An "average" year balances geographic areas of drought with other areas of plentiful rainfall. The famines of the nineteenth century took a severe toll; the great famine of 1876-1878 alone is estimated to have taken 5 million lives. As India's leaders sat around the bargaining table in 1947, hammering out the final details of independence from Great Britain, echoes of the tragic Bengal famine of 1943 (with its sacrificed lives variously estimated between 1.5 and 3 million) must have reverberated in the minds of all concerned.[1]

However, famine is not the only cause for worry; since the beginning of the twentieth century the equilibrium between rising population and agricultural production has been worsening. With only about one-fortieth of the earth's land surface, India in recent years has had about one-seventh of the world's population — a larger population than North, Central, and South America combined. The official population figure from the Government of India census of 1971 was 548 million, with a population growth rate of approximately 2.2 percent; the government's estimate in 1976 was just over 600 million. Many demographers feel that both of these figures are understated — the U.S. Department of Agriculture estimated the population of India in mid-1975 at 629 million and the growth at 2.4 percent; the Population Reference Bureau's 1976 figure was 620.7 million, but with an estimated growth rate of only 2.0 percent.[2] Taking one of the more conservative population increase figures given for the mid-1970s, about 13 million people a year (the equivalent of a new Australia) were being added to the country in these years — approximately two new faces every five seconds.

India presently faces the same Hobson's choice that confronts many less developed countries. On the one hand, mortality rates have declined sharply, for India needed no significant change in social structure to believe in the efficacy of inoculations and other modern forms of medicine and public health. But control of fertility is a different matter — this requires active involvement of the people and almost inevitably a significant shift in social attitudes.[3] The Indian government stepped up its efforts at population control during the so-called emergency period of 1975-1976, even resorting to such draconian measures as forced sterilization. Alleged excesses under this policy were contributing factors to Indira Gandhi's defeat as prime minister in the election of March 1977. The government formed by the new prime minister, Morarji R. Desai, sharply modified the birth-control program to emphasize its voluntary nature; the minister of health and family welfare maintained later that year that voluntary abstention from sex in the age-old Hindu tradition of renunciation might well be the best policy. Mankind's sexual drives being what they are, this seems to many to be more hope than reality. Even if there were a rapid movement to a zero-growth mode, the age composition of the country would not bring a stabilization of population for many years.

The Indian people are predominantly vegetarians, by belief and in practice.[4] Rice is the staple food of about 75 percent of the population. The United States Department of Agriculture estimated that in recent years the average daily per capita available supply in India (production plus imports of food grains, excluding pulses) has been approximately 300 grams, or 1,500 calories. In addition, the average Indian diet includes about 600 calories a day from pulses, sugar, oils, fruits, vegetables, milk, and small amounts of meat (mostly poultry), for a total of about 2,100 calories per person per day. With the importance of food grains in the diet, India needs a net addition to its food grain stock of about 2.5 million metric tons a year just to maintain present per capita consumption levels.

In the nineteenth century India was an exporter of cereals; around 1880 over a million metric tons a year were being sent abroad.[5] By the first decade of the twentieth century this figure had dropped to just over half a million, and by the 1920s India was importing upward of 150,000 metric tons a year. This jumped to over 1 million metric tons during the period 1930-1935 and skyrocketed to about 3 million in the post-World War II period.

Perhaps the burgeoning population could have been fed had the domestic yields increased commensurately; on the contrary, yields hardly varied during the three decades preceding the government's First Plan in 1950-1951. "Yield records were low not only when compared with Western Europe," noted Wilfred Malenbaum in his study of this period, "but even when compared to other preindustrial countries like Egypt and China."[6]

Given such disparities in yields, it was natural for the country's First Plan to stress agriculture. Thanks to beneficent conditions during this five-year planning cycle from 1951 to 1956—good weather and at least a modicum of increased agricultural efficiency—the historic patterns of food insufficiency, malnutrition, and famine seemed to have been arrested. At this point the central government made a far-reaching and much-debated decision: to turn the country's development emphasis to industrialization. Using a mixed-economy approach under a socialist rubric, Prime Minister Jawaharlal Nehru exhorted the country to strive for giant leaps in the key industries that he and his planners saw as a salvation from India's centuries of poverty and despair. Despite the fact that over half of the national income was generated in the agriculture sector and some three-quarters of the working force employed therein, government expenditures for agriculture plus irrigation accounted for only 20 and 23 percent of the total expenditures in the Second and Third Plans (in contrast to 31 percent in the First Plan).[7]

This stress on industrialization produced some notable results, at the same time many inefficiencies and shortfalls. Sadly, preoccupation with heavy industry was played out within a framework of tremendous pressure from a swelling population, large numbers of whom were underemployed or unemployed and who nevertheless needed to eat, and a series of tardy and insufficient monsoons (with 1957-1958 a particularly bad year). By the late 1950s development headlines around the world again trumpeted INDIAN FOOD CRISIS.

In the jaded and often cynical world of the late 1970s it is not easy to engender response to yet another crisis in India. But back in the late 1950s a group of experts *was* able to dramatize the Indian food situation enough to waken both the country itself and its friends around the world. The remarkable report of this group — the Agricultural Production Team, sponsored by the Ford Foundation on the joint request of two central government ministries (Food and Agriculture, and Community Development and Cooperation) — "marks a watershed in the history of India's agriculture," to quote Sudhir Sen, one of India's respected contemporary economists. It served as a major catalyst in turning the planners and the country as a whole toward heightened emphasis on food production.[8] In their short initial chapter the Ford Foundation experts graphically stated the situation: 5 million people were added each year during the first Five-Year Plan, 7 million more per year would be added during the Second Plan, another 10 million per year through the Third Plan — an explosive increase that would raise the total population in the country from 360 million in 1951 to 480 million by 1966. That terminal year of the Third Plan, 1966, was just seven years away, they noted; when it came, they estimated 80 million *more* people, enough by themselves to be one of the half-dozen largest countries in the world. Even though their arithmetic was slightly inflated (a precise extrapolation was closer to 71 million), their point was eminently believable.

With grain the dominant food in India, providing two-thirds of the average caloric intake, the Ford Foundation experts estimated that on the order of 110 million metric tons of grain annually would be needed by the end of the Third Plan. But with existing plan supply targets, the gap between need and fulfillment would actually grow wider and balloon to a 28-million-ton shortfall by 1966. At the very minimum, there had to be a production *increase* that would average over 8 percent per year during the eight years remaining to the end of the Third Plan. The analysts were blunt: solutions had to come from within the agricultural structure of India itself, for "no conceivable programme of imports or rationings could meet the crisis of this magnitude." The inevitable conclusion was that an all-out emergency program was required.

The various parts of this program had to go forward together, the Ford team believed, and include these high-priority efforts:

(a) A public works program for increasing village employment.
(b) Stabilization of farm prices by a guaranteed minimum price, readily available markets, and suitable local storage.
(c) Intensified irrigation and drainage programs.
(d) Special intensive efforts on selected crops in selected areas.
(e) Heightened security of land tenure, and programs for land consolidation.
(f) Immediate large-scale credit through cooperatives.
(g) Progressive reduction in the numbers of cattle.
(h) Mobilization of community development efforts and various technical ministries toward concentration on food production.
(i) Establishment of a high-level coordinating food production authority.
(j) Top priority for procurement, production, and distribution of high-analysis chemical fertilizers.[9]

The Ford Foundation experts' ten recommendations together form an integrated set of practices, needed in concert to bring about the sharp jumps in agricultural production that were contemplated. This "package" concept soon led the Government of India, again with the direct participation of the Ford Foundation, to a world-renowned innovative program called the Intensive Agricultural Districts Programme (IADP).[10] The central tenet of the IADP was this concept of a "package of practices." The action programs suggested by the authors of the 1959 report had ranged over the whole agricultural panorama—fertilizer and other input supply increases, credit plans, water management, farm management assistance, and so on. No one of these, though, would work at full efficiency without the presence of other equally effective inputs. In essence, a *combination* of inputs must be applied in necessary quanta to give a "critical mass" synergy that will allow a takeoff in innovation.

The rationale of the IADP stemmed from one of the ten recommendations of the 1959 team—that certain crops would be selected in certain areas for special intensive efforts. From India's 320 districts fifteen were selected—one from each major state. The choice was based upon the presence of a full set of already existing strengths—a well-organized Community Development Programme, successful credit, supply and marketing cooperatives, the presence of assured rainfall over the district and adequate irrigation facilities, the absence of land ceiling imbalances or farm consolidation problems, and finally, abundant local leadership assumed to be receptive to change.

In broad outline, the IADP program built on a set of existing assets, using the critical-mass concept to demonstrate and educate on the potentials of rural change. The various people involved in carrying through IADP efforts — the cooperative managers; local, state, and central government officials; the Ford Foundation experts — all impressed on the cultivators the principle that to improve and modernize their farming they needed to use a number of practices in proper combination, in conjunction with services. Fertilizer, water use and management, and marketing outlets all had to be brought together in combination to make the kinds of gains in yields and prices that could readily come from such a program.

This project of bringing requisite new knowledge about agricultural innovations to the Indian countryside was profoundly aided by one of the most imaginative of all organizations that India has formed since independence — the Community Development Programme.[11] When the program came into being as a key component of the First Plan, a new administrative unit standing between the old British "district" and the village was established — the "block." Each block covered some 100 villages over about 650 square kilometers, with a total population of approximately 80,000. At the block level a cohesive administration was established and charged to take a "system" stance in regard to village development: to recognize the interdependence of all the services to the village and the need for their coordination. The program was entered upon with great gusto, and by the mid-1960s it covered, in just over 5,000 blocks, almost all of rural India. Several of these were consolidated to rule out overlap and administrative inefficiency, so by 1972 there were 4,893 blocks, serving a rural population of some 438 million and all of the country's 569,000 villages.[12]

The block is headed by the block development officer (BDO), and he in turn has a hierarchy of technical specialists. The key figure for agricultural inputs is the agricultural extension officer (AEO); generally there is one AEO for each block. Virtually all the cultivators were and are highly immobile (travel even today is still mostly by bullock cart, with a practical maximum range of 3 to 8 kilometers), and technical advice and aid must be brought to them. To meet the need for an officer at a level lower than the block, the village-level worker (VLW) was appointed. By the middle of the 1960s the number of *gram sevaks*, the Hindi name for the VLW, had risen to 52,000 — about ten per block, each with an assignment of ten villages and perhaps 8,000 people.

The visionary thinking that went into the Community Development Programme pictured the VLW as the embodiment and exemplification of the "multipurpose" extension worker, who was at once familiar with the village, knew the people and their needs, and had the combination of personal knowledge and contact with higher technical authorities to fill these needs. This mirrored the dreams of Mohandas Gandhi's "village swaraj," his concept of village self-sufficiency as a prime virtue of the New India.

In practice, the low pay of the VLW, combined in many cases with disjointed training, tended to emphasize quantity at the expense of quality.[13] One of the central assignments of the VLW was to bring to the farmer the best of information about the agricultural inputs. Some did very well in this assignment; others were not as knowledgeable or as motivated, or became overly fragmented by the many other tasks assigned them. Their advice became more desultory and ineffectual. The BDO and the AEO helped, to be sure, but the territories they covered precluded the intimate daily contact needed, for example, in the planting season. The location of institutions serving a set of 108 villages in three states was analyzed in a Natonal Institute of Community Development (NICD) study of agricultural innovation[14]; Table 1 shows the pattern that emerged.

In 90 percent of the sample villages the VLW was located within 8 kilometers — the effective range within which the farmer with his bullock cart could be reasonably mobile. Within this same range the *panchayats* (the village governing units) were found in 96 percent of the villages, cooperatives in 94 percent. About half of the villages also had a godown (storehouse) and a veterinary center within this radius. The block office, on the other hand, was within 8 kilometers for only a quarter of the villages.

The NICD team studied the overall process of innovation in these villages and concluded that "the four factors which are of major importance in explaining differences among villages in adoption of agricultural practices are village leaders' contact with change agents, the secular orientation of village leaders, change agents' use of impersonal techniques in disseminating information — especially the demonstration — and the electrification of the village." In a later study that centered on the farmer himself, the NICD team reaffirmed the hypothesis many social scientists have held, that the general socioeconomic status of the farmer in terms of his level of living, education, and caste rank was strongly and positively related to innovativeness.[15] Beyond this, though, the NICD report put special emphasis on linkages of the farmer with the outside world. In particular, closeness of contact (especially personal contact) between the farmer and outside change agents heightened the likelihood of innovation.

With the IADP and community development efforts working in tandem with other stepped-up central government and state agricultural programs, the food grain picture seemed to be moving forward apace in the early 1960s. The critical figure to watch each year has always been the final production of

TABLE 1   Location of various institutions in India in relation to the villages they serve. An analysis of 108 villages in three states is given. Figures are percentages of villages sampled and may not add to 100 because of rounding.

Service	Inside village or within 1.0 mile	Between 1.0 and 4.9 miles	Between 5.0 and 9.9 miles	10.0 miles and over	No infor- mation
Educational institutions:					
Primary school	100.0	0	0	0	0
Middle school	37.0	46.3	13.0	1.9	1.9
High school	13.9	50.0	22.2	13.9	0
Health services:					
Primary health center	4.6	22.2	30.6	38.9	3.7
Subsidiary health center	15.7	37.0	18.5	8.3	20.4
Dispensary	24.1	38.0	11.1	17.6	9.3
Hospital	0.9	18.5	24.1	56.5	0
Communications:					
Post office	52.8	39.8	5.6	1.6	0
Telegraph office	3.7	25.0	31.5	39.8	0
Economic institutions:					
Cooperative	75.9	18.5	4.6	0	0.9
Godown	19.4	33.3	27.8	12.0	7.4
Bank	0.9	15.7	32.4	50.9	0
Insurance agent	0	11.1	16.7	71.3	0.9
Wholesale market	2.0	27.8	38.0	31.5	0
Retail market	37.0	44.4	13.0	4.6	0.9
Village store[a]	82.6	—	—	—	—
Political institutions:					
Panchayat	89.8	6.5	2.8	0.9	0
Political party headquarters[a]	61.1	—	—	—	—
Voluntary organizations:					
Youth club	65.7	12.0	3.7	0	18.5
Community center	24.1	8.3	20.4	13.0	34.3
Library	47.2	27.8	12.0	7.4	5.6
Extension services:					
VLW office	48.2	41.7	8.3	1.9	0
Block office	3.7	21.3	38.0	37.0	0
Veterinary stockman center	10.2	38.9	30.6	18.5	1.9

TABLE 1 (cont.)

Service	Inside village or within 1.0 mile	Between 1.0 and 4.9 miles	Between 5.0 and 9.9 miles	10.0 miles and over	No infor- mation
Administrative offices:					
Police station	1.9	26.9	50.0	21.3	0
Revenue office	0.9	17.6	32.4	49.1	0
Court	0	6.5	15.7	75.9	1.9
Religious institutions:					
Temple, mosque, church	85.2	4.6	3.7	1.9	4.6
Other:					
Cinema	3.7	18.5	29.6	48.2	0
Bicycle repair shop	19.4	40.7	23.2	16.7	0
Engine repair shop	0	18.5	24.1	56.5	0.9

SOURCE: F. C. Fliegel, P. Roy, L. K. Sen, and J. E. Kivlin, *Agricultural Innovations in Indian Villages* (Hyderabad: National Institute of Community Development, 1968), pp. 87-88.

[a]Data on distances were not collected.

"total food grains." This had risen to 89 million metric tons in 1965 (the crop year ending June 30), up from 66 million in 1958; the growth rate seemed within reach of the Ford Foundation target. Yet a look around the rest of the world at comparative yields was proof enough of the continuing backwardness of India's agriculture. Nevertheless, that strangely recurrent euphoria so characteristic of good crop years in India set in once again.

A meaningful way to see this relationship is to take the top half-dozen producers and compare their yields. Table 2 does this; India and the five other highest-producing countries are compared for the crop year 1965-1966, just before the Green Revolution significantly changed the supply of wheat and rice. Although single-year figures can sometimes be misleading, this particular crop year of 1965-1966 was reasonably good around the world and serves to give rough comparisons.

The same process of comparing the highest with the average should also be done for crop yields within India, for they tend to vary widely. Table 3 compares the top half-dozen states for the country's two most important cereal crops during the same period as in Table 2.

TABLE 2   Comparison of yields of major crops in India and the five other highest-producing countries, 1965-1966 (100 kilograms per hectare).

| | India | | Five highest other countries | | |
Crop	Rank in total production	Yield (100 kg/ha)	Country	Rank in total production	Yield (100 kg/ha)
Wheat	6	9.1	U.S.S.R.	1	8.5
			United States	2	17.9
			Mainland China	3	N.A.
			Canada	4	15.4
			France	5	32.7
Rice (paddy or rough)	2	13.0	Mainland China	1	N.A.
			Pakistan	3	16.5
			Japan	4	49.5
			Indonesia	5	18.0
			Thailand	6	15.6
Maize	8	10.0	United States	1	45.4
			Brazil	2	13.8
			Mexico	3	11.2
			U.S.S.R.	4	25.3
			Yugoslavia	5	23.2
Cotton	4	1.1	United States	1	5.9
			U.S.S.R.	2	7.9
			Mainland China	3	2.7
			Brazil	5	1.7
			Mexico	6	8.1
Sugar cane	1	430	Brazil	2	445
			Cuba	3	330
			Pakistan	4	399
			Mexico	5	651
			Mainland China	6	575

SOURCE: Food and Agriculture Organization of the United Nations, *Production Handbook*, vol. 21, 1967.

Any jubilation about the 1965-1966 crop year was short-lived, though. The total dipped the following year to a disturbingly low 72 million metric tons, as a catastrophic drought over many sections of the country caused an unprecedented drop in the harvests. Only massive imports of cereals, estimated to be more than 10 million metric tons in 1966, kept the situation from becoming a national disaster.[16] The next crop year was also discouraging, with only 74 million metric tons of food grains. This time the aggregate failure of the monsoon was a little less, but more concentrated geographically, affecting especially the states of Bihar and Orissa (each recorded famine deaths that year).

The First Generation of the Green Revolution

At this point the Green Revolution came to India's shores. In 1963 Dr. Norman Borlaug personally brought to India 100 kilograms of dwarf Mexican wheat from the soon-famous research organization in Mexico sponsored by the Rockefeller Foundation, the International Maize and Wheat Improvement Center (CIMMYT). Over the summers of 1964, 1965, and 1966 additional quantities were imported from Mexico and widely planted. Likewise IR-8, the first of the semidwarf varieties of rice developed at the International Rice Research Institute (IRRI), a Ford Foundation-sponsored organization in the Philippines, had been released for international use; 2 kilograms of seeds were taken to India in a suitcase in 1965 by the manager of the National Seeds Corporation.[17] The pace of adoption was dramatic, as Table 4 indicates.

In just two years, with the combination of full monsoon rains and the newly realized early stages of this Green Revolution, total food grains in India had risen to over 95 million metric tons at the end of the crop year 1967-1968.

TABLE 3   Comparison of yields of wheat and milled rice for the six highest states in India in terms of total production, 1965-1966.

Crop	State (in order of total production)	Yield (100 kg/ha)
Wheat	Uttar Pradesh	9.1
	Punjab	12.4
	Madhya Pradesh	5.5
	Haryana	12.8
	Rajasthan	8.1
	Gujarat	10.8
Rice	West Bengal	10.5
	Bihar	8.1
	Andhra Pradesh	12.6
	Tamil Nadu	14.5
	Orissa	7.7
	Uttar Pradesh	5.6

SOURCE: Fertiliser Association of India, *Fertiliser Statistics, 1967-1968* (New Delhi: December 1968).

TABLE 4   Increase in planting of high-yielding varieties of wheat and rice in India, 1965 to 1971.

Year	High-yielding wheat planted (thousands of hectares)	Percentage of total wheat	High-yielding rice planted (thousands of hectares)	Percentage of total rice
1965-1966	3	Negligible	7	Negligible
1966-1967	541	4.2	888	2.5
1967-1968	2,942	19.6	1,785	4.9
1968-1969	4,793	30.0	2,681	7.3
1969-1970	4,918	29.6	4,344	11.5
1970-1971	6,480	35.5	5,589	14.9

SOURCE: Dana G. Dalrymple, *Development and Spread of High-Yielding Varieties of Wheat and Rice in the Less Developed Nations* (U.S. Department of Agriculture, Foreign Agricultural Economic Report no. 95, July 1974), pp. 28, 47, 72.

They dipped to 94 million the next year (the state of Tamil Nadu experienced a severe drought and contributed notably to the loss), but for the crop year 1970-1971 total food grains climbed to 108.42 million metric tons. This 15-percent jump in just two years was heady progress. At this point top Government of India officials, including Prime Minister Indira Gandhi, proudly boasted of self-sufficiency. Over 12 million hectares were already under the high-yield program, with both wheat and rice acreage already over 100 percent of the targeted goal for that year.

The surplus in food grains in 1971 made it possible not only to feed the incredible crush of refugees from East Pakistan during that entire year (estimated at upward of 10 million people), but also to adequately meet the food needs of India's own rapidly growing population. The short, successful war with Pakistan in late 1971 was followed by large-scale assistance in the form of food grains to the new country, Bangladesh, in the early months of 1972.[18] If the euphoria bordered on complacency, it was not just the Indians' view, for the *New York Times* was reporting in early 1972 on India's "grain surplus" and its search for export markets for the expected 8 million tons of additional surplus that the year 1972 would bring. India's minister of food was quoted by the *Times* on April 30 as maintaining that at this rate India would "out-strip the United States in seven to eight years" in wheat output. As late as April 1972 there had been reports that India was going to achieve a new record for the crop year 1971-1972 — and perhaps exceed the 108 million metric tons by 5 million more. Even the Fourth Plan target of 129 million metric tons by 1974 seemed possible — another 15-percent jump on top of this projected 5-million-ton increase. As it happened in 1970-1971, the harvest would actually be 129.95 million metric tons. The effects on yields, too, were pronounced. In the five crop years from 1966-1967 to 1970-1971, wheat production (in 100 kilograms/hectare) rose from 8.8 to 11.0 to 11.7 to 12.1 to 13.1; the corresponding figures for rice were 8.6, 10.3, 10.8, 10.7, and 11.2.[19] (These figures actually simplify a more complex set of equations, for the traditional varieties also increased in yield during this period, and the amounts of new lands and double-cropping of old lands bring different factors into play.)

It will be helpful for the reader at this point to compare a number of agricultural statistics for India and the United States. Pertinent figures are given in Table 5.

The Importance of Agricultural Inputs

The so-called miracle dwarf wheats and rices developed in Mexico and the Philippines were ideally suited for the IADP package concept. Both required more care all along the input cycle—more meticulous sowing and seed-bed preparation, assurance of water at the right times, better cultivation, and more efficient plant protection (through the use of chemical pesticides and fungicides). Both the wheats and the rices were highly responsive to fertilizer. Thus fertilizers (particularly chemical ones) came to be critical ingredients in the Green Revolution. In India they were especially important.

Back in 1959 the Ford Foundation team had recommended that by the end of the Third Plan in 1966 chemical fertilizers amounting to 1,500,000 metric tons of nitrogen, 750,000 metric tons of phosphoric acid, and 200,000 metric tons of potash be available for domestic consumption—a nine-fold increase in the use of nitrogen over the immediate past, and even larger increases in the other forms of fertilizer. In truth, the very use of chemical fertilizers was a departure from past practice. For thousands of years Indian farmers had depended upon organic sources such as animal manures and green manures to replenish the soils. Hosts of Indian farmers were biased against inorganic fertilizers; they believed organic matter to be the life of the soil. An ancient Tamil proverb put it this way: "Better to manure than to plow the land."[20] However, there simply were not enough organic sources to provide food for the burgeoning population in India. The unpleasant reality was that the soils were badly impoverished and deteriorated annually—a fundamental cause of the country's low crop yield. Many factors entered into this deterioration, including the lack of proper application of scientific methods, recurring problems with both drought and wet weather, insufficient irrigation, poor seed, diseases, insects, and weeds. The infertile soils demanded regeneration through careful soil management, but this could not be achieved with the high costs for, and limited supply of, organics.

TABLE 5   Agricultural comparisons for the United States and India, 1972. (Indian agricultural production is for the crop year 1971-1972.)

Item	Unit	United States	India
Total population	Millions	208	560
Farm population	Millions	9.5	448
Share of population involved in agriculture	Percent	4.6	80.1
Total land area	Thousands of square miles	3,600	1,267
Cropland	Millions of acres	430	403
Irrigated cropland	Millions of acres	41[a]	75
Area sowed	Millions of acres	293	345
Number of farms	Millions	2.9	50
Value of exports per farm	Dollars	2,748[b]	13.6[a]
Food supply per capita	Calories per day	3,240	2,140[a]
Amount of fertilizer (plant nutrients) per acre sowed	Pounds	182	18.7
Number of tractors	Millions	5.6	0.1
Production of —			
Rice	Millions of metric tons	3.9	42.7
Wheat	Millions of metric tons	42.04	26.5
Sorghum	Millions of metric tons	22.5	7.8
Corn	Millions of metric tons	149.0	5.0
Beans and peas, dry	Millions of metric tons	0.9	11.1
Peanuts	Millions of metric tons	1.5	5.7
Oilseeds other than peanuts	Millions of metric tons	40.1	2.6
Tobacco	Millions of metric tons	0.79	0.41
Cotton	Millions of metric tons	3.0	1.3
Yield of —			
Rice	Hundredweight per acre	46.8	10.2
Wheat	Bushels per acre	32.7	20.6
Sorghum	Bushels per acre	60.8	7.4
Corn	Bushels per acre	95.5	14.1
Cotton	Pounds per acre	495	149
Peanuts	Pounds per acre	2,212	704
Tobacco	Pounds per acre	2,074	821

SOURCE: Office of the Agricultural Attaché, United States Embassy, New Delhi, *Brief on Indian Agriculture,* 1973, p. 45.

[a]Estimated.
[b]Fiscal year 1972.

The Ford Foundation team encouraged the fuller use of manures, composts, and green manure, but concluded that "at the very best they can substitute for only a small fraction of the chemical fertilizers needed during the next seven years." High-analysis types of fertilizers were especially important, they said; unhappily, India had traditionally favored low-analysis fertilizers, such as ammonium sulfate and superphosphate. The team further advocated that the fertilizers should be concentrated on food grains rather than nonfood crops and on sugar cane.[21] The Ford Foundation team thus set the stage for a much-heightened emphasis on chemical fertilizers for the 1960s.

The domestic fertilizer industry had produced approximately 84,000 metric tons of fertilizer in 1959-1960, so the Third Plan targets of the Ford Foundation study team as "the very minima" seemed awesomely high. It soon became evident that in order to build up the indigenous fertilizer manufacturing industry, substantial investment capital from overseas must be encouraged. Private entrepreneurs, especially if foreign, were rather unpalatable to the socialist-minded central government: several proposals for investment from the outside during the 1960s that ran against the ideological grain of the Indian government failed to come to fruition.[22] Finally, one of the earliest of the foreign private-sector proposals, under discussion for eight years, fared better. In 1966 Coromandel Fertilizers (Private) Limited opened its plant in the state of Andhra Pradesh under a collaboration agreement between two American companies and a private Indian company. Soon after, another Government of India public-sector plant was built near Bombay, in this case financed partially by United States government assistance. By the end of the 1960s the addition of other new plants had raised Indian installed production capacity to about 1,500,000 metric tons of nitrogenous fertilizers and about 500,000 of phosphatic fertilizers. These plants ran at less than capacity most of the time because of production breakdowns and other inefficiencies, so that the actual production in 1970-1971 was 1,050,000 metric tons of nitrogenous fertilizers and 300,000 metric tons of phosphates. Consumption of fertilizers was well above this, at 1,439,000 and 541,000 metric tons respectively. Deficits through all of these years were made up by a massive program of fertilizer importation. Even with these vastly increased figures for production and consumption, both were still far short of the optimistic estimates of planners in the mid-1960s. A midterm appraisal of the Fourth Plan goals for fertilizer production drastically revised downward the target for the end of the Plan (1969-1974), so that the new goal actually fell below the target initially established for 1970-1971. By 1971 consumption was well below plans—in fact, the age-old cultivator caution in the use of chemical fertilizers appeared to be causing a new softness in demand that had the fertilizer companies quite concerned about how to best promote their products.[23]

Distribution Channels for Fertilizer

Let us now assume that a group of cultivators want fertilizer. From whom do they get it? For the moment we define a fertilizer distributor as anyone selling through an agricultural depot. Because of the physical immobility of the average cultivator, he will obtain his agricultural inputs (at least the heavier ones) by using his bullock cart to go to the nearest depot. With the cultivator's practical range about 8 kilometers, a rather large number of depots is involved. A common rule of thumb is that an agricultural input depot should serve about 1,000 to 1,500 farmers. When the latest official census in India was conducted in 1971, out of a total estimated population of 548 million people just under 80 million of these people were classified as cultivators, another 44 million as agricultural laborers.[24] With their relatives and friends they comprised the total of approximately 438 million rural people living in the 569,000 villages mentioned earlier.

Let us pause at this last figure to comprehend its enormity. There are over half a million separate towns and villages in India. What may have easy answers in the hundreds or the thousands may become enormously complicated in the millions, as we can see from the fertilizer depot illustration: simple mental arithmetic tells us we need 60,000 to 80,000 depots.[25]

With this many depots it matters very much just who their managers are. Nitrogenous fertilizers, dominating the chemicals, had been distributed in the 1950s and into the mid-1960s by the Central Fertiliser Pool, under direct control of the central government. Imported nitrogenous fertilizers were pooled with all the domestic manufactures, and this limited total supply was then allocated among the various states at a constant railhead price. The government determined via a central monopoly where and by what channels the fertilizers were to be distributed. The pool also stipulated monopolistic selling channels in the various states. In most cases, up to the mid-1960s, the agricultural cooperatives were the vehicles; in a few states some of the fertilizer was marketed through the state agricultural departments, in others a scattering of private trading was allowed.[26]

The performance of the cooperatives as fertilizer distributors during this period was dismal. With only a few bright exceptions most were not large enough, strong enough, or interested enough to be effective marketers. In 1965 a blue-ribbon Government of India Committee on Fertilisers, the well-regarded Sivaraman Committee, faulted the cooperatives' marketing efforts; lack of marketing experience, they said, was compounded by inadequate credit facilities, difficulties in developing adequate profit margins in fertilizers, and overall problems of small size and small sales turnover. The committee's choice of words in their conclusion was interesting: "fertiliser distribution has proved unprofitable to many cooperative agencies."[27]

The committee could not describe in cold print some further difficulties. The cooperative movement throughout India had long suffered from an "in-group mentality," with those in control exerting favoritism to the few.[28] Often this evolved into straightforward malpractice. Bribery and corruption were the norm; with fertilizer in short supply at various times, black-marketing was all too frequent. These same malpractices and others—for example, wide-spread adulteration of fertilizer—were characteristic of many private traders as well. Fertilizer distribution was clearly not in good hands, whether public, cooperative, or private.

From the Sivaraman Committee report came a number of suggestions for strengthening cooperative marketing efforts in fertilizer (for instance, broadening of their agricultural input base to include pesticides, implements, seeds, and consumer goods to reduce their overhead costs). In retrospect, though, the most important recommendation concerned that of the private sector. The committee bluntly called for the elimination of monopolies and recommended acceptance of a system in all of the states whereby private agencies would also be allowed a central role as fertilizer distributors.[29]

Over the years since this 1965 report, the states have reacted in varying ways to the Sivaraman caveat. The practices in two of the key agricultural states are illustrative. In Punjab, the state government has responded cautiously to any private efforts and has uniformly favored the state's cooperative marketing organizations as the preferred vehicle.[30] In Tamil Nadu, on the other hand, private distribution has been allowed for a number of years and has been actively encouraged since the late 1960s. With Tamil Nadu as the primary location for our study, we shall be emphasizing private-enterprise fertilizer marketing. A brief look at this important state in 1971 to 1973, the time of this study, will be useful.

Observations about the State of Tamil Nadu

The south of India has a special identity of its own. Some differences stem from climate and geography (for example, the east coast of South India has not only the southwest monsoon in the summer but also a northeast monsoon in the late fall). But the divergence between South India and the rest of the country is more fundamental than these factors alone.

In ancient days the Dravidians were pushed into the south by Aryan arrivals from West Asia. The Dravidians are different from the people in the north, darker skinned and with sharply differing languages. Subsequent great waves of invasion that swept over North and Central India, bringing bitter clashes between Hindu and Muslim religions and traumatic tensions in the total society, never really reached the south. It is true that many of the southern coastal regions became stopping places for the European empire builders and colonists. Still, this European intrusion into the south was largely confined to a few seaport towns—the Goa of Portugal, the Pondicherry of France, the Madras of England. Thus, over the earlier years, outsiders had been in the nature of blips on the horizon of the south rather than dominant central figures. The result is an intriguing survival there of ancient India, a mosaic of traditionalism, stability, and conservatism right to the present. The four Dravidian languages—Tamil, Telegu, Kannada, and Malayalam—provide a set of Dravidian cultures that set the south apart as a unique region of the country.

Present Tamil Nadu is, literally, "Tamil land." Historically it was the state of Madras, an outgrowth of the Madras presidency of the British colonial period, one of the major British administrative units, stretching all the way from the southern tip of India up along the east coast through the present state of Andhra Pradesh. Part of the state of Madras was lopped off in 1950 to become, with the princely states of Travancore-Cochin, the state of Kerala; another part became a segment of the present state of Andhra Pradesh (Telegu speaking) in 1953; and other sections were transferred to the present states of Kerala (Malayalam speaking) and Mysore (Kannada speaking) in 1956. Shortly after the present borders of the state were set in the late 1960s, the Dravida Munnetra Kazhagam government then in power changed its name to Tamil Nadu. It is the seventh largest state in the country (41 million people in the 1971 census) and eleventh in area, with just over 130,000 square kilometers.[31] Thus there are something over 300 people per square kilometer, making the state the fourth most densely populated in the country.

The population growth rate is rising (it was estimated at the time of this study at well over 2 percent per annum), because of the combination of a declining death rate and a strong in-migration, especially of Tamilians from Sri Lanka and Burma. The birth rate is declining (marginally), but is still 27 per thousand (India overall is listed officially at 39.9). About 90 percent of the population is Hindu, just over 5 percent is Christian, and about 4.5 percent is Muslim. Tamil Nadu's literacy rate is 39 percent, second highest in India (the all-India figure is 29 percent).

About 30 percent of the population is urban; Madras at 3 million is the largest city, and the state capital; Madurai, Tiruchchirappalli, and Coimbatore are each about half a million. Tamil Nadu is one of the more industrialized states of the country; all four of its largest cities have a well-diversified set of medium and small industries.

Yet the state is predominantly rural; for example, there are some 28,000 villages with a population of less than 1,000. And agriculture contributes almost twice as much to state product as does industry.[32] There are strong pluses and minuses for agriculture. The net area sowed is about 48 percent of the total land in the state, with a particularly rich deltaic region in the

Cauvery River basin. Water is a problem in many parts of the state, however, and irrigation has overriding importance in state agricultural plans.

Rice is the state's most important food crop, grown on some 2.7 million hectares (out of the total gross cropped area of 7.5 million). More than two-thirds of this paddy is under the "high-yielding varieties programme." Although little wheat is grown in the state, there are substantial amounts of the millets — *cholam* (in Hindi it is called *jowar,* in the United States sorghum), *cumbu* (*bajra* in Hindi, pearl millet in the United States), and *ragi* (the term for finger millet used all over India). There is an active HYV (high-yielding variety) program in the state for the first two of these. Groundnut (peanuts), sugar cane, cotton, and plantation crop tea are widely grown as cash crops. Seed multiplication schemes abound at the state seed farm, and several private seed producers are active.

The growth in use of the inputs necessary for the HYV program has mirrored the rapid increase in the grains themselves. By 1970 over one-third of all the pump sets in the country were in Tamil Nadu — almost one-half million of the total 1.2 million. The cultivating practices in Tamil Nadu are largely bullock and hand based; the rather small number of tractors in the state reflects the small-unit, monsoon paddy culture. The total number of tractors in India is rather small, given the total cropped area in the country. In 1972 there were just 67,000 in the country; by way of contrast, Japan had some 270,000, China 115,000, and the United States 4,387,000.[33]

In the area of fertilizer distribution, though, Tamil Nadu's comparative performance stands out. In the 1972-1973 crop season Indian farmers as a whole consumed 2.7 million metric tons of fertilizers (down to 2.5 million in 1973-1974). Tamil Nadu, at 324,000 metric tons, took some 12 percent of this total — the second state in usage. Its consumption of fertilizers per unit of crop area, at 46.5 kilograms per hectare (1974), was second in the country, exceeded only by Punjab with 71.6. The all-India average was just under 17 kilograms per hectare of crop land. (For comparison: in 1971, when India's consumption was 13.2 kilograms per arable hectare, most countries in Europe were over 200, with the Netherlands at 749; even in Asia, India was the lowest of the major countries — Taiwan was 295, the Republic of Korea 243, Japan 385.)[34]

There has been a special problem in the use of fertilizer in India — "a nitrogen mania." Over the recent years of stepped-up fertilizer usage in India, urea became especially popular, as it has a pronounced immediate effect. The Government of India promoted it heavily in order to bring about rapid increases in yield and thus persuade cultivators to switch from organic to chemical fertilizers. The other two ingredients of the tripartite set that make up balanced chemical fertilizers — phosphorus and potash — were considerably slighted. International comparisons of fertilizer content are a bit misleading, for soils vary widely around the world. Yet it is noteworthy that in the 1971 United Nations figures, India's average chemical fertilizer balance was 6.6-2.0-1, whereas in Belgium it was 0.8-0.8-1, in West Germany 0.9-0.8-1, and in Japan 1.4-1.1. In a recent statement the Commissioner of Fertilisers of the Government of India reiterated the word "mania" and said that preoccupation with nitrogen was setting a dangerous trend—there appeared to be widespread phosphorus deficiencies and a profitable response to nitrogen could not be obtained without the use of phosphates and potash. In Tamil Nadu the imbalance was even higher than for the country as a whole—somewhere in the neighborhood of 8-2-1 (in Punjab it was even worse at 18-4-1).[35]

Tamil Nadu's strengths in these inputs—relative to the rest of India, if not to some of its neighbors—are mirrored in the fact that its rice yield in 1972 averaged 2,010 kilograms per hectare, highest in the country; in 1971, when India as a whole was averaging 1,710 kilograms per hectare, Europe as a whole was averaging 4,600, the Soviet Union 4,000, the United States 5,200, and Japan a bit over this; the world average was 2,280. As only about 40 percent of Tamil Nadu's area sowed is also irrigated, some part of the rice and practically all of the other food grains are grown under rainfed and dry-land conditions. The overall food grain yield for the state at the time of this study was about 1,300 kilograms per hectare, considerably below the 1,800 plus of Punjab, which has 70 percent irrigation of its sowed area, but still second among the states. The all-India average for food grain yields in 1973-1974 was about 870 kilograms per hectare (the all-India area irrigated was about 22 percent).[36] In sum, Tamil Nadu has been one of the most receptive of all the states to the marketing and consumption of agriculture inputs, especially fertilizer.

In 1971, both in the country as a whole and in Tamil Nadu, the Green Revolution seemed to hold out the tantalizing hope that final solutions for the world's age-old food problems might be at hand. Subsequent to this high point is an untoward sequel, a less optimistic story that stems from important new developments linked to the so-called oil crisis. We shall analyze this set of developments in detail in Chapter 5. First, however, it is meaningful to look at the excitement of this Green Revolution through the eyes of those who saw it in the first years of the 1970s.

Scattered among all the people involved in the various agricultural inputs are certain individuals whose functional responsibilities lie at the nexus, and therefore whose efforts have a greater effect on change than others do. Some of these individuals have the personal qualities and mentality to become change agents, and to carry this change mentality to fruition with farmers and other persons. There are likewise functions on the output side that are particularly critical—certain dimensions of the processing functions, particularly important points in the distribution chain. Here, too, if one can identify the individuals holding positions at the critical junctures and identify the most change-oriented among them, once again an innovative change mentality may be fostered. The remainder of this book concentrates on the process of identifying the critical functions on both the input and the output side of agriculture, on further identifying the individuals within these critical functions who appear to have potential for a change-agent mentality, and on working with these individuals to heighten their knowledge and abilities with regard to this special talent.

Two particularly important actors on the stage of Indian rural development will occupy us. With fertilizer becoming a particularly critical part of the input package, the fertilizer distributor himself, handling both this commodity and a number of other modernizing inputs—pesticides, feeds, contract agricultural services, and the like—has been at the center. By his efforts in selling combinations of inputs he can readily be the catalyst for development. Likewise, on the output side, the processors of primary agricultural products have special impact. The village environments of this book are scattered through two states in South India. This is predominantly rice country, and rice milling is the crucial processing stage in the rice systems of the world. If the rice miller is innovative and makes use of modern equipment and methods, the ratio of output to unmilled input will be greater and the quantity of both rice and rice by-products more substantial. If he is not innovative, serious losses will occur despite production increases achieved from new, high-yielding strains of rice. The next chapter considers the fertilizer distributor; the chapter following it has a major section on the rice miller.

3

The Fertilizer Distributor as Change Agent

The sharp change in direction in fertilizer policy in India as a result of the Sivaraman Committee report had a ripple effect in the states. In Tamil Nadu it was a tilt toward private enterprise. By the late 1960s private-sector companies dominated distribution all through South India. (Only one public-sector company, in Kerala, was a significant competitor.) The dominant firms were two formerly British trading houses, E. I. D. Parry, Ltd., and Shaw-Wallace and Company, Ltd.

Inasmuch as the Sivaraman recommendations stressed private-enterprise efforts, these two companies were logical choices as the focus of our study of fertilizer distributors. Each year from 1968 through 1973 our group conducted extensive research in Tamil Nadu, interviewing in depth a group of 236 retail distributors who sold for the two companies. We spent many more hours in individual detailed case studies with some of our subjects. In order to put these fertilizer distributors in the context of the total agricultural picture, we spent substantial time with two other groups of South Indian businessmen — a group of rice millers and one of village businessmen, in a diversified sample of representative village business activities. For additional perspective, we interviewed some small-scale manufacturers in a suburban industrial estate, as well as a group of small-town textile and engine company executives. These fertilizer distributors and their counterparts in other businesses combine to give some special insight into small-town and rural change, and especially into the businessman as a village entrepreneur.

Here in Chapter 3 we present our largest sample, in order to generalize about fertilizer distribution over the whole state. Our sample comprised 180 distributors in three districts: South Arcot, Tanjore, and Coimbatore. (An intensive sample of 56 distributors in one *taluk,* which is an administrative subdivision of a district, will be analyzed in the next chapter.) For 142 of these men we have a complete set of performance data, and a number of the generalizations in this chapter stem from this sample size of 142. The samples are described in more detail in Appendix A. For this interviewing we devised a standard questionnaire to elicit information about the following:

The founding of the firm and the founder;

The presence or absence of innovations after the founding of the firm (in effect, the "stages of growth"), as well as further questions concerning the outlook for future innovations;

Facts about the entrepreneur;

Information flows;

Statistical and performance data on the firm;

Attitudinal and behavioral questions on a wide variety of topics, directed at the entrepreneur himself.

The questionnaire was administered personally to all 236 people during the summer of 1971 by my two senior Indian research associates and a trained team of five young graduates from Madras Christian College, each fluent in English and Tamil. In addition, during this summer and again in the summer of 1973, a number of case study interviews were conducted in considerable depth. Contact with these distributors totaled approximately 500 hours.

Who is a "typical" distributor? Our large sample allows us to generalize. The average man is forty years old, married, with 3.2 children. Nine out of ten are Hindus; Muslims make up the bulk of the remainder with a scattering of Jains (no Christians). More than half are either the only son or the first son, a higher percentage than among the rice millers, for example. More than one-third are from the two business castes, the Chettiar and the Mudaliar.[1] Just under one-third are Brahmin and other high-caste groups and approximately the same number are from predominantly agricultural castes and from the "scheduled" and untouchable castes. The distributors' average education is just over six years; most of them are concerned about this and express the feeling that they are undereducated for the job—that a high school education really is needed. The language facility of our distributors is surprising—generally they have at least speaking knowledge of one of the other Dravidian languages and of English.

Over half of the distributors were born in villages of under 2,000 population, and over two-thirds of them have remained either in their original village or in a small town of under 15,000. Only a few have ever lived out of their own district, and the average distributors interviewed had visited only two and a half other states in their entire lifetimes (about 5 percent have been out of the country). Just over half of their fathers are or were agriculturalists, almost always owner-cultivators; the others are or were small-town businessmen such as provision merchants or paddy dealers (only a few money lenders).

Starting the Fertilizer Distributorship

Although many of our respondents were businessmen before going into fertilizers, the fertilizer distributorships are truly new businesses—more than 50 percent of the firms in our sample are less than seven years old. The case history of one of the older distributorships will help explain why their numbers remained so low over these years.

Mr. *A* is today one of the most important dealers in a district near Madras city. He is a Marwari; his father emigrated from Rajasthan in 1919. The father was a money lender and ran a pawn shop. In 1947, at the age of seventeen, Mr. *A* took over the business when his father suddenly died. A year later two other businessmen in his town formed the first fertilizer distribution company in this area of the district, and Mr. *A* acted as commission agent for them. In 1952 Mr. *A* bought the company and thereby obtained a monopoly of the trade in the entire taluk. His monopolistic pricing policies and credit practices soon came under attack from the government in power, and in 1957 it suspended his exclusive license and appointed two more distributors for the taluk. Finally, in 1959, his license was canceled altogether and given to a cooperative society, as it had now become the government's policy to hand over licenses to the cooperatives whenever a particular area came under the newly established Block Development Scheme. In 1961 government antipathy toward the private sector eased somewhat; Mr. *A* was appointed distributor for one of the private fertilizer companies in his taluk and opened a main store and three branches. Again fortune proved fickle. Two years later this license also was canceled, and he was given a much more limited license that did not include any fertilizer from government sources. In 1966 he began the promotion of a cattle feed manufacturing unit, set up as a cooperative with some government aid. Finally, the following year, he was reappointed distributor for government fertilizer, but in 1968 a change of government brought general elections. He was removed from the cattle feed manufacturing unit and arrested on the charge of hoarding fertilizers and selling them at black-market prices. This charge, too, was eventually disproved; by 1969 he had his private distributorship back and again became centrally involved in the cattle feed manufacturing unit. The advent of the Green Revolution and the growing importance of private fertilizers soon made him one of the strongest dealers in the entire northern part of the state. Mr. *A*'s travails in the face of such capricious fortunes leave little wonder why so few businessmen in the rural areas were willing to persevere!

The more promising situation for the private dealer in the late 1960s, with at least acquiescence on the part of the government, soon led to many new dealerships. If one asks what qualities are needed in these distributors who emerged, several quickly come to mind. First, the distributor is serving the cultivator and should know something about farming. Second, the process involves marketing: goods are physically moved into the distributor's shop and have to be stored; sales effort is needed to market the product. Undoubtedly there will be strong pressures for extending credit to the cultivators—the financial dimension is a critical one. Finally, something much more profound will be required, for this man is at the center of rural economic development and change.

We wondered if the fertilizer distributor saw himself in this light—really considered himself an innovator when he founded his firm. So we asked a number of questions about his self-image. Virtually no one envisioned himself initially as a change agent. Rather, the distributors saw themselves as no different from their competitors already in the field. On the other hand, they seemed to have a well-formulated image of these competitors. When asked which competitor firm was run most ably, most of the distributors had ready answers and were able to describe exactly why—often with remarkably pungent comments about the other man's strengths and foibles. We received blunt comments in response to our question, "Do you think that people in the state show any special strengths or weaknesses as regards business?" One dealer who had migrated from the north said, "The people in this state are not so sharp at business. They are too good, very pious and religious minded. The people are honest. Tamil Nadu is a place for making good profit for the Rajasthanis." Another dealer commented, "The people here are hardworking but not business minded." Many of the distributors emphasized the inability of their business colleagues to look to the long run and to take any form of risk. The wide-ranging perceptiveness in these analytical comments about peers illustrates again the vast storehouse of native wisdom that village entrepreneurs always seem to have. The trouble is that this information is shared only incompletely, with periods of inattention, noncomprehension, and suspicion.

If the distributors' self-image was mundane, so too it seemed that the fertilizer manufacturing companies did not comprehend fully the implications of the distributors' role. We asked company officials, "What kind of a businessman makes the best distributor?" One executive answered: "My first choice would either be a rice miller, a commission agent, or a paddy broker. My second choice—several steps below—would be a kerosene agent. If I still did not have my dealer, I would look for a money lender, and I suppose my fourth choice would be a provision merchant. At the bottom—I would only pick one if I had to—would be an agriculturalist himself. I do feel that my second, third, and fourth choices are much too oriented toward the town business life and not enough toward farming, though." A number of other corporate officials articulated much the same order of choice.

Yet when it came to actually picking the distributor, the eventual choices were weighted heavily toward the fourth and fifth categories of the executive above—agriculturalists and grocery and provision dealers were far and away the two largest categories. Paddy merchants and other grain dealers were next, far below the first two groups. Then there were scatterings of many other professions and trades. In fact, the sum total gave a panorama of village and small-town business: bamboo and nail merchants; betel nut sellers; owners of piece goods emporia; jewelry shop operators; petrol, oil, and kerosene dealers; cement sellers, cotton seed merchants; tailors; cycle shop operators; chemists (druggists); and even one toddy shop (liquor shop) operator. (One can see the amazing range of possibilities for businesses by looking down the streets of Cheyyar, a typical South Indian town, charted in Figure 2.)

The choice of so many agriculturalists as dealers mirrored the income distribution patterns and the relative power base of the farmers. A great many of these dealers were relatively wealthy, large-scale farmers, who bought enough fertilizer themselves to justify pressing the company for quantity discounts that matched the price paid by any other dealer. Company sales executives, in turn, exhorted these farmers to take on an actual distributorship and recommended that the farmer sell to his immediate neighbors. The effect was to place all the farmers under the umbrella of "buying at wholesale," but not to implant much of a distributorship mentality in the rich farmer who initiated the process.

There are overtones of this choice by default in the case of the provision merchants also. These individuals run a general store and sell a wide variety of consumer products, most in bulk in tins and jars. Generally they have small godowns, or warehouses. The cultivators and laborers from the area come into the village on market days (and on many other days) to purchase their necessary provisions. Sales are generally in small amounts and credit is often extended, at very high interest rates of 24 to 36 percent. Thus, if fertilizer is regarded as another provision, to be purchased weekly along with salt and condiments, the provision merchant would seem to be the logical person in whom to vest the distributorship.

A closer scrutiny of the mentality of the provision merchant, however, discloses essentially a "sedentary peddler" behavior. There is no particular expertise implied in the products he has sold as a shopkeeper, and therefore there is no need for his own expertise in regard to their usage. How much does one need to know about salt technology to sell salt? Now he takes on a truly complicated product, one that is very often newer to him than to his customers. Until recently the farmer has not looked to the fertilizer distributor as his main source of technical information. In a 1971 study of fertilizer distribution in South India, conducted by the National Council of Applied Economic Research (NCAER), it was evident that while cultivators increasingly favored dealing with private fertilizer distributors, the reasons lay in better geographic locations, quicker service, better credit terms, and the like. Other recent surveys corroborate the peripheral role of the fertilizer distributor as a technical adviser. In a survey of more than five hundred farmers conducted by Madras Christian College in 1970, over 90 percent of the fertilizer distributors said

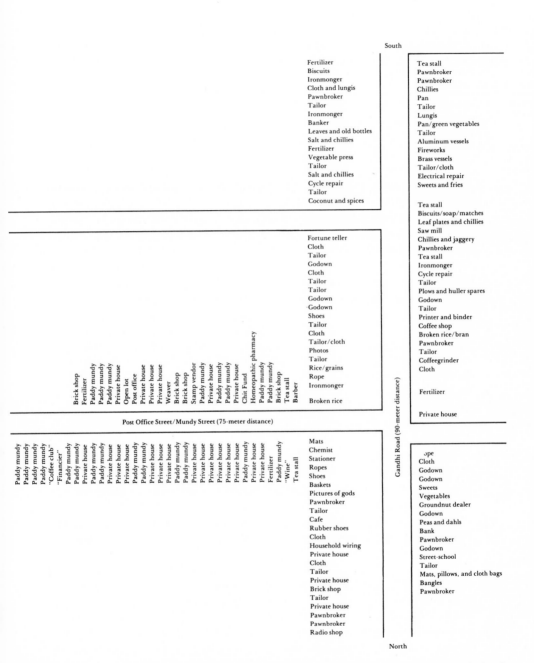

FIGURE 2   Map of the central business district of Cheyyar, North Arcot district (population in 1971 = 19,274), surveyed by Barbara Harriss, August 13, 1973.

that they "gave technical advice," but only 2 percent of the farmers preferred the private dealer mainly for this reason.[2]

The complexities of this technical advice are substantial, given the demands imposed by the new miracle seeds. If the distributor is to be effective, he must know the chemistry and the technology of fertilizers, as well as of pesticides. He must understand soil management and crop rotation and be able to provide the necessary services involved—particularly soil testing. These skills cannot be assimilated overnight.

The NCAER study also confirms the surmises of many other analysts, that manufacturers tend to pick their dealers overwhelmingly on the basis of financial soundness. Apparently the companies have a general impression that in the final analysis the volume of sales will depend upon the ability of the dealers to advance credit to the farmers. Other assets like past experience and ability to render agronomic services are passed over.

It is clear that with the rapid increase in the number of dealerships in the years 1969 to 1973 some of these dealers had been appointed indiscriminately, without proper assessment of their capabilities. Many people came forward to pick up distributorships, particularly in those years when fertilizer was in high demand. Frequently fertilizer trade was adopted as a secondary source of income, and the corollary was often a lack of insight into the real problems of fertilizer use by small farmers. This tendency has worsened since the oil crisis. With demand greatly exceeding supply, many dealers have attempted to license multiple outlets by using their wives and children as fronts. Then the already swollen totals are distended further by opportunistic small retailers dealing entirely with black-market fertilizer as a "diversification" of their regular trade.

There are a few dealers who have succeeded in establishing an image for the products that they sell and who have applied aggressive sales promotion in a most effective way. These men generally have a sound knowledge of the region in which they operate and maintain personal contacts with the farmers. Naturally, they are in great demand; manufacturers compete aggressively in offering incentives to induce them to accept their own company agencies. Despite manufacturers' efforts to develop exclusive dealerships, a substantial percentage of all dealers handle more than one brand. This percentage is particularly high among the more productive dealers. (In one survey it was found that more than 80 percent of the dealers sold more than one brand; one dealer handled products of seven different fertilizer companies.) When a marketer insists on an exclusive dealership, dealers often circumvent the requirements by maintaining various dealerships on the same premises but under different names of their family members. The concept of "exclusive dealership" has therefore eroded during periods of increased competitive behavior.

Some of the manufacturers have tried to counteract these twin problems of lack of expertise and eroding loyalty by giving the distributors technical information and by scheduling frequent visits from company sales personnel. One of the two large companies categorizes its dealers in the following way. An *A* dealer, selling over 200 tons of fertilizer per year, would be visited on alternate days. A *B* dealer, selling over 150 tons, would be visited every four days. A *C* dealer with 100 tons or more, would be visited once a week, and a *D* dealer, who might sell 50 tons per year, would be visited once a month. If the provision dealer has a trading area of some importance and does not have too much competition in fertilizers, then he may well be in one of the first two categories and would get technical backup from the company on a reasonably regular basis.

The *A* dealer, who sells upward of 200 tons per year, can make fertilizer sales alone close to a full-time operation. Many fertilizer distributorships in Tamil Nadu are run in conjunction with previously existing operations. Sometimes the new product drives out the old, and fertilizer becomes a full-time business in its own right. To gain a better understanding of this transition, we need to see the full picture of what a fertilizer distributorship can involve.

The Business Behavior of Fertilizer Distributors

Once launched into business and faced with the daily pressures of business life, the distributors soon exhibited varying performance patterns. By careful questioning, with surprisingly frank responses from the distributors, we were able to develop some key performance measures — total sales level, profit level, growth, physical volume (the actual tonnage sold), employee level, and statistics relating to new-product and new-function expansion within the firm. In addition we queried the distributors about their involvement in other endeavors beyond the distributorship itself.

In all of these performance measures there was substantial variability among the dealers, with some exhibiting high performance, others low. Furthermore, there were statistically significant correlations between these performance measures and other characteristics of the distributors — their biodata and their behavioral and attitudinal outlooks.

Some of the constraints and opportunities confronting a distributor are actually beyond his individual control. Two such environmental variables stand out as potentially important — caste and regional irrigation patterns (whether the distributorship is in an assured-water or a rainfed area).

South India tends to preserve many of its ancient and revered traditions, and caste is no exception. Particularly in small-town and rural South India, caste is always a known quality and almost without exception a potent constraint. We were fortunate in being able to obtain both main caste and particular subcaste (community) for 232 of our 236 fertilizer distributors. (Several did caution our interviewers that "caste is no longer allowed," but still were willing to tell us the community from which they came.) These were the castes in our fertilizer samples:

Chettiar	63
Gounder	47
Mudaliar	22
Pillai	17
Reddiar	14
Naidu	11
Brahmin	8
Other Hindu castes (15 different)	30
Muslim	20
Total	232

We were interested in a specific question with regard to caste, namely, does it affect the performance of various change agents? In other words, can one see distinctions among the performance variables of a fertilizer distributor— new products taken on, branches opened, firms started, and so on—that are found with higher incidence among one caste than another? To answer this question, we grouped the several dozen castes represented in this large sample into three separate combinations recommended to us by a number of South Indian businessmen, government officials, and other experts.[3] We decided to develop two separate groupings, or runs, of all the Hindu castes, and a four-group combination that included the Muslim group:

Run 1

(a) Chettiar and Brahmin
(b) Pillai, Naidu, Reddiar, and other
(c) Gounder and Mudaliar

Run 2

(a) "Business castes" (Chettiar, Mudaliar)
(b) "Agricultural castes" (Gounder, Pillai, Reddiar)
(c) Other caste groups

Run 3

(a) Chettiar and Brahmin
(b) Pillai, Naidu, Reddiar, and other
(c) Gounder and Mudaliar
(d) Muslim

We used discriminant analysis to test whether any of these groupings showed statistically significant differences on any aspect of performance. A few of the univariate one-way anovas (analyses of variance) are of statistical significance, but these are the expected ones. For example, urbanness can be clearly distinguished by caste. Likewise, certain ways of treating information vary by caste—a finding that is not quite so readily explainable. However, on overall discrimination on the nine key performance variables and nine other important biodata and behavioral-attitudinal variables, there is no association of statistical significance in run 1, run 2, or run 3. $F_{(36,214)} = 1.58$ and $F_{(36,240)} = 1.46$ for the three Hindu castes alone; $F_{(54,361)} = 1.50$ for the three Hindu castes and the Muslim group. In sum, caste does not seem to be related importantly to performance.

The second environmental dimension we explored was the presence or absence of assured irrigation in the area surrounding the dealer. Again we used discriminant analysis and split the dealers into three basic groups—those in an area dominated by assured-water lands, a second group that had some assured water along with substantial rainfed areas, and a third group in predominantly rainfed areas.[4] Here discriminant analysis turned up some intimations of statistically significant differences. $F_{(36,244)} = 2.64$ for overall discrimination on eighteen variables. The univariate one-way anovas particularly show that there were fewer efforts toward diversification in the dry-farming situation. This is an important association that we shall analyze in detail in the next chapter. Still, as we look down the other one-way anovas, we conclude that most of the "outside" differences both for caste and for irrigation patterns are minor in nature—that the main differentiations in performance lie within a set of factors internal to the firm and the specific actions of its people.

We probed the distributors in depth about their daily patterns of business behavior. We asked them what they read, to whom they talked, where they traveled, what they did outside the firm, what problems they faced at the moment, what plans they had for the future. We then analyzed these data by multivariate analysis.

From this analysis a set of patterns surfaces. The associations are strong in some cases, weaker in others. Field data of this nature are never neat and clean; they require us to make some assumptions in filling gaps and reconciling inconsistencies. We have made particular use of principal-component analysis. Our methodology and our assumptions and necessary compromises are elaborated in Appendix A.

When we put all this together, we catch glimmers of several subsets of distributors within the overall sample, each manifesting a different behavior and ending up with a different performance. We can see this most clearly by moving directly to some of the key questions of the study, those involving the process of innovation.

Stages of Growth in a Fertilizer Distributorship

Business growth very often takes place in discontinuous spurts. Thus one can usually identify discrete stages of growth. Often it is a large Schumpeterian innovation that provides the critical mass to make the spurt possible. We argued in Chapter 1 that in the rural environment of the less developed world these spurts may be viewed as imitative by developed-world standards but still be highly entrepreneurial. We called these steps meta-innovations. And these innovations, great and small, are the hallmarks of the change agent. Consequently, it is important to understand the growth process in fertilizer distribution, for its technology has a pattern with clearly definable incremental changes.

If the distributorship is a private one, generally the distributor will start out selling only one company's brands. This may not last very long, brand loyalty being notoriously weak. Particularly if it is a buyer's market, the distributor may be in a position to give up one brand or sell two competitive brands at the same time. Manufacturing companies naturally want to discourage this and try very hard to maintain their exclusive dealership concepts. But one of the very early stages in the development of a distributorship may well be the taking on of an alternative brand of fertilizer in addition to or in the place of the starting brand. In early months the distributor probably will stock superphosphate and urea and perhaps also carry a small quantity of the newer complexes. If the distributor is primarily serving only himself and his friends, his business may remain static over many more months — or may in fact dwindle down as other competitors come into the area.

Let us assume a rise in demand, and enough of an increase in supply to fulfill a significant portion of this demand. This describes the pattern in the early Green Revolution days of 1969 and 1970. As knowledge of the potency of fertilizer applications began to permeate among the cultivators in the districts, the sales of many of the distributors rose rather sharply. The D dealer at, say, 53 tons per year, might suddenly find his sales jumping to a yearly figure of 100 or 150 tons.

Two things now are likely. First, as fertilizer looms larger in his thinking, the distributor may diversify his product line, taking on more of the various fertilizer mixtures and compounds. In effect, he comes closer to a full line of fertilizers. Second, he will probably see the possibilities of adding other agricultural inputs. Cattle feed, poultry feed, and safety fuses for well digging are typical new lines. Pesticides are likely to be available from the manufacturer, and so small quantities of these may be sold. Though most of the cultivators' seeds are purchased from the National Seeds Corporation, there are opportunities for selling cotton seeds and other local varieties. All of these are direct agricultural inputs; the distributor may also take on closely related products used by the cultivator — cement, kerosene, and the like. Alternatively, or perhaps in addition, he may become involved in the processing side of agriculture — may open a rice mill or an oil cake operation, or may become involved in the output side as a betel nut seller, a groundnut seller, or a sugar middleman. Many of the distributors in our survey also began new retail businesses — general goods and provisions stores, cosmetics, cloth retailing, pipes and electrical goods, aerated waters, ropes, soaps, and even toddy. Only a few were already money lenders, or became money lenders after starting the fertilizer distributorship.

Characteristic of all these new products and related activities is ease of entry. For many of the products sold in a village, taking on a distributorship is not a very complex decision. "Soap is soap" goes the hoary village tautology. But there are, in addition, some products and services that *do* involve major commitments of capital and/or of technology. Selling and servicing pump sets for irrigation is a rather more difficult proposition than taking on the sale of soap. Likewise, selling and servicing agricultural implements is one of the major stages. One of the new technologies that appears most frequently is the purchase by the distributor of sprayers for the application of pesticides. Typically, he will keep control of the sprayer and provide a contractual spraying service for the cultivator. A few distributors have made the great capital commitment — in the range of 25,000 rupees (equivalent to just under $3,000 in the early 1970s) — of purchasing a tractor for hire by cultivators.[5]

The distributor has two alternatives for the hire of such equipment. He may choose to have the machines available at his shop, where the cultivator can come to rent one and take it away for a contract period, paying for it upon return and providing his own labor. Or the distributor may choose to have his own man travel to the cultivator's plot and do the application work direct. If the latter system is employed, it too demands a major input in technology. The dealer now not only assumes responsibility for providing the equipment, but is required also to become a manager and a scheduler. He probably must visit the field more often, and his orientation shifts from that of a seller of products to that of a provider of products *and* services.

Adding the new employee is another critical step. The new man may work only part time — for example, a pesticide sprayer — or the dealer may employ him as an assistant for a fuller range of responsibilities. The new man may become the dealer's field salesman. Alternatively, he may remain at the distributor's base while the distributor himself goes into the field for selling. There is a major conceptual difference between the one-man shop and the two-man shop.

There is another important variation on the two-man basis—the practice of setting up subdealers in nearby villages. In effect, a branch is opened and the dealer also becomes a middleman wholesaler. This has been a time-honored way for a dealer to bring one or more of his sons into the business. By deputing a son to another village for a small branch operation, the distributor is attaining several goals. Not only is he training his son for eventual takeover of the business, he is also giving him an autonomy, albeit of a modest sort, out of the physical sight of the father. South Indian farmers, however, are often grudging in their delegation of authority. More than once in our field work we were told by sons of their frustration at not "being given the key"—not being able literally to open the doors of the father's shop, even on holidays. Family squabbles and tensions had another effect here: sometimes distributorships were split up among various members of the family after a family argument, each faction taking one of the branches.

Another important stage of development may eventually come—door delivery of fertilizers and other products. Up to the present, few dealers have provided this service. We have explained that the cultivator typically brings his bullock cart to the village or town where the fertilizer distributorship is located and himself transports the fertilizer back to his farm. Only a few fertilizer distributors ever send out their own bullock carts. Most cultivators only buy a few fifty-kilogram bags at any particular time, so it would clearly be unrealistic to use one of the typical Indian seven-ton trucks for this delivery. Smaller-size delivery trucks are not yet widely used in rural India. Some dealers who own a tractor *and* a rubber-tired wagon might be able to contemplate motorized delivery. Often the condition of the roads to the village is so bad as to make it impractical, given the heavy capital and maintenance costs. Still, door delivery is the logical companion to field selling. One large-scale dealer in Pondicherry, selling over 500 metric tons a year, sends men out on motorcycles for sales contact. One can readily imagine some larger version of the cycle being used by this same person as a delivery vehicle. Door delivery may well be a live option in the near future.

The Package of Practices Concept

Whatever the stages of development of the distributor, there is a subtle psychological point at which the dealer may shift from being a sedentary, passive purveyor of a product to a service-oriented consultant to the farmer. The former attitude all too frequently characterized the mentality of both manufacturer and seller in the early days of fertilizer shortage and in the seller's market in the middle and late 1960s. Sadly, it is probably to be expected that whenever there is an overwhelmingly seller-dominated market, there will be this "take it or leave it" attitude on the part of all concerned with the selling side.

But there have been recent periods where vastly increased supply caused a reversal. In the years 1969 to 1972 fertilizer manufacturers all began to preach the service mentality, and some of them followed through on it to a degree. Just about all the companies developed in these years some printed literature that went beyond the promotional and became supportive technical information. More and more frequently, the regional sales representatives were trained for at least rudimentary technical consulting skills, and the larger companies began to do more extensive field experiments in conjunction with trained agronomists from the home office. Some companies stood ready to make soil tests for the customers of their individual dealers—an important need, and one just beginning to filter into the consciousness of most cultivators. Thus the fertilizer distributor, backed by the services of the company (or companies) he represents, has increasingly been given at least the opportunity to provide a set of services that has come to be known as a "package of practices" (the concept coming directly from the Ford Foundation's Agricultural Production Team in its 1959 *Report on India's Food Crisis*).[6]

Multivariate Analyses of the Sample Data

It would be unwise to assume that these steps are inevitable, with the fertilizer distributor broadening his mentality in the process of broadening product lines and coming naturally to the package way of life and the service mentality it brings. A favorable outlook for this innovative response by the distributor depends on answers to some additional questions. First, is the process of selection of these men the right one? If so, what should be their relation to the cultivators and how much can they modernize this rather traditional group of people? What is the record of performance to date in innovation by the dealers, particularly in the face of recent black-market patterns? How might the distributors be trained to increase not only their knowledge and understanding of agricultural inputs, but also their abilities to be change agents? Might skilled trainers be able to inculcate these unique entrepreneurial dimensions in these individuals, who would in turn by a process of emulation and "demonstration effect" plant entrepreneurial skills in a whole additional set of their neighboring cultivators, small-town businessmen, and others?[7] Our data provide some answers.

Product Expansion Within the Firm and Without

In our determination of how innovative the distributors in our sample have been within their own firms, the gross totals give us a frame of reference: just over one-half have added one or more product lines; about 10 percent have tried a new function such as contract plowing, door ordering, or spraying; slightly under 15 percent have opened one or more branches. A startling 50 percent of the fertilizer distributors have also been involved at some point in their business life in starting one or more other new firms. This would be a high percentage even among urban Indian entrepreneurs, and seems especially noteworthy given the rural locale of most of the distributors in our sample.

There is a rich variety among each of the four basic forms of product expansion, and multivariate analysis brought out important associations. We constructed four performance variables: the number of *new products* taken on over the life of the firm that could be considered in the same general product line (mainly new varieties of fertilizer); the number of *new functions* adopted over the life of the firm (contract spraying, contract plowing, spray set rentals, and the like); the number of *new branches* for fertilizer distribution opened over the life of the firm; and last, the number of *other firms* started by the fertilizer distributor in his own lifetime. We put these four variables together with a further set of performance variables (relating to sales, profits, growth) and a set of variables quantitatively describing the man himself and his business life (age, education, and other biodata, together with facts that related to his information sources, planning, behavioral and attitudinal views on himself, and so forth). In total, there were approximately fifty variables. First by cluster analysis, then by a process of stepwise regression, we found these variables related in statistical significance to the product expansion variables. We then used principal component analysis, first both to split and to combine some of the existing variables and relate them to the performance variables, then to find those particular sets of variables operating together that gave strong varimax factor loadings. A set of distinct patterns emerges.

Let us look first at the four product expansion variables alone. On the one hand, there is a reasonably strong link between adding products and adding branches — one would expect this, given that the branch generally extends the existing product line. Further, there is a clear link between expansion of existing product lines and formation of outside firms. Thus there seems to be a group of dealers who find their outlets for expansion in existing endeavors, and when they innovate, it is outside the firm rather than inside. There appears to be a completely separate group who emphasize movement into new functions *within* the firm. This second group is the one most likely to open branches. These relationships can be seen in Tables 6 and 7.

We have identified two critically important groups here. The two categories describe two types of dealers, and these two groups of people have a number of other recognizable distinctions — in other words, there is statistically significant association with a number of other key variables. To see the full panoply of these relationships, it is best to take them a step at a time. To help keep score as we move through these several steps, we shall identify at the

TABLE 6   Relations among fertilizer distributors' product expansion variables (correlation coefficients, with $n = 142$).

Variable	Same endeavors	New functions	Branches	Other new firms
Same endeavors	1	.149*	.264***	.288***
New functions	.149*	1	.179**	–
Branches	.264***	.279***	1	–
Other new firms	.288***	–	–	1

*Significant at .05 level, one-tail distribution.
**Significant at .01 level, one-tail distribution.
***Significant at .001 level, one-tail distribution.

beginning of each section the regnant hypotheses in each — those that relate most directly to our paramount concern for understanding entrepreneurship. Here is the first, a result of the material just discussed:

Entrepreneurial hypothesis 1:

There is a group of distributors who find their outlets for expansion in existing endeavors, and when they innovate, it is outside the firm rather than inside. Another group emphasizes movement into new functions within the firm; this group is more likely to open branches.

Modernization: A First Look

Our second hypothesis compares the "modern" distributors with the "traditional" distributors.

Entrepreneurial hypothesis 2:

The "modern" distributors tend to be those who emphasize the combination of expansion in existing endeavors and movement into new firms.

Alex Inkeles and David Smith trenchantly note on the opening text page of their recent important study, *Becoming Modern,* that the operative word *modern* "has many denotations and carries a heavy weight of connotations. It is applied not only to men, but to nations, to political systems, to economies, to cities, to institutions such as schools and hospitals, to housing, to clothes and to manners. Taken literally, the word refers to anything which has more or less recently replaced something in the past which was the accepted way of doing things." There is considerable research evidence to suggest that the

TABLE 7   Factor pattern (after varimax rotation) showing correlations among four original variables of fertilizer distributors' product expansion and two new composite factors.

Variable	1	2	Row SS
Same endeavors	.39	.72	.88
New functions	.75	− .03	.56
Branches	.80	.06	.64
Other new firms	− .18	.86	.77
Column SS	1.39	1.27	2.06

widely used dichotomy of traditional and modern greatly oversimplifies a complex set of relationships. Theorists on modernization have drawn attention to the subtleties involved and have pointed to a considerable modernizing influence among highly traditional people. Several writers on India have pointed to this manifestation; for example, the two Rudolphs have shown how in Indian political affairs modernity and tradition infiltrate and transform each other. And Milton Singer faults Max Weber and others in their assumption that the caste system cannot coexist with modernization: "After much evidence is given to show how flexible and adaptive Hinduism and the caste system have been in the face of economic and social change, the conclusion is illogically drawn that a major precondition for economic development and modernization is the elimination of most traditional institutions, practices, and beliefs."[8] Such conclusions, Singer argues, are "dogmatic, sweeping, bizarre and paradoxical."

Inkeles and others have granted that these inconsistencies and complexities do exist, but nevertheless have been willing to classify behaviors dichotomously and from this process develop explicit modernity scales. In effect, they have adopted the following scenario:

Certain individuals in less developed countries are able to solve their own personal identity crises and in the process they develop strong egos. Their fear and anxiety is reduced and they are able to develop the ability to trust other people. This reduction of fear and anxiety then allows the individual to interact with other persons who are neither members of the extended family nor in the closely knit set of personal friends. This broader interpersonal interaction increases the cooperative orientation of the individual and he or she develops empathy, other-directedness, and reliance on broader societal norms and values. In the process the individual becomes more willing to join both formal and informal groups outside his own immediate purview. This expands the individual's loyalties, and he learns to work for longer-range goals and to consider sacrificing some of his

immediate material gains for the interest of these larger groups. All of this facil-
itates the development of a market economy, community organizations and
other interest groups and in this process of greater participation and institution-
alization the society becomes more complex, differentiated, and generally more
"modern."[9]

Three assumptions are implicit here:

Assumption 1: Key personality traits are either necessary to or at least
greatly facilitate societal modernization and are therefore causal.

Assumption 2: These personality traits are isolatable, and a set of research-
able traits can be put together to form modernity scales.

Assumption 3: This syndrome of attitudes, values, and behaviors, identified in the scales as "modern," will provide a "universal" generalization,
across cultures. Inkeles has made a particularly strong statement on this admittedly controversial point:

> "Strong" institutions would bring about the same changes in individuals regard-
> less of the fact that those institutions have been introduced into diverse societies
> and were staffed by people with distinctive cultural traits . . . Without denying
> the uniqueness of each culture, we wish to affirm the common human nature of
> the people who make up each of these diverse societies. Separate cultures may
> give the individual personalities in each a distinctive content, but we believe
> those cultures do not alter the basic principles which govern the structuring of
> personality of all men. We believe certain panhuman patterns of response per-
> sist in the face of variability and culture content. These transcultural similarities
> in the psychic properties of individuals provide the base for a common response
> to common stimuli . . . The skepticism of anthropological critics notwithstand-
> ing, we believed valid cross-cultural generalization was possible.[10]

Critics have challenged each of these assumptions, commenting variously
that (a) "more modern" personalities, if such things do exist, are more likely
to be effect rather than cause; (b) modernity scales tend to measure mostly
attitudes rather than the more basic values and might be circular in their use
of value-loaded questions that are in turn used as definitions; and (c) individual cultures are more subtle and complex than any single generalization
about them.[11]

These criticisms are penetrating and perceptive, and one must be properly
warned by them. After the arguments are in on all sides of these questions, we
find the basic underlying hypothesis to be believable—that a generalized concept of modernity can be developed and that this concept has research viabil-
ity. Thus we decided to draw on the concepts of Inkeles and others for our
own research; we have taken the leap of faith that modernization is a valid
concept.

A set of beliefs akin to this modern-traditional split seems to be at work on the fertilizer distributors, where significant numbers of them appear to exhibit modernizing attitudes while still operating within a quite traditional context. We established what we believe are viable measures of this modernization. For this, we are much indebted to Professor Inkeles for considerable help with data and advice about possible measures of this important dimension. The six-nation study of Inkeles and his colleagues, conducted in Argentina, Chile, India, Israel, Nigeria, and Pakistan, and involving a battery of over 150 interview items on modernity obtained from 5,500 men, resulted in some well-validated subsets of attitudinal items. These had been analyzed and intercorrelated by the Inkeles team, and several simple overall measures of modernity had been developed by the time we began our first pilot study in 1970.[12] All of these data were freely made available to us, and from this well-researched set of questions we selected twenty-six for inclusion in our pilot questionnaire. Most of these were on one of two composite Inkeles "OM" scales, felt by the Inkeles group to best represent overall modernity. The remaining questions we chose were those relating specifically to questions of innovation and change, but not included on the OM scales.

These twenty-six questions, together with additional attitudinal questions that we had developed concerning risk and planning, made up the 1970 pilot questionnaire administered to the ninety-seven fertilizer distributors and rice millers. We analyzed these items through a nonmetric multidimensional scaling process developed by our colleague, Victor E. McGee.[13] By cross-referencing our results with the intercorrelation patterns of the original Inkeles data, we picked eight of these as our own representative OM scale (these are reproduced in Appendix A). We then constructed a modernization index, based on the combination of these attitudinal questions. These are coded on a traditional-modern dichotomy and thus are subject to the criticism of oversimplifying complex aspects of culture. We use the shorthand variable "modernization" only to identify certain attitudinal tilts of the individuals we interviewed. The fact remains that some of the distributors answered these attitudinal questions in a modern way and others did not. Our index reflects this. It in turn shows statistically significant patterns of association with other variables. We note two in Table 8; after we introduce additional variables, we shall return once again to this modernization scale.

Maximization of Sales, Profits, and Growth

Entrepreneurial hypotheses 3 and 4:

"Sales maximizers" seem less willing to take risk, evidence less modernity, and are those who emphasize new functions within the business.

"Profit maximizers" are more modern, more risk accepting, and more linked with movement into other firms. Growth within the firm is related negatively with profitability.

We are ready now to add those universally recognized measures of performance — sales, profits, and growth. Though all three *are* universal, the underlying rationales of the people bringing them about vary widely, not only across cultures but also within cultures at different time periods. We need to understand the distinctively Indian flavor imparted to all three. Further, we must distinguish the recent period involving the oil crisis (beginning in early 1974), with its attendant massive disruptions of the whole agricultural scene in India, from the immediately preceding four years, during which the promised Green Revolution fruits were beginning to flower in a somewhat more stable environment.

During the first stage of the Green Revolution a complex system of prices existed for the numerous varieties of fertilizer, with many short-term retail price shifts. The distributor operated under a system of commissions that varied by product, with the popular urea and ammonium sulfate carrying small margins, the mixtures carrying considerably larger margins, and the others falling in between. For the mixtures the distributor would generally make a gross margin of Rs. 33 to Rs. 42 per ton (the rupee was about 13.3 cents at that time). The margins on the complexes were comparable. The ammonium sulfates and ammonium phosphates and superphosphates were somewhat lower and the margin on urea the smallest. Special price concessions from the manufacturers were often the rule for certain distributors with large sales, and the convoluted structure of credit to the distributor added a further complication for him in realizing his actual gross profit. Sometimes the distributor was required to take a certain amount of the slower-selling products in order to obtain his share of the high-demand fertilizers.

TABLE 8   Relations among fertilizer distributors' product expansion and modernization variables (correlation coefficients, with $n = 142$).

Variable	Modernization (Broehl OM scale)
Same endeavors	.224**
New functions	—
Branches	—
Other new firms	.213**

**Significant at .01 level, one-tail distribution.

In turn, his selling practices to the cultivator involved all sorts of price shaving, varying credit terms, tie-in arrangements (for example, a cultivator might be told he could have urea only if he also took some complex), rationing to favored customers in peak periods—a whole gamut of often discriminatory, sometimes Machiavellian business strategies. Some dealers had a conscious policy of cutting the already low commissions on the popular brands in their urban headquarters (where there were many competitors), while charging the full commission in branches in smaller villages. In sum, the environment of retail fertilizer sales has been complex; individual decision making makes a real difference—"right" decisions (however one defines them) result in substantial profits, and "wrong" ones in significant losses.

Most dealers operate on a rudimentary single-entry bookkeeping system—or even on a straight cash in-cash out basis—and probably have only a very incomplete understanding of just what their expenses are. One of the fertilizer manufacturers made this estimate in 1973 for a dealer with an annual turnover of 250 tons:[14]

	Rupees per month
Rent (godown and selling premises)	100
Sales assistant's salary	120
Travel expenses	50
Electricity	15
Stationery and telephone	50
Entertainment	20
Total monthly expenses	355
Total annual expenses	4,260
Annual financial charges for bank guarantee for Rs. 20,000 at 1½%	300
Total costs for year	4,560
Cost per ton	18.24

At this time the distributor's margin ranged from about Rs. 33 to Rs. 42 per ton, depending on the particular variety. Thus the net income for the dealer might approximate Rs. 20 per ton, or Rs. 5,000 per year. This does not include other income from sale of pesticides, cattle feed, and the like, but these other-function activities tended to be minor and peripheral during this period. This Rs. 5,000 income would have put the distributor in the upper financial bracket of the village or town. Even the dealer selling only 150 tons would net Rs. 3,000 per year, an income in line with that of the district officers. If the dealer was also a businessman or a cultivator, his total income would probably be substantial by village standards. If a dealer sold only 100 tons per year, his income dropped to Rs. 2,000 a year, low by town or even village standards. So there was a break-even point somewhere around 150 tons, below which it would not pay a man to engage in fertilizer distribution alone. M. S. Randhawa, the eminent vice-chancellor of Punjab Agricultural University, calculated this even more precisely: "For a one man sub-depot, the operator would need to handle 152.4 tonnes of fertilizer in a year to earn a reasonable amount of commission (we assume Rs. 250 per month)."[15] There were many dealers below this 150-ton level—the average in our largest sample was 138—so it is clear that many of these dealers were looking upon fertilizer distribution as a secondary, probably seasonal, business, a way of supplementing their income. On the other hand, dealers at 250 tons or above could see the fertilizer business as a lucrative full-time endeavor.

There is great secrecy in India about both sales and profits. Deeply ingrained in the minds of an impoverished consuming class is an implacable antipathy toward "profiteers." Many analysts have commented that Indian businessmen, particularly the retail merchants, manifest a "subsistence-type" business orientation; that is, they seem to be content with a small profit as long as it covers their subsistence needs, rather than risk their capital in what might be potentially more profitable, but probably more risky, business ventures. The merchant becomes fearful of committing his capital to any single product or single enterprise and prefers instead to carry small quantities of a highly varied set of products.

This same loss-minimization rationale is widespread among subsistence farmers in developing countries, and some recent critics of the Green Revolution have pointed to it as being potentially in conflict with the use of the high-yielding seeds. One commentator put it this way:

> The yields of a peasant's crop are very low but so is the risk: His field, in which he usually grows many varieties and several different crops, nearly always produces something, however bad the pests or weather. The peasant farmer's first goal is not to maximize his profits; it is to minimize his risks. Yet Green Revolution crops perform to meet the Western commercial criteria of large production and high profits. They are bred and designed to be grown as monocultures and in monocrops, the whole field being planted to the same single variety of the same crop.[16]

This seems to stereotype as too starkly different the choice between traditional and high-yield varieties of grains. Although these imputations of conservative cultivator mentality are well taken, they have been overdrawn. The surprisingly rapid adoption of the high-yielding varieties in the developing world (for example, dwarf wheat in Punjab) certainly challenged some of the conventional wisdom about the presumed rigidity of the peasant farmer. On the other hand, the embryonic move back toward the traditional varieties in the face of the oil crisis equally challenges some of the more simplistic claims for the Green Revolution.

All too many times a companion practice of loss minimization has been adulteration, cheating, or black-marketeering. Richard G. Fox in his classic study of business practices in a North Indian market town summed it up this way:

> Thus the profit motive among the local merchants and particularly Baniyas takes an involuted form of a high rate of savings and business chicanery rather than an outward manifestation in large business investment and expansion. This does not mean that given a black market situation, the merchant will not maximize his profits, will not charge "all the market will bear." Indeed, it is precisely only this sort of situation which the merchant anticipates as a source of profit and toward which he channels his business energy. He views his daily business profit as providing for his bare subsistence in times of black market or scarcity. He therefore is satisfied with a profit set at a minimal level.[17]

Given the pervasive feeling among Indian peasants that this summary precisely describes the merchant's attitudes, it is easy to understand why the Indian businessman will instinctively attempt to hide or at least downgrade his profits. It is part of the ancient fear in small-town and rural India of looking too personally ostentatious. (For example, there is a practice in the building and construction industry, probably going far back into antiquity, of hanging a dilapidated effigy of a human figure from the front of a new building to show symbolically that the owners really are not as wealthy as the new building seems to imply!)

This preoccupation with secrecy is accentuated by an ingrained fear of "the government." In times of hoarding and black-marketeering in the recent past, the central government and/or the state governments frequently responded by swooping down on the alleged hoarders, seizing stocks of goods (especially foodstuffs), and in the process fining and often jailing the presumed culprits, the businessmen. Even in more normal times the businessman tends to operate under a constant fear of tax collectors and possible government exactions.

Thus the Western concept of long-run profit maximization is far distant conceptually from the small-town Baniya merchant whom Fox describes, or indeed, from a considerable portion of the small-town and rural South Indian businessmen. The short run dominates — and it is almost so short as to be just the particular moment. Probably the Baniya merchants in the town studied by Fox would agree with Lord Keynes' statement that "in the long run we are all dead."

There are some countertrends. The larger Indian business houses (at least a significantly growing portion of them) are embracing more explicitly the ideology of gearing business practices to the longer run. Were we to ask an average Indian city dweller which firms these were, we would find surprising unanimity — the more responsible, ethical firms are well known. If the present world economic convolutions can be harnessed, and Indian business life return to something resembling normal times, this modest trend toward socially responsible businesses may grow. On the other hand, if economic tensions and inflationary pressures stemming from the oil crisis continue, the temptation for hoarding, black-marketeering, and other sharp business practices, and the concomitant heavy-handed government response, will probably set this movement backward.

Concepts of profit maximization will pervade the remainder of our analysis. When we use the term, it is in its Western sense of long-run profit maximization. We feel that this is a legitimate way to look at profit maximization in an Indian context, given two cardinal assumptions: first, that the heightened interest in responsible business behavior on the part of both Indian businessmen and Indian government administrators continues, and second, that inflation and instability stemming from the oil crisis can be somehow neutralized. Long-run profit maximization can readily be shown to be good business practice for the short run, provided the long run can be seen and planned for in a stable way. We hope such vision will characterize India's (and the world's) future.

Our analysis centers on the private sector, and therefore we discuss profit in its private-enterprise sense. Still, we are really talking of profit maximization in its more deeply based frame of optimization. Government corporations, too, are striving for profit in the sense we use it here. Cooperatives need a profit-maximizing mentality, even though profit per se is not part of the rubric of cooperation. *All* business institutions may be thought of as optimizers of "long-run profits," even though the rationales of their particular organizational forms may vary widely.

We were fortunate in that we received surprisingly good cooperation on our queries about sales and profits, in spite of the widespread Indian patterns of secrecy and suspicion. Had we asked the dealers for explicit rupee figures, probably we would have faced the same evasiveness noted by so many observers. Instead, we asked the dealers to place their firm's sales and profits at a particular level in a six-category interval scale, for each of three years (1969, 1970, 1971). The interval scales were constructed so that the profit levels were 10 percent of sales levels, and thus a comparison allowed a reasonable approximation of profitability. In addition, we asked the dealers for their tonnage for each of the three years. We were able to cross-check their statements of tons sold with company figures of fertilizers sold *to* them. The two sets of figures correlated surprisingly well — the distributors, apparently not threatened by statistics on physical volume, gave us straightforward responses. By a careful process of reconstruction we were able to check the sales levels; the distributors tended toward understatement but this did not significantly alter their positions on the interval scale. Likewise, we drew upon the manufacturers' field representatives for corroboration of relative profitability. The latter process, although more subjective than that used for sales, again confirmed the interval scale statements on profit levels. With reasonably dependable physical tonnage figures for those consecutive years, we were able to construct simple growth curves. Even though all of these calculations are imprecise, nevertheless we feel that all three indices are valid measures of the distributors' performance for these three years. Significant patterns of association with other variables ensue from this set of performance figures.

At this point, we wish to adopt two key working definitions and make explicitly clear just what we are and are not saying, for we shall be referring to these terms throughout the remainder of this chapter. First, those with the highest sales levels are defined as "sales maximizers." Patently, this is a simplification — high sales level does not necessarily go hand in hand with high motivation for sales. The natural counterpoise to sales maximizing is profit maximizing; thus our second key definition is for those with the highest levels of profit — the "profit maximizers." Again, taking profit *level* alone does not automatically define a motivation for a profit-maximizing decision. To make this more precise, we constructed a "profitability" variable by taking the residuals between sales levels and profit levels and plotting them. The differences in variance are small, but there are statistically significant relationships between this profitability variable and other important performance, behavioral, and attitudinal variables. To repeat, there are no behavioral implications in the definitions per se of sales level, profit level, and profitability — not *until* we make inferences about the three variables as they link in statistically significant ways with other variables that carry behavioral and attitudinal connotations.

We begin by looking at the relation between sales level, profit level, profitability, the four product-expression variables just analyzed, and a set of other important variables. Table 9 is a three-vector factor-analysis solution involving seven performance variables. Table 10 shows some important correlations between sales and profit and other important variables.

From these associations we draw some preliminary inferences, some tentative insights that we shall check further with later associations before general-

TABLE 9   Factor pattern (after varimax rotation) showing correlations among seven original variables of fertilizer distributors' performance and three new composite factors.

Variable	1	2	3	Row SS
Same endeavors	.42	.64	−.20	.63
New functions	.67	−.15	−.02	.47
Branches	.79	.02	.24	.69
Other firms	−.14	.82	.11	.70
Sales	.63	.30	−.25	.55
Profitability	.09	.34	.71	.63
Growth	.08	.27	−.66	.51
Column SS	1.68	1.38	1.11	4.17

izing from them. The patterns seem to point to the fact that the sales max-imizers seem less willing to take risk, evidence less modernity on our scale, and tend to be the group that not only is maximizing sales in the various fertilizers but also is carrying through the newer functions within the business. The group that we can distinguish by their profit levels and profitability residuals as being profit maximizers are more modern, more risk accepting — and ap-parently *less* involved in moving into newer functions *within* the business. Rather, they seem to be linked more directly with movements into other firms. Growth had a modest positive relation to sales level but, as the factor analysis showed, its most direct relationship is a negative one with profita-bility, a not uncommon situation for a growing company.

Why does the profit maximizer not wish to innovate *within* the firm? There

TABLE 10   Relations among fertilizer distributors' sales and profits measures and other key variables (correlation coefficients, with $n = 142$).

Variable	Sales level	Profit level	Profit-ability
Education	.196**	.164*	—
Index of travel	.207**	—	—
Medium risk	—	.194**	.141*
Modernization	—	.209**	.173*
Growth	.156*	—	—

*Significant at .05 level, one-tail distribution.
**Significant at .01 level, one-tail distribution.

are some clear reasons for this seeming inconsistency. We need to understand some additional patterns, though, before addressing this central issue.

Patterns of Information Flows

Entrepreneurial hypothesis 5:

> *Individual information sources, taken alone, have little link to performance. In-formation networks, on the other hand, have an important correlation. They are also positively associated with a number of other paramount entrepreneurial variables—leadership, planning, optimism, modernization, and risk.*

Entrepreneurial hypothesis 6:

> *Those distributors who are interested in news relating to personal interests and who utilize personal sources of news tend to exhibit higher performance.*

The most pronounced single set of influences operating on high performance stems from information flows. The successful entrepreneurs seem to be those who can grasp and treat information and then utilize it within the business. Further, it is not just the source itself that is important but, particularly, the *pattern* of information gathering. Those distributors who have wide-ranging news interest and have developed a wide net of information sources are also those who tend to be highest in total performance.

Indeed, some of the information sources we had expected to have impact turned out in our sample to be more marginal with respect to performance than we had first hypothesized (Table 11). Extensive reading of newspapers, listening to the radio, and visiting the cinema seemed to have practically no influence on high performance in any of the areas we measured. The amount of traveling the distributor had done appeared to have increased the sales level, but had no other association with performance. Knowledge of languages had some impact also on profit levels and on expanding the existing product lines. A number of these communication and information variables are correlated with one another (as logically they should be) and in turn are highly correlated with education and younger age. One would expect this. Still, if the use of one particular form of communication, say, the transistor radio, were increased, there would apparently be no direct influence on those performance measures particularly related to innovation and change.

The *network* of sources, on the other hand, has considerable influence. A pattern of linkages of information seems to be far more important than any individual source taken alone. This can be seen clearly in our data. We ask the dealers to describe to us exactly how often they got news and information from five key places — relatives and personal friends, business friends, business associations and trade journals, government, and the religious community. Then we constructed from these patterns a composite index, which we called "other information sources." Similarly, we asked the dealers to be specific about which kinds of news interested them most — news of hometown and village, of the state, of the nation, of business or industry, of world events, of sports, or of religious and cultural events. Again we built a composite index called "news interest." Both of these had significant correlations with several of our performance indices (Table 11). Of particular interest was the correlation of other information sources and the developing of new functions within the business and the correlation of both of the indices with the formation of other new firms. In other words, these two overall linkage variables were the only communication variables directly associated with innovation itself.

Further, both of these indices were linked in a highly significant way with a number of other variables directly related to the process of mapping and executing new business plans (Table 12). The other information variable was linked at a statistically significant level with four of our key planning variables — initial planning problems, current planning problems, short-term plans, and long-term plans. The news interest variable was also statistically linked with two of these. Both of the variables were also linked significantly to our modernization variable, and both were linked directly to a variable we constructed relative to the distributor's level of leadership in organizations. The news interest variable also linked directly with medium risk.

This striking difference between all of the other communications variables taken singly and the two composite linkage variables encouraged us to do further analysis of the two composites. We ran principal-component analysis for each; each variable split in half, with the four resulting parts logically explainable. For the "other information" variable, three of the five parts were

TABLE 11   Relations among fertilizer distributors' information and performance variables (correlation coefficients, with $n = 142$).

Variable	Travel	Newspaper	Radio	Cinema	Languages	Other information sources	News Interest
Same endeavors	−	−	−	−	.190*	−	−
New functions	−	−	−	−	−	.159*	−
Branches	−	−	−	−	−	−	−
Other new firms	−	−	−	−	−	.163*	.216**
Sales level	.207**	−	−	−	.277***	.326***	−
Profit level	−	−	−	−	.183*	.191*	−
Profitability	−	−	−	−	−	−	−

*Significant at .05 level, one-tail distribution.
**Significant at .01 level, one-tail distribution.
***Significant at .001 level, one-tail distribution.

TABLE 12   Relations among two key fertilizer distributors' information variables and a set of performance variables (correlation coefficients, with n = 142).

Variable	Other information sources	News interest
Initial planning problems	.210**	–
Number of meetings attended	.167*	–
Leadership index	.274***	.205**
Current planning problems	.316***	–
Short-term plans	.148*	.225**
Long-term plans	.274***	.301***
Rating of optimism	.155*	.279***
Modernization	.215**	.358***
Medium risk	–	.278***
Medium risk (business)	–	.289***

*Significant at .05 level, one-tail distribution.

**Significant at .01 level, one-tail distribution.

***Significant at .001 level, one-tail distribution.

brought together in a factor pattern we called "personal sources"—information from relatives and personal friends, from business friends, and from the religious community. The remaining parts—information from business associations and trade journals and information from government—we called "organization sources." For the news interest variable, the first four parts linked together in one factor pattern—news from hometown, state, nation, and business (again the more personal interests). We called it "political interest." The remaining three in the news interest variable—world events, sports, and religious and cultural events—we felt were more broadly "cultural interests." After obtaining these four new variables from the original two, we ran a set of correlations, regressions, and factor patterns and saw further the power of linkage variables (see Table 13). It turns out that the first half of each of the two variables—the more personal sources—are the parts of the overall variables directly related to the performance variables concerning innovation. (This finding, incidentally, runs counter to recent evidence on the *diffusion* of innovations; we disclose this incongruence in our concluding chapter.)

Several other information variables appear to have modest and selected influence. For example, the number of people contacted in the previous period is linked with the opening of branches and with high sales and profit levels. As one travels around his immediate district (we charted such trips by our subjects and found most to be of short duration), one would likely be looking for opportunities to increase sales levels. There is corroboration for this in a related variable, the number of places a person had lived over his lifetime. The fact that a distributor made a practice of moving around seems to tie in with the opening of branches — previous contacts in past residences might well make good branch personnel. Our variable on the distance involved in recent trips tied most directly with the opening of new firms. This, too, has logic — branches would not likely be far distant, a different business might. Incidentally, the overall index of travel that included the total number of states visited was qualitatively different from these more business-oriented trips and proved to have no association with performance variables.

As we put all of these communication and information dimensions together, we were struck again by the overriding importance of linkages among sources. Perhaps most significant is linkage among sources of particular types. It is general travel and usage of generalized sources that has much influence on performance, particularly the innovating performance we are analyzing. Rather, it is the person who can put together a number of information links *directly related to his environment* that seems to be the person also exhibiting more innovative behavior.

In sum, it seems clear that the patterns of information flow are fundamentally important to business performance and business innovation among the fertilizer distributors. Those distributors who were able to develop a set of links to information — by a combination of their own efforts and aid through

TABLE 13   Relations among two key fertilizer distributors' information variables, each split by factor analysis, and a set of performance variables (correlation coefficients, with $n = 142$).

	Other information		News interest	
Variable	Personal sources	Organization sources	Political interest	Cultural interest
Same endeavors	–	.140*	–	–
New functions	.170*	–	.146*	.152*
Branches	–	–	–	.142*
Other new firms	.156*	–	*	−.216**
Sales level	.295***	.138*	.147*	
Profit level	.150*	–	–	
Profitability	–	–	–	

*Significant at .05 level, one-tail distribution.
**Significant at .01 level, one-tail distribution.
***Significant at .001 level, one-tail distribution.

information brokers (either within their own family or close friends) — were most likely to be the successful entrepreneurs in terms of profit, growth, and innovation. These networks remain highly personal, pragmatic, and reasonably narrow in any "worldly" sense.

Planning and Innovation

Entrepreneurial hypothesis 7:

Conscious planning is an important indicator of performance. Short-term planning associates more with expansion of existing lines and opening of other new firms. Long-term planning associates more with new functions and opening of branches.

A second pattern of business behavior that links closely to performance is that which involves planning. There is a pervasive feeling of fatalism among many of the distributors that appears to discourage any significant planning. For example, one man answered the question, "What is the best number of children for a man like you to have during your lifetime?" by saying that he wasn't particular: "We are not the authority." These comments reinforce the widely held tenet that Hinduism is a passive and quiescent religion, that it leads to a lack of concern for the long run of at least this life.

But others *did* plan. We asked the distributors to describe both the problems they had at the start of the business and what they considered to be their current problems. Next, they were asked if they planned any major changes in the next six months — if so, to describe these. Some of these short-term plans evolved around the life of the family, rather than the business. For example, more than one respondent spoke graphically of the short-term problems of obtaining enough cash to marry off a daughter. One man told us of specific plans to open two new branches, but said that he could "do nothing on this until I see just how my daughter's marriage costs come out." Our question concerning longer-range plans was asked this way: "Can you describe how you think your firm will have changed five years from now?" A number of the respondents were completely nonplussed by this kind of question — the time frame was simply too long. As one man put it, "I can't say anything — everything is in the hands of the gods."

We found that the distributor's ability to describe and analyze his problems, and his perception of the future, gave us substantial insight into his ability to plan rationally. And our planning variables turned out to be important indicators of business performance. Modernization associates strongly with these variables, and our earlier description of the more modern, more profit-oriented distributor seems logically to fit with these planning horizons — particularly specific short-term and long-run plans for the future. Likewise, the various information sources are statistically associated, as shown in Table 14.

We also see ties to performance. Short-term planning abilities seem especially important to starting other new firms, as well as expanding the existing fertilizer line. Conversely, distributors who focus on new functions within the business and the opening of branches seem to evidence a better articulation of long-run plans (Tables 15 and 16).

Risk and Performance

Entrepreneurial hypothesis 8:

Risk is positively associated with performance. High risk tends to link with existing endeavors and high sales levels, medium risk and business risk with the opening of other firms. Both link with profit measures.

One important ingredient remains before we can discuss overall typologies and sketch some pictures of composite dealers. Risk has always been closely associated with innovation, and our data clearly confirm this. Table 17 shows that the strongest associations are between risk and formation of new firms, expansion of existing fertilizer lines, and the basic profitability of the distributorship. The patterns in this table and in Table 18 are evocative in several of the previous patterns we have sketched.

TABLE 14   Relations among fertilizer distributors' planning variables and those involving information and modernization (correlation coefficients, with $n = 142$).

Variable	Short-term plans	Long-term plans
Other information sources	.148*	.274***
People sources	.165*	.367***
Organization sources	–	−.145*
News interest	.225**	.301***
Political news	.186*	.318***
Cultural news	−.218**	–
Modernization	.224**	.201**

*Significant at .05 level, one-tail distribution.
**Significant at .01 level, one-tail distribution.
***Significant at .001 level, one-tail distribution.

TABLE 15   Relations among fertilizer distributors' planning and performance variables (correlation coefficients, with $n = 142$).

Variable	Initial planning problems	Current planning problems	Short-term plans	Long-term plans
Same endeavors	–	–	.357***	–
New functions	.177*	.230**	.184*	.253***
Branches	–	–	.157*	.204**
Other new firms	–	–	.351***	–
Sales level	–	–	.143*	.233**
Profit level	–	–	–	.196**
Profitability	–	–	–	–

   *Significant at .05 level, one-tail distribution.
  **Significant at .01 level, one-tail distribution.
 ***Significant at .001 level, one-tail distribution.

Splitting the Data Set

Entrepreneurial hypotheses 9, 10, and 11:

Differences in the age of the firm and the age of the distributor have little association with performance variables. Rural dealers tend to sell less and have substantially diminished profitability.

We split the data set along three interesting dichotomies: younger and older firms, younger and older respondents, and rural and urban distributorships. Fortunately, the large size of the set allowed us to eliminate a substantial number of people in the middle range and thus highlight whatever differences there might be.

The dissimilarities brought by age of firm were modest and predictable. The respondents in the newer firms seemed more willing to take risk, but had not yet moved into as many different endeavors within the firm or opened other businesses. The newer firms were somewhat lower on sales level and considerably below the older firms on profitability. In the principal-component analysis the older firms were very similar to the patterns in the composite sample. The younger firms, too, were generally similar, except that the information variables tended to link closely with sales levels, much less so with profitability. These are all relationships that one might expect—the distributors who have recently founded firms and are struggling to attain reasonable profitability have not yet had time to move into other functions or other new businesses.

TABLE 16   Factor pattern (after varimax rotation) showing correlations among four original variables of fertilizer distributors' planning, three original variables of performance, and two new composite factors.

Variable	1	2	Row SS
Problems at start	.69	.05	.48
Current problems	.66	− .03	.44
Short-term changes	.39	.68	.62
Long-term changes	.68	.00	.47
New functions	.58	.02	.34
Other firms	.06	.86	.74
Profitability	.05	.40	.17
Column SS	1.80	1.35	3.24

Next we composed two new data sets, one with young distributors and the other with older men. As we would expect, the younger men were considerably more modern in attitude and substantially higher in education. Yet when overall patterns in the two groups were compared by principal component analysis they looked quite similar, and each was also quite comparable with the composite data set. For example, sales levels and profit levels were reasonably close for both young and old. The only significant difference on the performance variables was the fact that the younger dealers appeared to

TABLE 17   Relations among fertilizer distributors' risk preference and performance variables (correlation coefficients, with $n = 142$).

Variable	High risk (composite)	Medium risk (composite)	High risk (business)	Risk (quadratic equation)
Same endeavors	.289***	−	−	.210**
New functions	−	−	−	.225**
Branches	−	−	−	.178*
Other new firms	.137*	.176*	.255***	−
Sales level	.234**	−	−	.175*
Profit level	.272***	.194**	−	.156*
Profitability	.154*	.141*	−	−

*Significant at .05 level, one-tail distribution.
**Significant at .01 level, one-tail distribution.
***Significant at .001 level, one-tail distribution.

TABLE 18   Factor pattern (after varimax rotation) showing correlations among two original variables of fertilizer distributors' risk preference, three original variables of performance, and two new composite factors.

Variable	1	2	Row SS
High risk	.49	.45	.45
Medium risk	.68	− .04	.46
New functions	− .27	.73	.61
Other new firms	.58	.06	.37
Sales	.21	.74	.59
Profitability	.55	− .06	.31
Column SS	1.47	1.29	2.76

have moved much more substantially into the newer endeavors within the business (but the two groups were similar on founding of other firms). The overall conclusion here is that while there are some meaningful differences in the biodata of the two groups, there is no significant difference caused by age with regard to the various performance variables.

More substantial differences exist between the rural and urban distributors. The rural dealers are more averse to risk and use fewer information sources. Their planning horizons are about the same as the urban dealers; they are about as modern as the urban dealers. The numbers of new endeavors within their businesses, as well as the numbers of outside businesses, are just about the same as for the urban dealers. Other performance variables, however, are lower. The sales levels of the rural dealers are below their urban counterparts. The differences in profitability are more striking: not only is the rural dealer lower on the level of profitability, but there is a negative correlation between profitability and movement into new businesses (as well as in use of information). There is a logical reason for this; the rural dealer may well be starting other firms, but in doing so is operating in a much more difficult information system, and in an environment that makes profitability more difficult.

Modernization Revisited

Entrepreneurial hypothesis 12:

The performance of the "modern" dealer differs in a number of ways from that of the "traditional" dealer—he innovates more within the business, has higher sales and profitability, and has faster growth. Modernization is positively associated with information usage, leadership, planning, and risk assumption.

The data discussed in conjunction with entrepreneurial hypothesis 2 persuaded us to split the distributors into subsets of less modern and more modern. We then compared them on nine prime variables—those we found overall to be most meaningful. In our discriminant analysis we found the two subsets to be significantly different at the .001 level: $F_{(9.92)} = 4.03$. We have shown several of these graphically in the histograms in Figure 3.

Modernization would be expected to show heterogeneity of the men, and the two data sets confirm this. The more modern man is better educated, reads more newspapers, and goes to more cinemas. He is considerably more interested in information sources and utilizes them more widely and more readily. He goes to more meetings and takes a stronger leadership role in his organizations. Interestingly, his language facility is about the same as the less modern man, he has actually done *less* traveling than the less modern man, and he listens less to the radio. In general, the two typologies stand up to expectations.

Another presumption of modernization measures is that more modern people tend to have higher performance. This is strikingly confirmed in our data. On all seven of the basic performance measures the modern distributor is noticeably higher. He innovates more within the business, opens more outside firms, has higher sales and profitability levels, and exhibits faster growth. He has a keener sense of both short-term and long-term planning and is more willing to take medium risks in his business (whereas the less modern distributor is more willing to take high risks). In sum, our concept of modernization is an important predictor of various performance indices of innovation.

Can the Fertilizer Distributor Be a Change Agent?

Field data of this nature, administered in a cross-cultural environment to a group of generally untutored villagers, are likely not to fall together in completely neat packages. We find a large number of statistically significant correlations, and these hold up remarkably well as descriptors of overall fertilizer distributor logic. While there is no single set of correlations, regressions, or principal-component analysis that fully describes all the generalizations of this chapter, a relevant two-vector factor-analysis solution that incorporates the two central characters we discuss throughout the chapter, the sales maximizer and the profit maximizer, is shown in Table 19.

Now that we have a sharper focus on these men, we can return to our initial question, "Can the fertilizer distributor become a change agent and thus be a catalyst for rural economic development?" If we look first at the traditional, sales-oriented dealer, we are immediately faced with an anomaly. On the one hand he is the dealer who appears to be maximizing total sales levels—selling the largest amount of a combined total of fertilizer and other products and

FIGURE 3 Traditional ($n = 46$) and modern ($n = 56$) distributors: histograms of six variables.

```
                        NEWS INTEREST
                   Traditional      Modern
                        Category
                        midpoint
                     *     8
                           9
                    **    10
                          11
                          12
               *******    13   *
                   ***    14
                     *    15   ***
                 *****    16   **
                ******    17   ***
                  ****    18   ****
                 *****    19   *********
                   ***    20   **************
                 *****    21   ************
                   ***    22   ***
                          23   ***
                          24   ***
                     *    25   *
Means                 16.98        19.64
Standard deviations    3.60         2.29
                   F(1,100) = 20.15
```

```
                      OTHER NEW FIRMS
                   Traditional      Modern
   *********************************   0   **********************
        *************   1   ***********************
                   **   2   **********
                        3   **
                        4   **
Means                 0.37         0.98
Standard deviations   0.57         1.01
                   F(1,100) = 13.28
```

```
                      SHORT-TERM PLANS
                   Traditional      Modern
   *****************************   1   ********************
        *************   2   ******************************
                   **   3   *******
Means                 0.37         0.77
Standard deviations   0.57         0.65
                   F(1,100) = 10.35
```

LONG-TERM PLANS

	Traditional	Modern

Category
midpoint

```
************************    0    ****************
  *****************         1    *******************************
        ***                 2    *********
         *                  3    *
```

Means	0.57	0.91
Standard deviations	0.71	0.71

$$F_{(1,100)} = 5.81$$

PROFITABILITY

	Traditional	Modern

```
                       - 1.4
                       - 1.2
                       - 1.
      ******           - 0.8   **
        ***            - 0.6   *****
     ********          - 0.4   *****
        ***            - 0.2   *********
       *****             0     ******
   **************         0.2   **************
         **             0.4   *****
         **             0.6   **
        ***             0.8   *
                        1.    **
                        1.2   *****
                        1.4
                        1.6
                        1.8
```

Means	- 6.66 E-2	0.11
Standard deviations	0.46	0.51

$$F_{(1,100)} = 3.42$$

OTHER INFORMATION

	Traditional	Modern

```
          *       5    *
        ***       6    *
    *******       7    **
  *********       8    ****
     ****         9    *****
      **         10    ******
     ****        11    *******
    ******       12    **********
     ****        13    *********
      ***        14    ***
                 15    **
       **        16    **
                 17    **
```

Means	9.76	11.41
Standard deviations	2.82	2.60

$$F_{(1,100)} = 9.24$$

TABLE 19   Factor pattern (after varimax rotation) showing correlations among one original variable of fertilizer distributors' planning, one original variable of risk preference, one original variable of modernization, three original variables of performance, and two new composite factors.

Variable	Profit maximizers	Sales maximizers	Row SS
Long-term change	.13	.73	.55
Medium risk	.64	.06	.41
Modernization	.60	.26	.44
New functions	− .21	.70	.54
Other new firms	.62	− .08	.40
Sales level	.17	.62	.41
Profitability	.56	− .04	.30
Column SS	1.57	1.49	3.06

services. Yet at the same time we have pictured him as traditional, narrow in his uses of information, overly concerned with problems, and with only a smattering of new short-term plans. He seems to mirror his constituency, the cultivators. In some respects this is a happy circumstance: find a man closely related to the cultivator (a cultivator himself, a local provisions dealer, or some such man) and let him sell fertilizer on his own, without worrying too much about whether he is really stressing modernizing inputs or just responding to the cultivators' short-term interests. It seems unlikely, though, that either the dealer or the cultivator will be thinking in terms of a package of practices and opting for new and truly innovative agricultural inputs.

The modern dealer is more likely to be a profit maximizer, rather than an undiscriminating maximizer of total sales. Even some of the very small dealers exhibit a keen profit maximization sense. One dealer, for example, calculated the rate of interest for his invested capital, made an allocation for rent and mortgage payments among his various business activities (he was also in the provisions business), and explicitly allocated his own time. As a result of this calculation he decided to drop the fertilizer business and concentrate on his more lucrative provisions business.

Our sample tells us that the profit maximizing dealers sense a break-even point and while they continue to add other products in the same line, they eschew much movement into new functions. There is logic to their actions. In the height of the period we call the first-stage Green Revolution (from 1970 through 1973) many of the new functions had not been allowed to be financially attractive for a novice entrepreneur. Contract spraying, for instance, was difficult to make profitable, given the government subsidies of both their own contract spraying efforts and those of the cooperatives. Likewise, the use of a tractor as a contract plowing service was fraught with difficulties — the long waiting list to obtain the tractor, the temptation to use the tractor on only the fields of family and friends, and so on. The incentives for other new functions within the fertilizer business also tended not to be strong. The government was a direct competitor for a great many of these activities, generally on a subsidized basis that kept the price low to the cultivator but in the process made the margin unattractive to the private operator. There is nothing inherently wrong with subsidizing agricultural inputs in order to encourage their use. However, it does seem myopic to extend such subsidies only to government and cooperative units, for this tends to discourage those private-enterprise businessmen we have identified as being more modern and innovating. One can make a strong case that private agricultural input manufacturers also should assume these subsidy costs, that to do so would enhance long-run profit maximization by stressing the full package of practices. To date, however, most private manufacturers have been hesitant to do so.

Thus the profit-oriented dealer has concluded that his time and money are better used outside the firm and so has made his entrepreneurial moves, not in fertilizer, but in other new firms. These new firms might not themselves be particularly "innovative," at least in a Schumpeterian sense. There are few equivalents of the aerospace electronics companies in village India. The new firms were, instead, cement dealerships, gasoline and oil outlets, provisions houses, even an occasional machine shop, or perhaps a simple engine and pump assembly company. There are additional clues in our data to suggest that the dealers would tend to take this reasonably conventional approach. Although these modern dealers were noteworthy for their use of a network of information sources, the sources tended to be those we define as personal — family, friends, relatives, business associates, and the like. The dealers were not interested in cultural and world events; their perspective was personal and immediate.

Still, we must not gainsay the entrepreneurial element in the founding of *any* firm. Some of these new firms involve what we have denoted meta-innovations — products or processes that are new to their particular (in this case rural) environment. For example, gasoline for automobiles and diesel fuel for trucks are marketed in India via "petrol bunks." These generally have certain characteristics. First, they are today located rather infrequently in the rural areas (as a result, an automobile trip requires careful planning). Second, the rural bunks (and most of those in the towns) offer no services other than pumping — no comfort stations, no vehicle service. An owner of a rural Tamil Nadu bunk (in a village of under 2,000) decided to combine automobile servicing and repair with gasoline pumping. (Sorrowfully, we must report that still no comfort facilities were provided.) Not an innovation by any developed-world standards, yet it was considered an oddity in its area. This was a non-conformist act by an individual who sensed a relationship not seen before. Manifestly, a meta-innovation.

This still begs the question of real innovation *within* the fertilizer firm. There are logical incremental steps that can readily be taken by the fertilizer distributor to adopt not only new products but new functions within his business. Some of these are conventional, commonplace moves. Others are true meta-innovations. Door order (and, possibly, door delivery) is a case in point. The shift in locus from the cultivator to the distributor is more than a mere alternative-choice, cost-benefit transport decision. It involves the physical presence on the land of a formerly sedentary tradesman (albeit perhaps one of his employees). This is a departure from existing moves, one with promise but fraught with unexpected complications.

Another case: Tamil Nadu has witnessed a veritable explosion of pump-set installations over the past few years. The market became saturated (no pun intended!), and the pump-set installers began a commission war of attrition. Business in spares was dwindling, and the stocks of rice mill huller parts they also sold were being leapfrogged by the millers' purchasing direct from wholesalers in the cities. As the local demand declined, a few of the more innovative dealers began to canvass on a wide radius, promising a high degree of customer service. In the process they redefined the very conception of their business (and provided yet another example of the package notion).

Two steps seem to be needed to realize the promise of the fertilizer distributor as full-scale change agent.

First, profit maximization appears to be the key to motivating the modern, innovating man. The new functions must be made profitable in their own right, probably by a combination of subsidy from the manufacturers and/or the government and by the willingness of the government to reduce subsidies to the cooperatives and government corporations (a difficult political decision, to be sure). In essence, the fertilizer dealer must be freed to pursue profits aggressively across the whole spectrum of agricultural inputs. This is not a special pleading for the private sector per se. Rather, what we are emphasizing is the fundamental entrepreneurial mentality that must underlie the quest for profit.

The second step is to identify among potential fertilizer distributors those people who appear to have modern, profit-oriented mentalities, and to select among existing fertilizer distributors those men who have the potential for heightening their understanding and application of long-run profit maximizing behavior. In the next chapter we suggest some methods for doing this and give some specific examples. In Chapter 5 a specific training program designed to inculcate entrepreneurship is described. For both selection and training, these six basic objectives are sought:

(a) Strengthen and broaden information sources and flows and, in particular, inculcate the concept of combining ideas and facts;

(b) Sharpen the understanding of planning, with special focus on short-term planning;

(c) Deepen the perception of risk taking, and highlight the middle ground between a no-risk mentality and a gambler's syndrome;

(d) Focus thinking on personal goal setting, and carry each individual through his own practical application of it;

(e) Strengthen all of these goals with a pervasive achievement motivation that stresses long-run profit maximization;

(f) Emphasize the practical needs for change, vividly show some reasonable real-life change possibilities, and constantly reiterate the belief that individuals can cultivate the change-agent mentality.

4

Village Entrepreneurs
in Action

We can enhance our understanding of rural change and the special role of change agents by an intensive look at one particular locality—two community development blocks in Namakkal taluk in Salem district, in the center of the state of Tamil Nadu. The southern and western boundaries of Namakkal border the Cauvery River, one of the great watersheds of the south of India. The lands along the river basin have almost completely assured irrigation, except during periods of extreme drought. Systems of canals also bring dependable irrigation to other lands near the river. Farther out from the river basin are scattered garden lands under well irrigation and much dry-land cultivation. The countryside is hot (mean maximum temperature in March, April, and May is 37° C, with a nagging hot wind) and dry (average annual rainfall is 79 centimeters). There is also a small hill area in the eastern part of the taluk, sparsely populated and cultivated on a rudimentary basis. Thus, within the taluk are intensive cultivation, dry-land farming, and a hill country largely out of the regular economy.

We were fortunate in our choice of Namakkal, because a research team of the Pilot Research Project in Growth Centres had chosen two of the taluk's eight community development blocks for its study.[1] This growth center project in Namakkal is part of a substantial country-wide effort, the result of the Government of India's recognition of the need to accelerate and guide rural development in new ways in order to support the continued modernization of agriculture, to diversify economic opportunities, and to improve social progress and the quality of life of rural people. The project was the chosen vehicle for accomplishing this purpose. Twenty pilot study areas were picked, one or more located in each of the states of the country in a strategy similar to that of the earlier Intensive Agricultural Districts Programme. Action programs to improve the input and distribution system and to upgrade the public infrastructure and social services were to be the eventual products.

The Tamil Nadu pilot area covers the two community development blocks of Namakkal and Mohanur. Our intensive study of village entrepreneurship was a natural complement to the more broadly focused growth center project, so our research efforts were planned to encompass the same field ground. We interviewed in depth every one of the 56 private fertilizer distributors in the taluk (15 of whom were in these two blocks) and also interviewed a representative group of other village businessmen in both the two pilot blocks and the other six in the taluk. The growth center project personnel interviewed some 662 people, including 216 businessmen and 107 shopkeepers.[2]

The two pilot community blocks, Mohanur and Namakkal, are immediately adjacent to each other, in the center of the taluk. Together they extend over 474 square kilometers, an area equivalent to a square just under 22 kilometers on each side. Thus it is slightly larger than four townships in the United States. (Under the U. S. rectangular survey of public lands in 1789, townships were to be 6 square miles in area and contain 36 sections of 1 mile each.) If this were the Midwest farming area of the United States a few years back, we might expect these four-plus sections to average four 160-acre farms for each of the square miles, perhaps something under 750 farms in an area equivalent to the 474 square kilometers, or 183 square miles, of Mohanur and Namakkal blocks. If it were an agricultural area in the United States, there would perhaps be two or three small towns, even a slightly larger county seat. There would probably be about 10,000 people.

Naturally, the Indian countryside is different from central Illinois. The census in 1971 listed the two blocks as having a total population of 154,751, so at that time there were approximately 321 people per square kilometer. These people lived in 255 separate hamlets, comprising fifty-nine inhabited settlements, all except one classified as villages. The exception was the town of Namakkal, with a population of just under 35,000, the headquarters of the taluk. Only ten of the villages were under 1,000 in population; if we exclude Namakkal and the next largest settlement (the town of Mohanur, with a population of just over 8,000), the other fifty-seven villages had an average population of 1,195 people.

Nearly 99 percent of the population were Hindus; Muslims and Christians constituted a very small percentage of the total population in this part of the state. In the 1971 census 36 percent of these people were classified as literates, slightly below the level for the state.

Though there is no rail connection anywhere in the taluk, the two blocks are fortunate in having a good road system. One of the state's "national highways" comes down to Namakkal from the north and continues westward from Namakkal. Two other highways go south from Namakkal, and every one of the fifty-nine settlements in the two blocks has an all-weather road into it. Almost half the villages have a regular or request bus stop; for those that do not, none is farther away than 4 kilometers. In general, Tamil Nadu has a better road system than most of the states of India; the pilot blocks here are two of the best situated in the state.

Land and Agricultural Patterns

There are just over 33,000 hectares of net sown land in the Namakkal and Mohanur blocks (1,959 hectares of which have been sown more than once). Thus the 15,497 householders owning land averaged a holding of just under 2 hectares. (There were also 13,449 landless households.) Only 16.5 percent of the area sowed had assured irrigation, and the price was more than eight times that of rainfed dry lands (Rs. 75,000 per hectare and Rs. 9,000 per hectare respectively). There is an interesting panorama of crop production; Table 20 shows the production, yield, and marketing patterns. In general, the yields per hectare are substantially above that of the country as a whole and in most cases above the average for the state of Tamil Nadu.

We see the relationships between traditional and modern agriculture most clearly at the point of application of the agricultural inputs necessary to bring about this production. Table 21 indicates the agricultural inputs for Mohanur and Namakkal in 1972.

When we remind ourselves that these two blocks are progressive ones in an agriculturally progressive state, we are struck with the small quantities of modernizing inputs that have been used. The average amount spent per farmer on all inputs was under Rs. 150; as the average holding was just under 2 hectares, the farmers were spending perhaps Rs. 70 per hectare—approximately $10 per hectare or about $4 per acre. Pump sets were the most expensive input, averaging Rs. 2,430, or just over $300. The machinery and equipment purchased was rudimentary, averaging only Rs. 10 per farmer; clearly, most of it was nonpowered "machinery," such as scratch plows.

The small amount of fertilizer used is the item that best reveals the modest progress of modernization in the two blocks. Only 18 percent of the farmers used fertilizer, applying about 34 kilograms per hectare; this was below the Tamil Nadu state average of 45, though double the all-India average of 16.[3]

The land we are considering varies in its quality, and there are several patterns of irrigation. One can build a matrix of these classes of land, chart precisely the crops being grown on them, and from these figures establish within close limits the "standard" applications of nutrients necessary for growing each crop. Such a process was carried out by government officials for our two blocks, and a sophisticated calculation was made of the approximate amount of fertilizer necessary for adequately growing the crops there. Actual use in 1972 was 1,177 metric tons; the estimated total tonnage needed in the proper combination of the three basic nutrients was 35,547. Thus the farmers in the

TABLE 20   Crops produced and marketed in 1971 in Namakkal and Mohanur blocks.

| Crop | Total area (hectares) | Yield per hectare | | Percent sold |
		Quintals	Rupees	
High-yielding varieties:				
Bajra	959	13	780	36
Brinjals	1	20	N.A.	55
Cotton	11	10	2,200	97
Groundnut	250	18	2,124	84
Rice	364	40	2,640	55
Sugar cane	116	998	7,984	98
Local varieties:				
Bajra	6,898	9	540	26
Banana	508	161	4,830	98
Castor	94	4	364	84
Chillies	79	7	N.A.	92
Cotton	610	11	2,420	98
Groundnut	9,450	11	1,298	87
Jowar	10,820	10	660	29
Onion	108	70	N.A.	98
Potato	19	25	1,500	10
Ragi	54	10	610	2
Rice	1,639	27	1,782	44
Sesamum	75	4	812	78
Sugar cane	615	992	7,936	98
Other (betel leaf, tapioca, onions)	342	Various		98

SOURCE: Pilot Research Project in Growth Centres, table 1.9A.

two blocks were purchasing and applying fertilizers that filled only about 3 percent of their real needs.

This is not even the whole picture, for the input patterns vary within the blocks themselves. To see this, let us return for a moment to the pilot project.

The Growth Center Concept

A growth center is the spatial application of the concept of critical mass. The first step is the process of integrated area planning, where all aspects of development in a given geographic area are analyzed and a regional plan evolved. Namakkal's plan is part of the two-region "Salem-Cuddalore" plan.

TABLE 21   Agricultural inputs purchased in 1972 for Namakkal and Mohanur blocks.

Item purchased	Quantity		Value in rupees		Farmers involved	
	Total	Per unit	Total	Per unit	Number	Percent of total
Fertilizers	11,770 (quintals)	0.34 (per hectare)	942,050	27 (per hectare)	2,837	18
Improved seeds	237 (quintals)	0.01 (per hectare)	50,065	1.4 (per hectare)	1,854	12
Pesticides/fungicides	67 (quintals)	0.002 (per hectare)	66,320	2 (per hectare)	N.A.	—
Pump sets	234 (number)	1 (per farmer involved)	566,150	2,430 (per farmer involved)	233	2
Machinery/ equipment	5,656 (number)	1 (per farmer involved)	40,822	10 (per farmer involved)	4,131	27
Cattle	888 (number)	1.4 (per farmer involved)	330,700	537 (per farmer involved)	616	4
Cattle feed	10,040 (quintals)	0.30 (per head)	218,280	6.6 (per head)	5,937	38
Total			2,214,387	143 (per farmer)		

SOURCE: Pilot Research Project in Growth Centres, table 1.8.

A number of growth centers are identified — small towns or large villages that have the potential of becoming nuclei for future economic, social, and political development in the surrounding areas. In India the region likely to be served by each growth center would probably include some fifty to a hundred villages, with a total population in the neighborhood of 100,000. The area might be conterminal with the existing administrative boundaries — for example, the block — or it might not. There have been suggestions that the community development block might need to be redefined in terms of a more integrated tie to these growth centers.[4]

Within the growth center area a hierarchical ordering of communities is made and two or more levels of "service centers" are identified, all coming under the ambit of a growth center. The analytical process of using central place theory for the calculation of these levels can involve quite sophisticated techniques; in the case of the Namakkal pilot research project the definition of the service centers was on a more rough-and-ready basis.[5] A straightforward listing of the services available in each of the villages was calculated, and the hierarchy was modified to take into account kilometer distances between possible service centers and the villages served by them. A total of seven service centers was identified, at three separate levels in the Namakkal centrality hierarchy. At level 1 was the town of Namakkal itself, present population just over 30,000, the taluk headquarters, and the designated growth center. At level 2 were two other towns (Mohanur and Velagoundampatti), both with present populations of about 10,000. (The latter town lay just over the northwest border of Namakkal taluk, yet was a logical service center for that area — another example of the possible need to redefine the block.)

Our interests in this chapter lie particularly with those villages at the third level — the smaller service centers, with populations of 1,000 to 4,000, and perhaps ten to fifteen villages within the orbit of each. There are four of these in the Namakkal plan:

Village	Population	Population rank ($n = 59$)	Centrality rank ($n = 59$)
Valayapatti	3,867	5	4
Sengapalli	2,633	18	3
Keerambur	2,679	16	6
Aniyapuram	1,028	50	27

The first two were next in rank on the centrality measure. The latter two were located in two strategic spatial areas not yet covered in the two blocks and along available transport links, a combination that persuaded the Namakkal growth center analysts to choose them over other towns ranking higher in the hierarchy. Table 22 shows patterns of concentration in terms of specific functions for Namakkal, for Sengapalli, and for Idumbankulam (the smallest of the ten villages in the Sengapalli service center area, population 685).

When the full set of service functions for each service center area is listed, we can immediately spot gaps. The action programs that stem from the pilot project research are designed to identify the best mix of these functions and to suggest additional functions called for to fulfill the critical mass for change. Let us use patterns of fertilizer distribution in Sengapalli subarea as an interesting case in point to identify needed additions.

As seen in Table 23, the seven service centers in the two blocks exhibit spotty patterns of nutrient distribution, even when we take into account the varying incidence of irrigation within each of the seven subareas. We see these deviations more strikingly when we lower our sights from the totality of the two blocks to the individual units in the Sengapalli subarea.

A Ten-Village Pattern of Agriculture

In Tables 24 and 25 we see patterns of irrigation, fertilizer application, cropping, and yields for the ten small villages in Sengapalli subarea, all in a

TABLE 22   Service functions available in three towns of Namakkal and Mohanur blocks.

Sengapalli (population 2,636; centrality rank 30.7)	Namakkal (population 29,984; centrality rank 325.9)	Idumbankulam (population 685; centrality rank 6.4)
Cottage industry	All those in Sengapalli,	Cottage industry
Temple	*plus* —	Temple
Potwari headquarters	Credit cooperative	Potwari headquarters
Home village of panchayat	Insurance office	Retail shop
president	Political party office	Bus stop, wet season
Panchayat headquarters	Government office	Bus stop, dry season
Retail shops	Library	Bicycle repair shop
Bus stops, wet season	Community center	Industry
Bus stops, dry season	Wholesale shops	
Primary school	Bank	
Middle school	Hospital	
High school	Kanoogo office	
Bicycle repair shop	Hardware store	
Industries	Chemist/pharmacist	
Branch post office	Block headquarters	
Carpentry/blacksmith shop	Telephone exchange	
Fertilizer/seed depot	Telegraph office	
Periodic market	Agricultural implement	
Village-level worker head-	representative's office	
quarters	Technical school	
Veterinary facilities	Dramatic clubs	
Family planning/maternity	Dairy/milk center	
and child welfare center	Tractor repair shop	
Producer cooperative	District headquarters	
Consumer cooperative	Tehsil headquarters	
Cinema	Pump set repair shop	
Sports club	Home village of block officers	
Oil depot		
Primary health center		

SOURCE: "Preliminary Draft Plan for Integrated Area Development, Mohanur and Namakkal Blocks" (New Delhi: Department of Community Development, Government of India, May 8, 1973).

TABLE 23   Irrigated land and fertilizer purchased as a percentage of recommended amount by service center, Namakkal and Mohanur blocks, 1972.

Service center	Percentage of irrigated land	Percentage of fertilizer purchased
Namakkal	12.3	1.4
Mohanur	16.1	24.0
Sengapalli	23.4	27.1
Velagoundampatti	18.7	2.6
Aniyapuram	5.7	1.2
Keerambur	13.5	1.8
Valayapatti	14.9	2.4

SOURCE: "Preliminary Draft Plan for Integrated Area Development, Mohanur and Namakkal Blocks" (New Delhi: Department of Community Development, Government of India, May 8, 1973), table 3.9.

rectangle about 6.5 by 9.7 kilometers, just about the area a village-level worker might cover. Once again, fertilizer purchases correlate more closely with the amount of irrigated area than with the amount of total cropped area. But there are other factors at work too. Observe the first six villages in Table 25. They are the ones where fertilizer purchases come closest to "standard." They are uniformly the villages with the higher yields across all crops. Further, they are the villages that are using the high-yielding varieties of seeds —all six are using HYV rice, none of the other four do so; the high-yielding varieties of sugar cane, groundnut, and bajra (pearl millet) also are found only in these six villages. The more remunerative cash crops—sugar cane, banana, and betel—are found only in the six villages (with two exceptions).

Some of this higher performance is accounted for by the fact that three of the six villages have higher percentages of irrigated land. It is remarkable, though, that the local-variety yields are also uniformly higher and that diversification of crops is present predominantly in these six villages. Some contemporary critics of the Green Revolution feel that concentration on only one or a few crop varieties over a large geographic area is courting disaster—that a genetic weakness may occur that would confer susceptibility to some pathogen.[6] Such harbingers of doom might be discounted were it not for the fact that just such an epidemic occurred in 1970 in the United States when the southern corn blight destroyed about one-fifth of the crop. In this instance the damage was held in bounds only by the skill and prompt action of American plant pathologists and breeders. The pessimists point to the greater vulnerability of the less developed countries, which would be unable to act as quickly. These same critics worry that the concentration on high-yielding varieties is greatly diminishing the rich choices available among local varie-

TABLE 24   Agricultural production and marketing in Sengapalli subarea, Mohanur block — area and yield for seven major crops, 1972.

	Village									
	Sengapalli (pop. 2,636)		Punjai Edayar (pop. 3,530)		Nanjai Edayar (pop. 3,852)		Manapalli (pop. 4,122)		Kumarapalayam (pop. 2,869)	
Crop	Area (ha)	Yield (kg/ha)	Area (ha)	Yield (kg/ha)	Area (ha)	Yield (kg/ha)	Area (ha)	Yield (kg/ha)	Area (ha)	Yield (kg/ha)
Rice										
Local	65	3,500	68	2,700	81	3,000	155	2,500	287	3,500
HYV	40	5,500	12	5,000	15	5,000	120	3,500	32	5,500
Bajra										
Local	25	1,500	268	1,600	—	—	130	918	—	—
HYV	101	1,900	—	—	—	—	—	—	—	—
Jowar (local only)	113	1,700	187	1,700	—	—	210	1,000	2	1,700
Banana (local only)	—	—	14	400	75	266	18	400	24	400
Sugar cane										
Local	22	99[a]	56	a	31	a	101	a	—	—
HVY	—	—	—	—	—	—	—	—	79	99[a]
Groundnut										
Local	110	1,400	92	1,400	—	—	180	1,200	—	—
HYV	40	1,800	70	1,800	—	—	—	—	—	—
Betel (local only)	29	649	14	630	15	630	11	630	50	631

SOURCE: "Preliminary Draft Plan for Integrated Area Development, Mohanur and Namakkal Blocks" (New Delhi: Department of Community Development, Government of India, May 9, 1973), tables 3.7 and 3.8.

[a] Average for all sugar cane areas.

ties. Evidence from the Sengapalli subarea, although fragmentary, does suggest that diversification of crops and diversification of varieties can go hand in hand with other progressive, remunerative efforts.

One last fact about Sengapalli should be noted — four of the six high-performing villages have their own fertilizer and seed depot, and one of the other two is situated less than 2 kilometers away from a depot. The sixth, Idumban-kulam, is a special case of a sugar cane area where individual fertilizer orders are large and delivery is most often by truck. Thus a natural hypothesis emerges: that ready availability of agricultural inputs tends to link to high-performance areas.

Namakkal's Fertilizer Distributors

Our focus is on the fertilizer distributor, so we interviewed in depth all of the fifty-six private distributors in Namakkal taluk, fifteen of whom are in the

| | Village | | | | | | | | | |
Idumbankulam (pop. 685)		Valavanthi Sircar (pop. 2,245)		Perumandapalayam (pop. 2,065)		Kuttalamparai (pop. 2,148)		Kalipalayam (pop. 1,244)		Percent sold
Area (ha)	Yield (kg/ha)	Area (ha)	Yield (kg/ha)	Area (ha)	Yield (kg/ha)	Area (ha)	Yield (kg/ha)	Area (ha)	Yield (kg/ha)	
196	3,000	60	2,500	11	2,100	36	2,000	3	2,000	58
8	6,000	—	—	—	—	—	—	—	—	64
13	1,600	171	1,100	343	1,100	270	900	130	900	30
—	—	—	—	—	—	—	—	—	—	40
198	1,500	186	1,300	306	1,000	325	1,000	87	1,000	33
38	425	8	400	—	—	—	—	—	—	100
190	a	—	—	4	a	—	—	—	—	100
—	—	—	—	—	—	—	—	—	—	100
—	—	110	1,200	390	1,000	420	1,100	248	1,200	86
—	—	—	—	—	—	—	—	—	—	83
—	—	—	—	—	—	—	—	—	—	100

two pilot blocks. As we read through the respondent answers and interviewer comments for the fifty-six distributors, located within 24 kilometers of one another, we are struck by the rich and varied lives of these people and the sharp differences among them in experience, attitude, and outlook. Some have become large-scale businessmen, economically successful and manifestly powerful in their communities. Others have a much narrower view of life, are cautious about their affairs and pessimistic about their future. Namakkal's fertilizer distributorships tend to be small; the individual firm's tonnage is about 70 percent of those in our larger sample. While the age of the men in the two samples is almost exactly the same, Namakkal's firms are on the average over 50 percent older. Its dealers are less educated, less involved in organizations, travel less, utilize their sources of information less frequently. The older firms tend to be ones with new product lines and new functions, and tend also to have branches. Likewise, the distributors in these older firms are apt to be those who have been involved in the opening of other new firms.

TABLE 25   Agricultural input patterns for Sengapalli subarea, Mohanur block, 1972.

	Village			
	Sengapalli (pop. 2,636)	Punjai Edayar (pop. 3,530)	Nanjai Edayar (pop. 3,852)	Manapalli (pop. 4,122)
Distance to fertilizer depot (km)	0	0	0	0
Cropped area (% of 7,113 ha total for ten villages)	9.2	11.5	4.0	13.3
Irrigated area (% of 1,666 ha total for ten villages)	6.6	11.5	11.8	15.6
Fertilizer purchased (% of 624.8 metric tons total for ten villages)	5.6	10.9	14.4	8.9
Fertilizer purchased (recommended amount)	24.2	26.6	31.7	14.4
Average purchase of fertilizer (quintals)	2.3	3.9	9.5	3.1

SOURCE: "Preliminary Draft Plan for Integrated Area Development, Mohanur and Namakkal Blocks" (New Delhi: Department of Community Development, Government of India, May 9, 1973), tables 3.7 and 3.8.

Most of the key variables we identified earlier as being associated with performance stand out again. Modernization still associates directly with younger, higher-educated men, and with those who are willing to take risks, to be involved in leadership positions in organizations, and to have well-formulated short-term plans. Again the separate information variables (such as newspaper, radio, language facility) have very few statistically significant relationships with other performance variables, but the two information linkage variables do correlate again (at the .01 level).[7] Likewise, those parts of the two variables that stress personal sources and interests are those that have the most power with regard to performance variables.

With these statistical aids we can analyze the questionnaires carefully and find real clues to differences in attitudes, degrees of modernization, ethical behavior, and so on. We conclude again that some of the traditional ways of judging people—caste, family background, occupation—are not very good indicators of performance. On the other hand, a number of the behavioral and attitudinal discriminations seem to have important meaning. Patterns of information flows, attitudes toward planning, types of responses to modernization questions—these can be of significant help in assessing who might be the most prone to change-oriented thinking.

Our reasoning was that if the people we tapped happened also to be located

| Village | | | | | |
Kumarapalayam (pop. 2,869)	Idumbankulam (pop. 685)	Valavanthi Sircar (pop. 2,245)	Perumandapalyam (pop. 2,065)	Kuttalamparai (pop. 2,148)	Kalipalayam (pop. 1,244)
1.6	2.8	4.4	5.5	7.4	9.9
7.2	9.5	7.8	15.0	15.5	7.0
16.5	22.3	7.1	2.4	5.5	0.7
21.2	36.0	1.4	0.9	0.64	0.06
52.9	71.2	6.3	2.4	15.9	0.5
8.0	45.0	0.9	2.2	1.1	0.6

in or near villages and towns we had previously identified as needing a growth center emphasis, we might be able to position the distributors as change agents and thereby enhance the potential for rural change. Let us therefore narrow our focus again to the growth center pilot area, Namakkal and Mohanur blocks, where fifteen of the fifty-six distributors in our sample carry on their business. This is a small number, and in order not to breach our promises of confidentiality we shall use standardized scores in the following analysis.

Two of the four level 3 growth centers—those proposed at Keerambur and at Aniyapuram—have no present distributorship. Each has a retail shop, a couple of cottage industries, and a rice mill. Our problem was to determine whether one or another of the villagers operating these businesses would be the right person for the new fertilizer depot, or whether it would be wiser to import one of the younger distributors that we had identified as being change-oriented and as having the potential for becoming a major distributor. We can build a good choice system from the data.

First we tabulate the various responses of the fifteen distributors for the variables we identified earlier as being important predictors, then we tabulate the particular performance variables we identified as emphasizing a profit-maximizing rationale. The comparative rankings of the distributors are shown in Table 26.

TABLE 26   Simple rank comparison between five predictive and three performance variables for fifteen fertilizer distributors in Namakkal and Mohanur blocks, 1971.

	Predictive variables (z scores)							Performance variables (z scores)				
Dealer number	Other information sources	News interest	Leadership index	Short-term planning	Modernization	Total	Rank of top seven	New endeavors	Other firms	Profitability	Total	Rank of top seven
1	−.89	.58	−.71	−.56	.89	−.69	6	−1.37	−.54	−.69	−2.60	
2	−.56	−.42	−.71	.84	−.52	−1.37		.10	−.54	−.69	−1.13	
3	−.89	−1.09	−.71	−.56	.25	−3.00		.10	−.54	−.69	−1.13	
4	−.89	−.76	.66	−.56	.12	−1.43		.10	−.54	−.69	−1.13	
5	1.12	1.24	.66	2.25	−.14	+5.13	3	1.57	−.54	.09	+1.12	5
6	.11	−1.09	−.71	−.56	−3.10	−5.35		1.57	.04	.86	+2.47	4
7	−.22	−.42	−.02	−.56	.12	−1.10		−1.37	−.54	−1.46	−3.37	
8	1.12	.24	−.71	−.56	.25	+.34	5	−1.37	−.54	−.69	−2.60	
9	1.12	1.91	.32	2.25	.25	+5.85	2	1.57	.62	.60	+2.79	3
10	−.89	−1.09	−.71	−.56	−.01	−3.26		−1.37	−.54	−.69	−2.60	
11	−.89	−.42	−.71	.84	−1.04	−2.22		.10	.04	.09	+.23	7
12	2.12	1.24	.32	−.56	.76	+3.88	4	.10	1.77	1.38	+3.25	2
13	−.89	.58	−.71	−.56	.64	−.94	7	.10	−.54	.86	+.42	6
14	1.12	.91	3.07	−.56	1.41	+5.95	1	.10	2.93	−2.41	+5.44	1
15	−.56	−1.42	.66	−.56	.12	−1.76		.10	−.54	.69	−1.13	

This is a simple system, one that can be readily used by fertilizer management personnel in the field. In our case, on the basis of profit maximization, we predicted five of the seven high-performance dealers.

We gain more confidence in this rough-and-ready approach when we subject the data to more sophisticated statistical analysis. The most precise technique, we feel, is canonical correlation of the five predictive and three performance variables for the fifteen distributors. The results confirm our simpler system. Here are the canonical correlations and their squares:

Root	r	r^2
1	.873	.762
2	.832	.692
3	.632	.400

The first root was statistically significant at the .01 level, the second at .04. Incidentally, we ran canonical correlations for the same five predictive and three performance variables in the large sample of 142 fertilizer distributors with good results; the first root was significant at the .00004 level.[8]

Our subjects were people we met and knew, so we are privy to much more information about them than is usually the case. So many differences, such diversity among these close neighbors!

Mr. *A,* the largest dealer of the fifty-six, is one of the biggest fertilizer distributors in South India (sales in excess of 2,000 metric tons). He began the firm in 1945. The original business was rice milling and oil extraction, with oil cakes, ghee, and fertilizers as by-products. He took on kerosene in 1950 and began fertilizers in a major way after 1955, opened a petrol bunk in 1961, and started a wholesale sugar dealership in 1964. All through the 1960s he was an authorized wholesale paddy broker and trader. Seven branches of his fertilizer operation are in Namakkal taluk, five in other nearby taluks. He uses information from personal friends and business friends far more than other information sources and has great interest in information most directly related to his village and industry. A member of six local organizations and an officer in four (though without a leadership post as such), he employs over fifty people in the various aspects of his business.

Dealer *B,* on the other hand, has already discontinued selling fertilizer and become a partner with fifty-one other people in thirteen new toddy [liquor] shops just opened.

C, one of the smaller dealers, has so many overdues—and so little optimism about the future—that he will likely give up the business in the near future. ("I would rather concentrate on my own cultivation.")

D, in the next village, also has sizable arrears but has specific plans to open a new branch in Namakkal town.

E, one of the larger dealers, wants to move into poultry feed and develop his own poultry farm as well as a food processing unit.

F is contemplating a trucking business.

G is also in the banking business and finds the latter has so much less risk that he plans to place his effort there rather than in fertilizer.

We look further through the two blocks: *H,* in 1965, at the age of twenty-seven, became head of the family when his father suddenly died. The business had been only a rice and oil mill at the start, but had begun to handle fertilizers in the 1940s. (The family also owns nearly 120 hectares of cultivated sugar cane and rice land.) A fertilizer branch was opened in 1950, another rice mill in 1952. A cinema was being constructed at the time his father died in 1965. *H* completed it and further expanded to a traveling cinema in 1969. He is the only distributor in Namakkal taluk with a college degree in business. His news interest and use of news sources ranks at the top; he has visited every state in India except Assam and has traveled to Ceylon. Just a few weeks prior to the interview, he had traveled over 1,000 kilometers to the next state. He is managing trustee for the local temple and attends at least two or three meetings each month. The current year has been a difficult one for him—his fertilizer sales dropped by 50 percent and his profits were off considerably. He had extended credit in the previous season of over Rs. 300,000; one sugar mill alone owes him over Rs. 42,000 for fertilizers purchased. The fertilizer manufacturer was pressing him to clear the arrears, and he was in the process of selling part of his land to do so. Still, he has well-defined plans for opening a new theater in a town several miles away. His advice to young men: "Expand your business only cautiously—you should try to avoid credit sales to the largest possible extent." Yet he remains optimistic, modern in his attitudes, and risk accepting.

I is an elderly member of the Gounder caste, with a small firm in a small village. He has a modest grocery shop and also sells kerosene and aerated water. He has had no schooling, never reads newspapers nor listens to radio. He has lived in the same place all his life, his longest trip in recent months being only 25 kilometers. "No comments" on any future plans, no reply at all on a number of risk and modernization questions. [Our interviewer's report: "This is the only reply from him, persistently: what is there to advise?"] Uncooperative, highly traditional. [Our interviewer's final comment: "Response—*bad.*"]

J is also a Gounder, a smaller dealer in a small village. He began the firm in 1965 as a kerosene and oil agency (his father was then in charge), started selling fertilizers in 1967. He has expanded little since then and does not expect any improvement (in fact is considering asking the manufacturer to release him from the dealership). He has had some high school, but makes little use of information sources, has no involvement in organizations, people "hardly ever" ask him for any information. "I am too young to give advice" (twenty-seven at the time of the interview). Risk averse, he is very traditional in his responses.

K, from the Udayar community, is pessimistic about the future: "There is little opportunity to get ahead."

L has lived all his life in his small village, yet by and large has modern responses: "You must always be active and not be discouraged when there is no business; almost all problems do get solved, especially if you have good plans." He deals in fertilizer as a full-time job, has branched into pesticides and oil cake sales; he is also a private contractor for a water lifting scheme to (illegally) siphon water from the Cauvery canal to certain private wells alongside—a high-paying job but one that requires many political kickbacks. He is also involved in a new toddy shop, in partnership with several other members of his community.

M, from the Konar community, has little formal education and was a bullock-cart driver prior to starting the firm. He took on kerosene in 1963, cement in 1967, sugar in 1968, and stocked soaps from the mid-1960s on. He is sole agent for a popular brand of safety fuse, which he markets in three different districts. He opened four fertilizer branches in the mid and late 1960s, yet has visited only one other state in his lifetime.

N, a Chettiar in his early forties, in 1955 started a new fertilizer firm with his brother, but they had a major misunderstanding five years later and the firm was split in two. He speaks three languages, is keenly attuned to information flows, yet has a traditional view of life: "Men should get quite a bit more money than women for the same work"; "Young boys should pay strict attention to their work and not become involved in trying to develop new ways" (of growing rice, for example); "Popularity is the best basis for choosing village leaders."

O, a Gounder, was the branch postmaster from 1955 to 1965, when he lost the job in a political change. For a year he was completely out of work, then finally started the fertilizer firm in 1966 with money from one of his relatives. He purchased his present building and spent a very large sum to put it in good order, severely cramping his finances the first year. In 1967 he began selling pesticides, in 1968 cement, in 1971 cattle feed. In mid-1971 he assumed the news agency distributorship for two newspapers and five weekly magazines. His interest in news sources is high, and he is consulted frequently for information. He has plans for starting a small-scale industry, using as a role model an admired manufacturer in a nearby city, "an ordinary man who made himself into a great industrialist." His attitudes toward other businessmen are quite pungent: "My biggest competitor has adopted fraudulent means to increase his profit by cheating the farmers."

Our confidentiality constraints prevent us from identifying each of these with the dealer numbers in Table 26. Suffice it to say that these additional pieces of information from the interviews give us further insight into the patterns among the top seven and increase our predictive confidence. Were we to have a free hand to manipulate a block-wide game of musical chairs among these distributors, it would be easy to envision a set of moves among the fifteen, with a few additions from outside the two blocks, that would position fertilizer distribution in a more effective way in the pilot area. There are many other factors, of course, that lead to the kinds of imbalance between recommended and actual amounts of fertilizer applied — the patterns we saw in Tables 23 and 25. We hypothesize, though, that we could significantly affect this balancing process by this analytical approach to allocation and reallocation of fertilizer distributorships, using the system we have just discussed.

Now we are ready to look at several other interesting patterns in the two pilot blocks. These involve small retail businesses, small industries, and cottage industries.

Down a Village Street

To put these fertilizer distributors in Namakkal in perspective, we conducted a limited sample of other village businessmen. We went to a small town, arbitrarily started at a modest printing shop and sampled it and the next twenty-four businesses on that side of the street. Here is the lineup:

Type of shop	Number of employees
Printing	12
Ready-made clothes	1
Printing	5
Stationery and school supplies	2
Cloth	8
Groceries, toilet goods, food grains	7
Cycle hire and repairs	4
Crockery	1
Soda water and cigarettes	1
Sale and service of radios and fans	3
Groceries	2
Medical supplies	2
Brass utensils	1
Textiles	4
Provisions	6
Dry cleaning and laundry	5
Vegetables	2
Tailor	8
Children's garments	1
Nonvegetarian "hotel" (cafe)	18
Timber depot	7
Haircutting salon	4
Betel nuts	1
Pawnbroker and money lender	1
Electrical wires and bulbs	2

Curiously, this was the only sample of our many in India where the respondents asked for anonymity, both for themselves and for their town. Perhaps the contiguous relationship along that village street made it more difficult for the merchants to be open about business practices.

Discriminant analysis, comparing this group of heterogeneous businessmen with the homogeneous fertilizer distributor samples (both the Namakkal and the three-district samples), showed that there were only a few differences of statistical significance.[9] The univariate one-way anovas helped to pinpoint the variations. All three of the samples are quite similar with regard to education, lifetime travel, modernization, and profitability. This "village street" group, though, is considerably more sedentary—much less business travel for much shorter distances—and significantly lower on the number of other firms founded. The typical pattern for most of the twenty-five is to have been in this particular business only; generally they had inherited it through the family (whereas the fertilizer dealers were often trying a totally new business). The village streeters also exhibited considerably more risk acceptance than did the fertilizer distributors. Finally, there is an interesting pattern of use of information sources among these village street merchants. Evidently they have a close linkage among themselves for sharing information; they depend much more heavily on business friends than on any other group and correspondingly somewhat less on family. Likewise, the use of business associations and business literature is somewhat higher than for the distributors. As we have noted, this does not seem to make them any more innovative, even on our scales of modernization. It probably reflects more the close working arrangements, whereby they are inevitably in daily contact with their immediate neighbors. In fact, turning the point to its obverse, one might find it surprising that so many of the fertilizer distributors had built up these kinds of business links, given their more typically rural location, especially in Namakkal.

Processing and Related Industries

If the fertilizer distributor is the potential change agent, the point of critical mass on the input side, it behooves us to consider where to find a similar critical mass on the output side. There are many places — along the channels of processing, storage, transportation, and marketing. For our study we selected an important candidate, the rice miller.

In the two blocks of Namakkal and Mohanur was a total of eighty rice mills in 1972. Three-fourths were small "coolie" mills, whose primary efforts were geared to custom milling for householders (usually for some combination of cash and goods in kind); the remaining twenty were "wholesale" units, milling on a more continuous scale, both for government shops and for large private retailers. Of the half-dozen small-scale industries in the block (*none* were large scale), the rice mills were the largest in numbers, third in gross revenues (see Table 27). In addition, in the two blocks were over a thousand cottage industry units, as shown in Table 28.

The fixed assets are modest for all of these, ranging from an average of about $13,000 for the oil extraction plants and just over $5,000 for the rice mills to $100 for the hand loom shops and $25 or so for the mat weavers and the leather tanners. These are presumably net figures, but the concept of depreciation is not well understood among these small businessmen, and it is likely that the capital is actually worth something less. Still, they are in the range for such village industries in South India and do show relative figures for one industry against another.

Such aggregate figures can gloss over some sharply differing situations in given industries. For example, for rice mills and oil extraction mills there are

TABLE 27   Summary statistics for small-scale industries in Namakkal and Mohanur blocks, 1972 (averages per firm).

Industry	Fixed assets (FA) in rupees	Output (Rs.)	Value added (VA) in rupees	Number of employees	Wage rate (Rs./mo.)	Ratio of capital to labor— FA/empl.	Productivity per employee— VA/empl.	Productivity of capital— VA/FA
Agro-industries:								
Rice mills	41,460	61,811	11,809	5.8	65	7,148	2,036	0.28
(n = 15 of 80 in two blocks)								
Oil extraction mills	91,033	736,638	35,323	11.1	73	8,199	3,182	0.39
(n = 15 of 39)								
Sago starch mills	52,925	614,214	33,628	33.0	28	1,604	1,019	0.64
(n = 4 of 4)								
Engineering and allied industries:								
Light engineering works	32,360	12,540	11,788	5.2	74	6,197	2,257	0.36
(n = 10 of 18)								
Auto repair	3,050	12,180	10,128	5.6	50	545	1,809	3.32
(n = 10 of 15)								
Truck body builders	26,045	140,460	49,245	15.8	158	1,651	3,121	1.89
(n = 10 of 18)								

SOURCE: "Summary Statistics for Industries, Namakkal and Mohanur Blocks," Pilot Research Project in Growth Centres, table 1.

TABLE 28   Summary statistics for cottage industries in Namakkal and Mohanur blocks, 1972 (averages per firm).

Industry	Number of units in — Block	Sample	Fixed assets (FA) in rupees	Output (Rs.)	Value added (VA) in rupees	Number of employees	Wage rate (Rs./mo.)	Capital intensity — FA/output	Ratio of capital to labor — FA/empl.	Productivity per employee — VA/empl.	Productivity of capital — VA/FA
Forest-based industries:											
Carpentry	259	25	543	1,504	1,487	1.0	—	0.36	543	1,487	2.74
Mat weaving	260	25	209	3,000	1,345	1.9	—	0.07	110	708	6.44
Industries based on animal husbandry:											
Leather tanning, leather goods, and footwear	213	25	259	1,403	942	1.0	—	0.18	259	942	3.64
Building materials, ceramics and allied industries:											
Pottery	116	25	1,230	1,564	1,191	2.0	—	0.79	615	596	0.97
Textiles:											
Handlooms, spinning, weaving, dyeing, and printing	353	25	655	1,673	1,673	2.2	43	0.40	302	760	2.52
Engineering and allied industries:											
Cycle parts and repair	122	25	2,742	2,548	2,041	2.3	32	1.08	1,190	886	0.74

SOURCE: "Summary Statistics for Cottage Industries in Namakkal and Mohanur Blocks," Pilot Research Project in Growth Centres, table 4.

both coolie mills and wholesale mills; in the former, value added is a larger percentage of output than in the latter. Likewise, the spinning and weaving shops are classic examples of the "putting out" system, where the product is brought to the home of the spinner, left for processing, and taken away again by the owner after the processing fee has been paid. Here output and value added are the same. On balance, a more meaningful comparison is the value added both to assets (the productivity of capital) and to employees (productivity per employee). We have plotted these two ratios for all twelve industries in Figure 4.

It might be expected that in these types of industries the two figures would tend to vary inversely — firms with high productivity per employee would tend to have lower productivity of capital, and vice versa. There would be exceptions on the high side — firms that were productive on both scores — and there would be exceptions on the low side. This is precisely what has happened. Among the small-scale industries the truck-body builders have a high productivity per employee and the second highest productivity of capital. The sago starch mills are lowest on productivity per employee (note their larger number of employees), and the rice mills are on the low side for both. Among the cottage industries, mat weaving has a high productivity of capital but a reasonably low productivity per employee. Carpentry is high on productivity per employee. Pottery is lowest in productivity per employee and next to lowest in productivity of capital.

These figures are available only for one year, 1972, and only for a small number of firms, but the relationships make sense. The more efficient firms cumulate to be more efficient industries, as shown by the average interest rates paid by the firms in the sample (Table 29). The weak position of the pottery industry is indicative of its higher average interest rates. The sample numbers for the small-scale industries are low, so it is difficult to generalize, for example, from a single loan made to one sago mill. It does appear, though, that truck-body builders have a lower interest rate than most of their peers.

Rice Mill Modernization

The efficiency of rice milling is an important concern all over India (as it is in a number of developing countries with rice as a staple — Indonesia, Thailand, Taiwan, Korea, mainland China, and others).[10] Efforts to modernize the rice milling industry raise some of today's great enigmas about the levels of appropriate technology and the relationship between traditional methods and more modern approaches.

Removing the husk from a grain of rice, and polishing or whitening it to the satisfaction of the ultimate consumer (perhaps extracting some by-products in the process), can be done in a number of different ways. The simplest, age-old method is hand pounding, still widely used in India and other less developed countries. It is most often done by an individual family to meet its own consumption needs, but can also be done on a commercial basis. One of the great sights of recent years has been the great corridor that extends along one side of the Rameswaram Temple in southeast Tamil Nadu, where literally hundreds of hand pounders are gathered, extending from end to end of

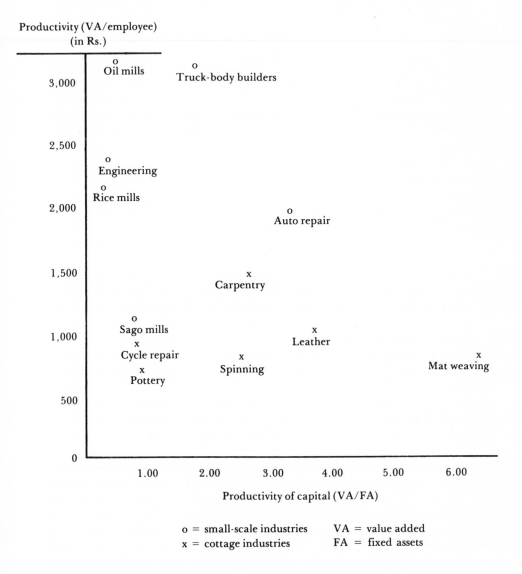

FIGURE 4 Productivity per employee vs productivity of capital for small-scale and cottage industries, Namakkal and Mohanur blocks, 1972. (Source: Tables 27 and 28.)

TABLE 29   Average interest rates by individual industry in Namakkal and Mohanur blocks, 1972.

Industry	Number in sample	Number with loans	Average interest rate (percent)
Small-scale industries:			
Rice milling	15	5	16.4
Oil extraction	15	11	14.9
Sago milling	4	1	12.0
Light engineering	10	10	17.2
Auto repair	10	6	19.7
Truck-body builders	10	9	16.3
Cottage industries:			
Carpentry	25	16	18.4
Mat weaving	25	16	16.4
Leather tanning	25	17	19.9
Pottery	25	16	20.6
Spinning and weaving	25	16	16.2
Cycle parts and repair	25	9	17.3

SOURCE: Pilot Research Project in Growth Centres, tables 3 and 6.

the enormous 1,200-meter hallway. Manual methods of rice processing are still dominant in several countries, where survival is associated with subsistence production. Yield and quality are normally very low, but so are investment requirements—only a crude mortar and pestle are needed. Labor costs, while significant, are usually disregarded by most farmers. Until the last decade the ratio of hand pounding to the total was quite high in many countries; the Food and Agriculture Organization (FAO) of the United Nations estimated in 1969 that about 75 percent of the rice crop in Bangladesh and 60 percent in Indonesia was hand pounded. The FAO figures for India were high, too; the 1969 figure was 50 percent. These statistics may lag behind the reality, though; for instance, a Government of India commission estimated the amount of rice hand pounded in West Bengal in 1954 to be 70 percent, but felt it had dropped to somewhere between 30 and 40 percent by 1967.[11]

The next step up in the chain of technology is the move to powered equipment. The simplest machine used is the traditional huller. A metal cylinder with serrated knives around it is rotated within another cylinder by a small powered unit of perhaps 5 to 10 horsepower. Generally the rice is parboiled before being put through the huller; if so, the outrun is better than if the rice comes direct from the fields. Still, the outrun of the huller is the lowest of all the rice milling machines, with a higher percentage of broken kernels and no way for the rice bran to be separated from the husks. The residue is a combination of husk and bran mixed together. While it is technically possible to separate them, the oil content of the recovered bran is much lower than that from modern rice mills (5 to 6 percent against 25 percent), so the huller residue is generally sold as poultry feed (with a considerable portion of the husk inedible). In the early 1970s the price of bran from modern milling processes ranged from Rs. 450 to Rs. 750; the price of huller residue ranged from Rs. 50 to Rs. 140.[12] In most of the artisan or coolie mills the huller is used by itself for both dehusking and polishing without any additional equipment such as sifters, separators, or aspirators.

A somewhat larger mill (like the wholesale mills in Tamil Nadu) might make use of several hullers together, in conjunction with a paddy cleaning machine, a paddy separator, and one or more emery-stone cone polishers. One of the hullers can then be set lightly enough just to take the husk off. A run through the separator removes these husks and separates out off-sized grains that were not husked at all. The latter are put through another huller set to effectively dehusk them. Brown grains all go to a series of polishers, which separate the bran from the rice grain and give the particular degree of whiteness desired by the mill's customers. There is an incredible variety of rice coloring, consistency, and flavor demanded by peoples around the world. Color alone is not enough—the consistency and taste, too, seem to call for an almost infinite variety of combinations. One of the significant problems of the earlier miracle varieties (particularly the original IR-8) was the difference in consistency and flavor that the new grain gave. Extensive consumer indoctrination was needed to shift taste in the direction of the newer variety.

The larger mills have the advantage, even when they use traditional items of equipment like the huller, of being able to combine these at various settings and control not just removal of the bran but also the outrun and the number of broken kernels. The broken pieces of rice grains can be eaten just as readily as whole grains, and the customer of the coolie mill often is not particularly concerned about the percentage of brokens. If, on the other hand, the grain is to move into the commercial market, the percentage of brokens has an increasingly negative impact. In fact, world standards allow only an infinitesimal percentage in a top-grade mixture. The rice mills of the developed world can reach this goal; mills in India, even the larger wholesale mills, that continue to use the older equipment cannot.

The next stage of modernization is directed specifically at this problem of brokens. Another device for removing the husk is a piece of equipment called the sheller. Instead of the husk's being cut off, as in a huller, it is kneaded off by being rubbed between two surfaces. In the older variety of sheller (the under-run disk sheller) the paddy grain was rubbed by rotating an abrasive wheel against a base so that the shell was in effect rolled off. The newer varieties of shellers are a major step forward, in that they use two rotating rubber rollers. This is by far the most effective way of shelling rice to give the lowest percentage of brokens. The rollers are expensive in developing countries like India and if not highly durable are subject to rapid wear. Thus the rubber-roller sheller is often thought to be overly expensive in an environment like India, even though it does represent the ultimate in modernization for the larger traditional mills.

The zenith in rice technology is the so-called modern rice mill.[13] This is a fully integrated, balanced unit with sophisticated equipment for both the processes and the physical movements between individual operations. The most modern version of each stage is used: beginning with the paddy cleaner, then the husker with aspirator, followed by the separator, the primary whitener, and the final whitener with a final aspirator and grader—all connected by a series of elevators and mechanical conveyors. These modern mills are made in large sizes that have a production capacity of 1 to 4 metric tons per hour (in the versions used in India) or even considerably more. By comparison, the larger wholesale mills have a capacity of around 1 metric ton per hour, the coolie mills perhaps 300 kilograms an hour. The modern mills are also more efficient on outrun; the single-huller coolie mills may have outruns from paddy rice that is not parboiled of less than 60 percent (by weight) with a high percentage of brokens (and no bran). The more efficient traditional mills with several-stage equipment can bring this percentage up to 63 to 66 percent, with substantially fewer brokens. The modern rice mill may be able to raise this to 70 percent and in the process reduce the brokens to the tiny percentage allowed for commercial, perhaps international, markets. If the paddy rice is parboiled before milling, the huller's percentage rises but still remains well below the modern mill.

The progress of rice mill modernization in the less developed countries over the past half-dozen years has been controversial.[14] India is a good case in point. Scattered through the country are at least 50,000 of the traditional hullers. It is not even clear exactly how many there are, for the government has very strictly limited their importation since 1958. At that time the central government prohibited the introduction of any new hullers; it followed this in 1970 with another law that required progressive retirement of existing hullers through a process of government-induced modernization. These attempts at control of the huller have not been very effective, and a black-market situation with under-the-table payments has allowed continuing use of hullers and their resale and expansion. Figures on other types of mills are also sketchy; it was estimated in 1969 that there were perhaps 3,000 shellers and 4,000 huller-sheller combinations.

In the late 1960s the Ford Foundation collaborated with the Indian Institute of Technology at Kharagpur to promote modern rice milling, especially the concept of the fully integrated modern rice mill.[15] The explicit strategy is important to note: it was to "modernize from the top." Rather than trying to aid the process of modernization among the 50,000 huller owners, or even to do much in the way of promoting individual modernizing pieces for the larger mills (such as rubber-roller shellers), the central government decided to introduce eleven of the modern mills at selected locations, to show the potential of this giant step in technology. A combination of German and Japanese machinery was purchased, in 4-ton, 2-ton, and 1-ton capacities. One of the 4-ton German mills was installed in Tanjore in Tamil Nadu.

Once installed, the mills had profound effects on the regions they served. There was already long-standing overcapacity in the rice milling industry in India. Mills operated for only a month or so at the end of each of the two growing seasons, with intermittent operations in between. Even in the busy season, the notion of operating beyond the eight daylight hours was uncommon. Now, with the high capital cost of the modern mills (the 4-ton version cost approximately $500,000 in 1972, including buildings and storage and handling equipment), high utilization was necessary to make the mill pay. Theoretically, it could operate round the clock (its estimated annual capacity was 25,000 metric tons). The Tanjore mill, installed in 1967, was operating at approximately 60 metric tons a day for 300 days. The 1970-1971 yield in the state was approximately 1,975 kilograms per hectare and approximately 50 percent, or 1 metric ton per hectare, came to market. So it would take 18,000 hectares of paddy land to produce the amounts required to keep the mill operating. With holdings in Tamil Nadu under 2 hectares per cultivator, this meant dealing, directly or indirectly, with many thousands of separate cultivators. The logistics of this—the transportation into the mill, the drying and storage, the marketing after milling—all involve numbers of these magnitudes. The impact of a modern mill is considerable!

In areas where there is excess capacity in the milling industry, such as in Andhra Pradesh, the competitive pressure from the new mill is instant and direct; even in areas where there is not enough capacity, as in the Tanjore district of Tamil Nadu, the pressure is soon felt by owners of the traditional mills.

One of the most fascinating of all issues relating to the less developed economies is determination of the optimum mix of the various levels of modernizing inputs as they are combined with the traditional. Not only are assumptions necessary about investment costs and their related amortization patterns under various levels of operation, major additional assumptions concerning employment effects are also needed. Each of the types of rice mills has its own direct employment requirements, hand pounding obviously being the most labor intensive, the mechanically integrated modern mill the least. There are also indirect employment effects brought about by such factors as differing patterns of transportation into the mill.

At the height of interest in the modern mill in India, in 1972, a major analytical paper that covered all of these technical and employment effects was published by Peter Timmer on rice mills in Indonesia.[16] He chose five varieties of milling: hand pounding, the small artisan huller, and three modern mills—a 1-ton, a 3-ton, and a 5-ton. Making some assumptions about investment costs and utilization of these five models, he came to the rather surprising conclusion that huller facilities should continue to make up the bulk of any modernization program for the Indonesian rice milling sector. This conclusion was accentuated by his belief that employment aspects (so important in Indonesia, as in India) would be enhanced by the widely scattered, cultivator-oriented transportation patterns inherent in the distribution of hullers throughout the countryside. Timmer's argument was buttressed by the fact that the more traditional units could be made indigenously, whereas the modern mills were all imported (into Indonesia, as into India). Timmer summed up:

> The only conclusion that seems possible is that the labor-intensive huller units have substantial economic and social advantage under a wide variety of Indonesian circumstances. Any rice milling modernization program should be planned to reap these advantages.[17]

Events moved rapidly in Indonesia, and in late 1974 Timmer wrote:

> Literally thousands of small rice mills were shown to be socially and privately optimal over a wide range of circumstances in between hand pounding and large rice mills . . . It is not hard to see, then, the reasons why few large rice mills (or bulk facilities) have been installed in recent years in Indonesia. Where market forces—low wages, high interest rates and cheap rice prices—have been allowed to work, the overwhelming superiority of small rice mills as a generic class has been apparent . . . and these facilities have indeed mushroomed.[18]

Timmer would have many disciples in India today with this reasoning. Over the past half-dozen years approximately two hundred modern integrated mills of various sizes have been built in India. About a score of these have been of the 4-ton size; the great bulk of them are 2-ton. Experience with these modern mills has been varied; some have been reasonably successful over the several seasons they have been operating, others have been used at far below capacity, with resultant high costs. The euphoria of the early 1970s about the revolution that would be caused by modernizing from the top with a string of high-technology rice milling units has been replaced by a more realistic approach that has put heightened emphasis on the traditional sector.

However, there are some compelling reasons for arguing that intermediate-technology modernization should proceed apace, with upgrading of the wholesale mills to include rubber-roller shellers and the like, and replacement of the traditional hullers by more modern equipment. Several rice milling machinery manufacturers have recently perfected small "mini-mills," one-pass units of approximately 1/5-ton capacity and powered by approximately 3- to 5-horsepower motors that in one operation will perform all the processes of husking, separation of husk and brown rice, whitening, and bran removal.[19] It was estimated in 1973, before the oil crisis, that these machines could bc delivered in India for Rs. 30,000, or approximately $4,000. The cost will jump considerably under recent complications imposed by galloping inflation. Several machines have already been tested in the Indian environment, with somewhat mixed reviews. The single-pass feature requires cleaned paddy and careful settings for the sizings of grain in order to obtain the expected quality of outrun. It seems clear, though, that in the foreseeable future just such a small modern mill will be within the financial reach of the small coolie mill owners who presently use one or two traditional artisan hullers. Timmer noted the arrival of the mini-mills in Indonesia in 1974 but was not able to obtain figures on their numbers. His category "small rice mills" included an undifferentiated combination of traditional hullers, new rubber-roller huskers combined with hullers, and new self-contained mini-mills.[20] Thus he in effect lumped together wholesale and coolie mills.

This is a mistake. The modest data on rice milling collected by the Pilot Research Project in Growth Centres already suggests that the traditional coolie mills are neither capital efficient nor labor efficient. Table 30 contrasts nine of the coolie mills in Namakkal and Mohanur blocks with five larger wholesale mills, of about equal size, in Namakkal town. Comparing the two types, one can readily see the sharp distinction between coolie and wholesale by the very large difference in average outputs for the two types of mills. Beyond this, these figures also demonstrate that the coolie mills are less efficient, in both productivity per employee and productivity of capital. We have again plotted these two variables in Figure 5. The five wholesale mills are ahead of all nine of the coolie mills on productivity per employee, and by a substantial margin. Likewise, the five wholesale mills are ahead of all except two of the coolie mills on productivity of capital. This is fragmentary evidence from a small sample for a single year; yet it argues eloquently that there are some profound differences among the various small rice millers.

We live today in a time of onrushing world food shortage. To the cost implications of various levels of modernization are now added actual food shortfalls — missing bowls of rice to feed starving people in India, Bangladesh, and many other places. The new mini-mills will have a substantially heightened outrun over that of the traditional hullers; even if used in precisely the same way by the coolie mills — that is, as custom hulling units primarily for home consumption — the total amount of food available will be larger, inasmuch as

TABLE 30   Comparison of coolie and wholesale rice mills in Namakkal and Mohanur blocks, 1972.

Village	Fixed assets (FA) in rupees	Output (Rs.)	Value added (VA) in rupees	Number of employees	Wage rate (Rs./mo.)	Ratio of capital to labor— FA/empl.	Productivity per employee— VA/empl.	Productivity of capital— VA/FA
Coolie mills (n = 9 of 60 in two blocks):								
Sengapalli	10,300	8,646	5,460	4	60	2,575	1,365	0.53
Punjai Edayar	6,000	3,600	2,988	2	N.A.	3,000	1,494	0.50
Nanjai Edayar	36,450	11,372	8,893	4	100	9,113	2,223	0.24
Aniyapuram	18,900	7,684	6,021	5	50	3,780	1,204	0.32
Aniyar	10,500	2,100	1,626	2	N.A.	5,075	813	0.16
Avalnaickenpatti	18,500	8,470	7,470	3	60	6,167	2,490	0.40
Nallipalayam	36,300	7,950	6,266	4	60	9,075	1,537	0.17
Valayapatti	34,600	9,683	7,380	8	53	4,325	923	0.21
Thummankurichi	45,200	8,900	7,240	3	45	15,067	2,413	0.16
Average/coolie mill	24,083	7,601	5,927	3.9	59.7	6,193	1,524	0.24
Wholesale mills (average for 5 mills in Namakkal; n = 5 of 20 in two blocks)	65,870	169,429	23,548	7.2	73	9,163	3,276	0.36

SOURCE: "Summary Statistics for Industries, Namakkal and Mohanur Blocks," Pilot Research Project in Growth Centres, table. 1.

the bran (a food for humans) will be segregated from the husks (the residue of bran and husks generally used for poultry feed). These increases in outrun efficiencies must, of course, be fitted to the total pattern of both the costs of the modernization and the employment and price effects. From the available evidence of Timmer and others, we feel assured that rice mill modernization is moving into a "second generation" phase, with the exciting prospect that a

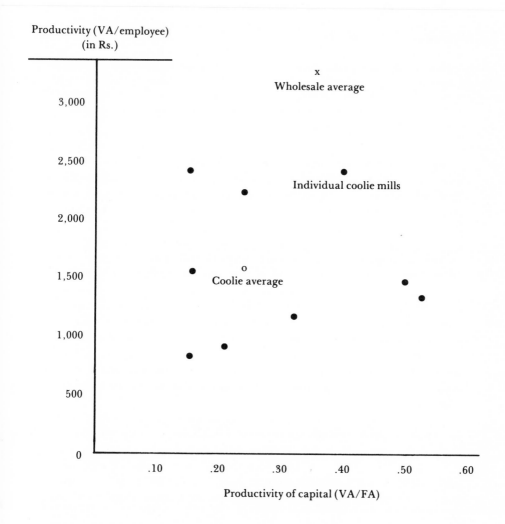

FIGURE 5 Productivity per employee vs productivity of capital for wholesale and coolie rice mills, Namakkal and Mohanur blocks, 1972. (Source: Table 30.)

new product of technology—the mini-mill—will hasten the long-awaited retirement of the traditional huller.

The groundwork for a new era in rice milling has thus been laid, one that we can hope will bring many thousands of small millers into the mainstream of modernization. It does take a conscious choice by the miller, however, for anything to happen. We need to ask:

Will the owners of coolie mills themselves be willing to modernize, or is it wiser to look on the outside for more change-oriented people (perhaps in a larger wholesale or modern mill?)

How change oriented are coolie owners in comparison to wholesale rice mill owners?

Are some of these owners—coolie or wholesale—more change prone than others and therefore more perceptive choices as change agents?

Notice that these are the same questions we asked ourselves in relation to fertilizer distributors. What does our research show for rice milling? There were fifty mills in our sample: twenty-four coolie mills and twenty-six wholesale mills.[21] The location was Tanjore district, a few miles down the Cauvery River from Namakkal. Tanjore is the rice milling center of Tamil Nadu and considered to be the most representative for analysis of that industry.

We first compared the total group of fifty rice millers with our large sample of fertilizer distributors, by means of discriminant analysis. A look at the means of individual variables for the two groups indicated that there were some marked differences. (A number of univariate one-way anovas gave F-ratios of statistical significance at the .01 level or lower). However, in the discriminant analysis, the patterns of variance were such that we had to reject the assumption of equality of dispersion: $F_{(78,28699)} = 2.50$. In effect, though the questions asked were the same for the two groups, the patterns of answering gave sharply differing variance relationships: it would be like comparing apples and oranges.

However, when we contrasted the large fertilizer sample with only the twenty-six wholesale mills for the same set of variables, we *were* able to accept the null hypothesis that the variance-covariance matrices were the same: $F_{(15,7721)} = 1.65$. With this assurance that we were matching legitimately comparable data sets, our discriminant-analysis F-test for overall discrimination showed us that the wholesale millers and the fertilizer distributors were not at all alike: $F_{(5,162)} = 6.83$. The univariate F ratios showed significant differences on the age of the firm (rice mills were older) and on the age of the respondents (rice millers were older). In addition, several key performance variables showed statistically significant difference (at the .05 level or lower): the "other information" variable, the number of meetings attended, the medium risk variable, the modernization variable, and the "other firms" variable. In all cases the rice millers were below the fertilizer distributors.

Then we did a discriminant analysis to compare the coolie mills to the wholesale mills. In this instance we were readily able to establish equality of dispersion for the combination of variables, so that our uniform set of questions could be compared across the two groups: $F_{(78,7174)} = 1.42$. And the F-test for overall discrimination clearly pointed to the two groups being significantly different (at the .001 level): $F_{(12,37)} = 8.58$. The univariate F-ratios showed the coolie mills to be lower on key measures: use of information sources, attendance at meetings and leadership roles, willingness to accept risk, attitudes toward modernization, opening of other firms, and of course sales and profit levels. Although the coolie mill owners in our sample are somewhat younger than the wholesale mill owners, they are less educated, more risk averse, operate considerably less profitable firms, and are not involved as much in organizations or leadership activities. Curiously, the coolie mill owners evidenced more interest in planning for both the short and longer term than did their counterparts. One wonders whether these plans were geared toward realistic and specific ends, or were more in the nature of concern and unease about their less-than-hopeful situation. Certainly the overall indicators point to persons less receptive to precisely the kind of attitudinal and behavioral variables we had earlier hypothesized as being integral to the process of becoming change agents.

What does this say about the second generation of rice milling modernization? Remembering that this is a highly complex question involving interrelationships among investment decisions, output decisions, physical logistics, and employment policies (among others), we can still feel reasonably assured of the hypothesis that the coolie owner is not a good candidate for a change agent. The wholesale rice mill owner is a somewhat better prospect. Even here, though, the wholesalers' levels of performance in those activities we consider indicative of entrepreneurial or innovative effort — the moving into other endeavors, the opening of new firms, profitability — are so low that we cannot predict which might be good candidates for aid in modernization. (We ran canonical correlations for the five predictor and three performance variables used earlier for both wholesale and coolie mills, with inconclusive results.) On balance, the more likely candidates would seem to be found among the innovative fertilizer distributors we have already identified as potential key men for rural change. There is a natural synergy, in fact, between fertilizer distribution and rice milling, clearly recognized by the fertilizer manufacturing executives; their first choice for a new dealer was almost always a miller or a paddy broker. Both functions at their best embody modernizing technology, and both are integral links in the agricultural system.

We do not mean to imply a simplistic, knee-jerk choice among gross categories of professions — that fertilizer distributors are somehow inherently more innovative than rice millers. Rather, we seek identification of *individuals* with some change potential. Our research has given us some likely places in which to look, and some analytical methods by which to choose.

The Agro-Service Center

Over the past decade there has been worldwide interest in constructing practical organizations that agglomerate the various agricultural services necessary for rural areas — all the inputs and all the related infrastructures — and in turn link these vertically upward to the processing, distribution, and related industrial dimensions of agricultural products. In Israel some highly innovative forms of agricultural organizations have been developed — the *kibbutz*, or collective village; the *moshav shitufi*, or cooperative village; and the *moshav avim*, or smallholders' cooperative village. In Yugoslavia the *kombinat* was developed recently to gather farm producers and processors into one large state enterprise. Similar aggregations, public and private, have been tried in a number of other countries.[22]

India is now beginning to experiment with just such a concept — called there the agro-service center. Again the essence is agglomeration; by bringing together agricultural services, their total impact is greater than the sum of the individual pieces alone. Many related services need to be part of this equation — small-town and rural banking and credit facilities, education and health services, rural electrification, transport facilities, communications, and retail trade outlets. Analysts generally agree that rural economic development needs this "all-sided" approach (the term used by Indian development specialists).

An Indian peasant being interviewed a few years ago by a United Nations mission reportedly said, "The first, the second, and the third thing needed in our village is better cultivation."[23] We do not wish to have quite this degree of tunnel vision, but we do want to plead the case that the structuring within the agro-service center itself is one of the most important of all the institutional groupings in rural economic development.

Let us sketch the possible ingredients of such an agro-service center. Some might be components of the actual entity of the center; others might be manned by independent operators; and, of course, some might not be found at all in a given growth center.

First, there is a set of agro-industries that are providing *agricultural inputs*:

Sale of commercial fertilizer mixtures and complexes, and custom mixing of
    fertilizer
Formulation of pesticides
Provision of pesticides and herbicides
Multiplication and processing of seeds
Sale of commercial seeds (HYV and others), with provision also for local varieties
Sale of cattle, pig, and poultry feed
Sale and installation of diesel pumps and electric pump sets
Sale of agricultural machinery and implements
Provision of farm hardware—fencing, safety fuses, containers, bags, cartons,
    crates, small tools
Sale of clay, tile, concrete, and sheet iron fabrications for use in farm buildings.

Inputs often involve products that have transport advantages when located near their markets; this is particularly true if the products are *heavy* (for example, brick and tile for farm buildings) or *bulk gaining* (equipment such as harrows, Persian wheels, chicken brooders, seed drills), or if the products themselves can be purchased in bulk and obtained in car-load lots (fertilizer ingredients, for instance).[24]

Next, there is a set of agro-industries that involve *processing and storage*:

Receiving centers (including possible mechanized weighbridges, dump pits,
    cleaners, elevators, and silo storage)
Processing operations, such as:
    Oil seed crushing and/or expelling
    Rice milling
    Rice bran production
    Flour milling
    Tamarind seed powder and tartaric acid production
    Ragi malt production
    Fruit and vegetable processing (and possibly packaging and canning)
    Poultry dressing plants
    Milk processing and creameries
    Animal rendering plants
    Cattle, pig, and poultry feed mills
    Banana powder extraction
    Glue manufacturing (from starch and the like)
    Molasses manufacturing
    Soap manufacture
    Processing of by-products (for example, manufacturing of cardboard boxes,
        baskets, or straw board boxes from sugar cane bagasse)
    Processing of coir, desiccated coconut, coconut shell powder
Commercial grading and packaging (for example, in jute bags, cardboard con-
    tainers, bottles, or cans)
Storage (perhaps refrigerated) in mud pots, mud brick cylindrical bins, metal

drums, and/or bulk storage, either flat or silo
Shipping facilities (such as conveyors or loading equipment).

The processing of the material input from agricultural or silvicultural operations almost universally involves *weight losing* or *bulk losing*; location near sources of raw material therefore has substantial advantage. Processing implies moving farther up the ladder of vertical integration and thus allows greater economic rewards to accrue to the village, particularly if most owners of the processing units live there. Storage and warehousing facilities for farm produce represent a particularly crucial type of infrastructure, with an extremely important economic effect on farmers. There is always danger of agricultural produce being injured by moisture or heat, eaten by rodents, or damaged by insects, worms, and other pests. The availability of ready storage frees the farmer from being forced to sell at the moment of harvest and forestalls the whipsawing of prices that often results from this forced choice. The late E. A. J. Johnson, an eminent location theorist, studied India's situation and concluded: "In a very real sense, then, warehousing can be called the protector of the national wealth in a country like India where agriculture is the main and important industry."[25]

Next, there are two closely related functions, *service operations* and *servicing of equipment*:

Custom hiring (with or without agro-service center operators) of major items of machinery for general cultivation, land development, plant protection, irrigation, harvesting, threshing, and processing
Land shaping and farm layout planning, together with water management where applicable
On-site soil and water testing
Contract hiring of outside services (such as aerial spraying) and rehiring to cultivators
Repair and maintenance of farm machinery
Maintenance and servicing of pump sets
Repair, maintenance, and new adaptations of processing machinery
Provision of spare parts for agricultural machinery and other equipment used on the farm, to be installed by the farmer for on-the-farm services.

The high cost of equipment relative to the cultivator's ability to pay makes some form of custom service operation very desirable. Strategic location of this kind of heavy equipment in agro-service centers makes for some difficult cost-benefit decisions that demand central scheduling and decentralized operations.[26] Given the hostile physical environment of many Indian villages (high temperature and humidity, dust and sand, rocky land that is particularly wearing on equipment), the servicing function assumes a special place.

The Indian cultivator has always shown much inventiveness in adapting simple equipment to his environment; when the equipment becomes more complicated mechanically, he is often not as skillful at coping with the problems involved.

Another set of functions of great promise for village-level adoption involves *manufacturing agricultural implements* of low and intermediate complexity. These might include many of the following, with emphasis on the simpler models:

Tillage—subsoilers, plows (scratch, moldboard, disk, chisel), harrows, cultivators, levelers, rollers, puddlers

Sowing—seed-cum-fertilizer drills, planter-cum-fertilizer distributors, special planting equipment, row markers

Plant protection—dusters, sprayers

Harvesting—reapers, combines, mowers, rakers, balers, forage harvesters

Threshing—threshers (stationary, Olpad, pedal), baling presses, sugar cane threshers, winnowers

Processing—maize shellers, groundnut decorticators, seed treaters, chaff cutters, seed cleaners, grain dryers, cotton gins, coir strainers, sweet potato slicers

Handling—grain bins, silos, elevators, loaders

Irrigation—low-lift water pumps, Persian wheels, diesel-powered and electric-powered pump sets, sprinkler irrigation equipment

Farm tools—carts and cart components, hoes and shovels, hitching and yoke harnessing.

Last, and in the final analysis probably the most important, is a set of *educational and "missionary" services* to the cultivators. These could readily include all of the following:

Consulting on soil analysis, fertilizer and pesticide selection, irrigation, and land improvement

Advice and record-keeping materials for farm management

Service as an information broker for market information, land and labor requirements and exchanges, and weather and crop reports

Aid in developing feasibility studies for new endeavors, either in farming or in agro-industries, and liaison to credit agencies (banks and others)

Assistance in systematizing job training on the farm and in the agro-industry

Provision of empathy and support to encourage the individual cultivator to be open-minded about new ideas and to be willing to take the first step in change.

Determination of exactly where to locate a given agro-service is an important decision both for its economic effects on the various villages and for its reshaping of the social and cultural parameters of these villages. Central place theory can give us some initial rules of thumb in making such a determination. If we know the populations of all the villages in a given area and know also the locations of the given functions we are studying, we can then compute a population threshold. Given a lower bound where all settlements lack the particular function and an upper bound where all settlements possess it, one can use one of several simple arithmetic methods to compute a median or average threshold. [27]

Generally, one does not wish to be below a population threshold. We need to make further assumptions, though, about the approximate levels of effective demand that will come forward from this particular population; for just as goods have their thresholds below which the total purchased is too small to justify sale, so too do services have their demand thresholds. The demand for heavy-equipment contour plowing and bunding is a case in point. The key to effective use of this kind of equipment is to minimize both the downtime and the travel time and maximize the time in field operations. Spotty, widely dispersed requests make this difficult. [28]

Similarly, the location of the service too far up the ladder is also a danger. For example, in the recent past all soil testing in Namakkal and Mohanur blocks has had to be done in laboratories considerably distant, mostly in Coimbatore town, about 160 kilometers away. The time between the taking of the sample and the return of the results was often three to four weeks or more. During this period crop conditions and weather patterns might have changed significantly and made obsolete the advice that was coming back so slowly. Soil testing services closer to the area of cultivation are now beginning to appear.

While this modest threshold model that relates only existing functions and populations is a useful starting point, it often gives overly simplistic results. In another growth center project pilot area, in a taluk very similar to Namakkal in Andhra Pradesh (the next state north of Tamil Nadu), the population threshold for fertilizer distribution centers was estimated to be 1,300, the seed distribution center figure was 650, and the agricultural implements distribution center was 730. Had the analysts there taken these static figures literally, the Andhra Pradesh taluk would have had 89 seed distribution centers, 50 fertilizer distribution centers, and about 75 agricultural implements distribution centers. It was obvious to them that this would be uneconomical and duplicative, so a practical process of modification was applied that balanced such factors as strengths of existing outlets, patterns of effective demand in the area, and availability of potential new entrepreneurs. From this set of dynamic factors judgments could be made about where to put increased concentration — as the analysts hopefully put it, "A few scientifically located centres would emerge." [29]

The threshold figures for these functions in Namakkal are similar, and were we to apply them literally, we would end up with fertilizer distribution depots in eight of the nine villages in the Sengapalli subarea. We, too, felt that this was too many—we would opt to strengthen the existing four dealers and perhaps aid them to open one or more branches in the smaller villages of the subarea.

We make similar threshold calculations to determine the requirements for various processing units—rice mills, oil extraction mills, and the like. Here the best method of calculation is based on the amount of production in the given growth center area. For example, the Sengapalli subarea produced 2,885 metric tons of local varieties of rice and 999 metric tons of HYV rice in 1972. We know also that 58 percent of the former and 64 percent of the latter were sent forward to market. Some 10 percent of the remainder was held back for seed, the rest consumed by the families of the area after it had been either hand-pounded at home or milled by a huller rice mill. If we assume for the moment that there were no competing rice mills outside the subarea, we need to determine how many rice mills would be needed. Let us use the capacity assumption that the Andhra Pradesh analysts adopted—that a mill would work 300 eight-hour days, two shifts for four months and one shift for four months. (Some mechanical drying is assumed.) Milling at 1 metric ton per hour would almost exactly take care of the Sengapalli subarea production of rice going to market. This could be accomplished by a 1-ton modern rice mill, or perhaps a sheller mill of the same capacity, leaving the home-consumption milling to be done by small huller mills. Alternatively, we might wish to use three to five mini-mills (depending upon the capacity we chose), which would take care of all of the market-destined rice as well as all of the home-consumed rice. To make the kind of practical choice the Andhra Pradesh analysts call "scientific," we would need to make further assumptions about numbers and locations of existing rice mills, marketing and transportation patterns, and so on. The lesson is clear, though: we could readily locate one or more modern mini-rice mills in Sengapalli subarea.

The case of agricultural implements distribution centers is more complicated, and should be discussed in conjunction with an additional factor of crucial importance in the developing world today, rural unemployment.

The age-old patterns of work in village India have long disguised an underemployment exacerbated by the long periods of idleness. A number of factors have contributed to this: (1) the seasonal nature of work and the large number of landless laborers; (2) the low land-to-man ratio, which has not provided each farmer with enough land to keep him continuously occupied; (3) the scarcity of capital, which has bred inadequate overhead and equipment; (4) the lack of alternative opportunities; (5) the existence of the joint family, which has often been likened to an unofficial agency for providing relief to the unemployed; (6) the lack of operational mobility that results from various social institutions, particularly the caste system; and (7) the immobility of the people and their unwillingness to move. Woven through these has been a rudimentary want structure — limited horizons and lack of aspirations, which have led to the farmer and his family being satisfied with a very low level of income and a very narrow life. By the late 1960s, in the Fourth Plan, the central government had generated a set of crash programs for dealing with this rural unemployment and its contingencies: the problems associated with backward areas, drought-prone areas, tribal areas, rural industry, and small and marginal farmers. A string of acronymic agencies was established — the Crash Scheme for Rural Employment (CSRE), the Small Farmers Development Agency (SFDA), the Marginal Farmers and Agricultural Labourers Programme (MFAL), the Drought-Prone Areas Programme (DPAP), and the Pilot Intensive Rural Employment Project (PIREP).[30]

Agricultural machinery is inextricably intertwined with these questions of unemployment. On the one hand, the tremendous promise of technology in alleviating the drudgery and inefficiency of small farmers has accentuated the pace of mechanization in agriculture all over the world. Many observers have argued that the only way to stem the exodus from the rural areas of the younger, more innovative people is to provide them with modernizing inputs congruent with their increasingly worldly values. On the other hand, mechanization has complex effects on employment in labor-surplus economies. Laboring people have long had a deep-seated, almost primitive fear of being displaced by machines. Luddite-like attacks on farm machinery, particularly threshers, are recorded as far back as the 1830s in England, with the perpetrators reputed to be led by a mythical Captain Swing. So it is not surprising that the Indian peasant, particularly if landless, would be hostile to the tractor and other machinery that might displace his hand labor. In 1970, for example, a "tractor stir" reminiscent of the Luddite tactics took place in the Tanjore district of Tamil Nadu; several tractors were smashed by mobs said to be landless laborers (encouraged, to be sure, by political agitators).[31]

But the realities are more intricate than any simplistic slogan like "tractors replace humans." There is burgeoning interest around the world in matching the proper pace of development with intermediate-level mechanization — in using what has come to be called appropriate technology. The precise balance point for given environments in this delicate mixing of modern and traditional technology has been the subject of some excellent recent analyses.[32] There are well-documented examples where the use of tractors increases farm output, incomes, *and* employment. In the Punjab a careful study showed that when tractor mechanization was accompanied by tube-well utilization, labor input increased by 25 percent, whereas when the latter did not accompany introduction of the tractor, a 30-percent decline in labor ensued. A number of other case studies show this pattern — that the effects depend very strongly on what happens in tandem with the arrival of the new tractors. If double-cropping can now be accomplished, for example, labor utilization can well increase. One analyst put it this way:

> There is urgent need for further studies . . . to formulate strategies of *selective mechanisation*—selective not in the usual sense of removing labour bottlenecks but in the sense of encouraging mechanisation which is income-increasing and either employment-neutral or, preferably, employment-generating and which does not increase rural income disparity. Otherwise, disastrous policies which give blanket encouragement to mechanisation are likely to continue.[33]

In India the interface between theories of appropriate technology and their practical implementations has shown up in the state agro-industry corporations. First in Maharashtra in 1965, and then a year later in Punjab, Bihar, and Tamil Nadu, joint ventures of the central and state governments were set up to enable farmers with meager resources to acquire costly equipment, particularly tractors, on a hire-purchase arrangement. A heavy subsidy by the central government was involved, both to enable low equipment prices and to provide foreign exchange for the large portion of tractors that was to be imported. By the early 1970s there were sixteen of these corporations around the country. Their primary function has been to provide a financing mechanism for tractor acquisition and to provide repair centers for the vehicles, once in the area. Several of the corporations also have developed custom service units —using the corporation's own crawler and wheel tractors for leveling, plowing, harvesting, threshing, and the like. Some of the corporations set up assembly units for the imported tractors. Several also purchased equipment for well drilling and perform this on a custom basis, most often to towns and villages but sometimes directly to individual farmers. Land reclamation and ground water exploration have also been undertaken by several of the units.[34]

In the main, the hire-purchase arrangements have created a reasonably effective vehicle for stepping up tractor usage in such areas as Punjab. Some of the imported tractors have experienced frequent breakdowns and persistent downtime. As one skeptic put it at a recent agro-industry conference, "At one time most of the agricultural tractors were lying in workshops in the nearest city awaiting repairs."[35]

There was a deeper problem, though. The agro-industry corporations tended to concentrate on setting up large units in large towns, with these units concentrating primarily on sales. The servicing was not only treated as an inconvenience, but all too often ineptly done. As a result, the concept of a service center was poorly received. In 1971 a major conference on this matter was held under the auspices of the Ministry of Agriculture of the central government, with an interesting cosponsor, the National Alliance of Young Entrepreneurs.[36] The same year saw a renewed concern about rural unemployment. Agro-service centers began to be viewed both as an answer to the failure in service on the part of the agro-industry corporations and also as a vehicle for helping to alleviate some of the rural unemployment. This is a logical juxta-position; there are skilled people in the rural areas, unemployed, who could be the nuclei for such service centers. Further, there was at that time (and re-mains today) an unsettlingly large group of young engineers unable to find work in their profession. In 1974 this number was estimated at upward of 100,000 engineering graduates.[37] It seemed only natural to channel young engineers into agro-service centers. In particular, if engineers specializing in agricultural chemistry, agricultural engineering, agronomy, entomology, plant pathology, horticulture, or animal husbandry could be persuaded to head these centers, a natural combination of technical skills and education would help reverse the rural brain drain. By 1973 the central government had carried its thinking to the operational stage and funded several pilot efforts, to be initiated through the agro-industry corporations of the states.

Immediately the question arose of just who would be in charge — would the centers be state owned, cooperative, or privately owned? The tilt of the govern-ment right along has been toward the first two options. In some states the state corporation set up the centers, in others encouragement was given to local cooperatives to assume this role. Many people had misgivings; as one of the influential papers in the south put it:

> There might be a temptation to entrust these programmes to voluntary agencies and cooperatives. That will probably be the surest way of denying the small and weak farmers their due. We know only too well that in many areas today there is a flourishing black market in agricultural inputs and equipment and there are any number of manipulations and other shady practices behind which one can easily trace the hands and interest of precisely those agencies that have somehow managed to earn the patronage of the political parties and some of the govern-ments.[38]

The influential *Economic and Political Weekly* faulted the cooperatives as being too weak:

> Between the politician and the bureaucrat, the cooperatives have remained a case of retarded growth. With the rise in the scale of procurement of food grains and supply of agricultural inputs, cooperative marketing societies have now a wide open field to emerge as viable bodies strong enough to withstand competi-tion from private traders without having to lean on official crutches. The prog-ress in this direction can be sustained only if the cooperatives are able, and are allowed, to build up a professional managerial cadre which would not be sub-ject to the passing whims of managing committees. Many of the marketing soci-

eties are presently managed by people from the Government who have neither the training nor the aptitude for marketing work in the real sense of the word. The present prosperity of the marketing cooperatives is not due so much to their managerial competence as to the monopoly conditions in which they procure food grains, sell fertilizers and earn fixed commissions. The real challenge for marketing cooperatives will come when, and if, these props are removed.[39]

Several of the private fertilizer companies have attempted to link new distributor appointments with unemployment concerns. For example, one of the large companies operating in the south has instituted on a test basis in the state of Andhra Pradesh a Scheme for Providing Entrepreneurship Facilities to Unemployed Agricultural Graduates.[40] The agricultural universities in Andhra Pradesh have been graduating large numbers of students in recent years and many have been unable to find employment. The company decided, as one of its "social objectives," to offer dealerships to a score of these men on a test basis, providing them with fertilizers, agricultural chemicals, and animal and poultry feeds, together with a power tiller, a few power sprayers, and several hand-operated sprayers — all on credit (with the help of the Union Bank of India). The plan is to bring these men together in a central location for a three-day training program that will show them how their university knowledge can be applied to the specific set of products available from the company, and how accounting and management of cultivator credit can be handled. Brief refresher programs later in the graduates' distributorships would reinforce the lessons.

It is too early to assess the potentials of this program. It involves heavy financial subsidy by the company, and company officials are concerned about how widely they can support such a plan. The state department concerned with cooperatives is also interested in agro-service centers and appears to be supporting them on an even heavier subsidy basis. For example, power sprayers have been rented by the cooperatives at a rate below their actual cost to the private-company distributor — a situation which would leave him no margin of profit whatsoever.

In Maharashtra another private-industry effort to build a set of agro-industry centers — the Agricultural Services Organization — has been initiated by a group of ten private companies, including manufacturers, fertilizer companies, and chemical companies, plus an insurance company. Small pilot efforts have been initiated, but the economic downturn has limited the organization's scope.[41]

Public, cooperative, private? In the final analysis it is not so much a question of what form of organization, but a concern about the behavioral and attitudinal set of the specific people who are involved. In Tamil Nadu are two cooperative marketing federations that have done an outstanding job in becoming full-scale change institutions in their areas. Near Coimbatore, a few miles west of Namakkal taluk, the Tudiyalur Marketing Federation has an outstanding record of serving its constituency, large and small, and has been unique in its ability to move into the agro-service arena. In consultation with CARE, Tudiyalur has set up an agricultural service center providing a full range of inputs. Likewise, in Tanjore district, the Tanjore Cooperative Marketing Federation has built a service center around the large 4-ton modern rice mill emplaced there in the early 1970s. Both of these cooperatives have had excellent full-time leadership, well-trained in both the technical side of the agricultural inputs and the marketing-oriented approach to the cultivators.

The issue, then, is not the sterile rhetoric of "socialism," "cooperation," and "private enterprise"; rather, it is the concern with finding the kind of mentality that will allow the proper mix of change and tradition that Indian villages need so badly. For example, it has proved difficult to persuade trained engineers to go back to the rural areas and become involved in an admittedly small operation like an agro-service center. A participant at the second National Seminar on Agro-Services held in 1973 put it bluntly: "They must be able to identify themselves with the rural environment and give up the comforts of city life."[42]

But the problems are not only financial. There is a philosophical dimension that we again wish to make explicit. We are talking not just about a set of physical services, but about an attitudinal and behavioral mind set. Change must be psychologically based. One development analyst put it this way:

> In order to arouse the villager from his age-old lethargy, to make him shed his fatalism, to make him adopt new rational attitudes towards himself and his surroundings, the effort has to be proportionately large and has to be carried out in a variety of directions simultaneously. Only continuous and pervasive intervention in the subtle course of his life and habits can wear down his resistance. It is as if we confront the villager with something new wherever he might turn. Let him be surrounded by buzzing activity in his fields, in his home, on the street, everywhere. Let him not retreat to any recess or corner where he can be left mentally undisturbed. That is the way to get him out of the morass of centuries into which he has fallen. If we thus generate a "psychosis" of change, a veritable conflagration to burn down his irrationality, we may succeed in putting him on his feet and in putting him on the path of self-sustained progress. Thus the all-sided activity with its multitude of new things happening all around may have great psychological value just as a "shock" treatment sometimes has.[43]

Perhaps we do not need to tread so heavily on the sensibilities of the villager; still, we do believe that the key to rural change is the change *mentality*.

We believe the agro-service center offers special promise as a catalytic agency for rural change. To make this a reality, though, a human catalyst must be involved. If the unemployed engineering or agricultural graduate has a change-agent mentality, so much the better. If, on balance, the difficulties are too great in bringing these people into the centers, or in making them effective once there, then we need to look to the rural population itself — such people as the fertilizer distributors we have studied. We need further to infuse the whole leadership of the center with this same mentality, that of the profit maximizer — the person who is willing to take medium risk, who will be a careful planner, who is by nature and inclination modern, and who has a calculating and profit-maximizing mentality. There are individuals like this in all three forms of the organizations just described. And, as we shall see, in all three there are real opportunities for upgrading the abilities, attitudes, and motivations of such people.

5

The Nurturing of
Change Agents

In the less developed world the gap between rhetoric and reality is sometimes very wide. The theorists in the academies and the practitioners in the administrative offices spin grandiose plans of what *ought* to be done — then often do not follow through. Dreams of rural change can become reality only when specific plans are brought to fruition. Thus we asked ourselves, once we had identified what we felt to be the key ingredients of the change-agent mentality, whether something could be done about using these insights in practical, action-oriented ways. In particular, having premised that we could identify from a group of people those who had the most promise as potential change agents, we wondered whether their innovative thinking could actually be increased and upgraded. Could change agents be "grown"? We sought to answer this question positively by planning and implementing a set of innovation seminars plus follow-up program in the summer of 1973 for a group of rural fertilizer distributors in South India.[1]

The Distributors for Change Program

The testing of our initial hypothesis concerning entrepreneurial behavior in the less developed world pointed to six central lessons. We felt we must address our efforts to accomplishing these things:

(a) Strengthen and broaden information sources and flows and, in particular, inculcate the concept of combining ideas and facts;

(b) Sharpen the understanding of planning, with special focus on short-term planning;

(c) Deepen the perception of risk taking and highlight the middle ground between a no risk mentality and a gambler's syndrome;

(d) Focus thinking on personal goal setting, and carry each individual through his own practical application of it;

(e) Strengthen all of these goals with a pervasive achievement motivation that stresses long-run profit maximization;

(f) Emphasize the practical needs for change, vividly show some reasonable real-life change possibilities, and constantly reiterate the belief that individuals can cultivate the change-agent mentality.

These are all complex subjects in their own right, and one can readily envision separate training programs to develop various facets of each. However, one of the most pronounced insights in the whole study was that individual pieces of information clearly are not as important as composites — the linking together of the information processes in an information pattern. To adopt this same "composite" strategy for the initial pilot training effort became one of our basic goals — to interweave to the maximum degree possible all of the research findings into one training package, what we called the Distributors for Change program.

We added several other considerations. First, we decided to concentrate only on private-enterprise fertilizer distributors, selected from the distributors of the two South Indian fertilizer manufacturing companies in our samples. We felt these private distributors had more of the modernizing, profit-maximizing rationale than did the public-sector distributors and the managers of cooperatives. We knew that there were undoubtedly many exceptions to this generalization; we invited top-level government administrators to observe the program, with the hope that we might be asked to try the same type of seminars with public-sector and cooperative distributors at a later date. We felt that fertilizer distributors were the best choices for an initial pilot program, as so-called appropriate technology had not yet reached the rice millers in our survey, and in any case they seemed less open to change.

Second, we chose medium-size and smaller distributorships and excluded the very largest of the fertilizer distributors, as their wholesaler focus was not really congruent with the small-town and rural distributor situation. Among these, we asked the two companies to help us identify those whom they felt to be in the middle in terms of entrepreneurial potential (more explicitly, approximately the second quartile) — not those of already-proven high-level entrepreneurial performance, nor those with no such apparent record. We administered our questionnaires to these people to corroborate our choice, using the predictive mechanism described in Chapter 4.

Third, we decided to bring them together as a group in a residential environment and thereby reinforce what we felt would be strong group support patterns. Since most were full-time proprietors who could spend only a short time away from their businesses, we planned a five-day seminar. We had a collateral training hypothesis that behavioral and attitudinal changes could be significantly affected in a short, concentrated program — and we wanted to test this belief.

Fourth, we decided that the program should be given in the language with which they were most familiar, Tamil. The faculty would be chosen from among the private fertilizer companies' management personnel, and these men would be trained to conduct the seminar straight through from start to finish. We would spend enough time with these faculty members to train them not only in the seminar methodology, but also in the underlying conceptual materials upon which the methodologies were based. To accomplish this required a period of many weeks, with carefully calibrated readings and a set of practice sessions where we played out each step of the seminar, then critiqued the performance and fitted this back to concepts from the reading materials. We particularly wanted to create a faculty that would be able to "train the trainers," that would be able to extend the seminar to other fertilizer companies and even to other industries, such as rice.

Fifth, the primary target goal would be to bring about change in the attitudes of these distributors toward organizing their work, and toward moving into new fertilizer service functions. An important secondary goal, though indirect, would be to promote by demonstration the effects of the fertilizer distributors' innovative attitudes on the change attitudes of the farmers served by the distributors.

Sixth, emphasis would be placed on the group's self-image and self-motivation by stressing that they were a specially chosen pilot group that would be the "first to learn valuable new methods of business operation." Thus a set of cognitive and group supports would be infused. The program would focus strongly on action outcomes—end results that would bring about innovations in the distributors' business practices and heighten their practical ability to be change agents.

Finally, a careful follow-up would be conducted over a period of approximately eighteen months after the program; too frequently in development programs everywhere there has been a pattern of grandiose beginnings that seep away like water on sand for lack of follow-through, and this is a flaw we wished to be careful to avoid.

Influence of Earlier Work

Social scientists typically share their information, crossing over disciplines and through individual projects to cull the best, in the hope of coming up with one further bit of knowledge. In our case there is a good deal of research that has indirectly influenced the seminars we are about to describe.

David C. McClelland and David G. Winter have long been interested in "motivating economic achievement" (the name of their important 1969 book, wherein they describe their own entrepreneurial seminars in India, conducted many years before ours).[2] Beyond their direct input into our project during its early stages of formulation, their joint book and other substantive contributions to the basic concepts of achievement motivation have indirectly influenced our seminars. We tailored some of the long-standing McClelland lessons to our particular moment in India's rural development, the summer of 1973, and built on much of his conceptual thinking.

Another whose work we incorporated is Eugene Staley. His extended interest in the development of small-scale entrepreneurs added major conceptual strengths to the training methodology we used.[3] At the time our Entrepreneurial Research Project began, Staley was in India on a research project aided by the Ford Foundation. The focus was development of curricula at the primary and secondary school levels for work-oriented education.[4] The training methods he suggested for adoption in one of the Western states had considerable relevance to our own program with mature fertilizer distributors in Tamil Nadu, farther south.

Our ERP colleague V. G. Patel provided other ideas. His entrepreneurial training program at the Gujarat State Development Corporation involved both starting a business and managing it, and considered the underlying achievement and attitudinal bases for this management process.[5]

Last, we drew upon several of the training concepts in achievement motivation promulgated by Acción Internacional in Venezuela.[6] The antecedents of the ERP lay in our own earlier studies of entrepreneurship in Venezuela, and the collateral work of Acción stimulated our comprehension of the special problems of entrepreneurship in developing countries.

The particular format of our seminar — both its underlying conceptual base and the particular training methodology — is our own. Because we feel that the particular combination of ideas used in the seminars has its special relevance and integrity, it is worthwhile to elaborate in some detail precisely what happened at each stage of the program. In addition, Appendix B gives the complete schematic outline presented to the various authorities in India prior to the seminars.

The Seminars

Teaching abstract concepts of change is difficult under the best of circumstances; here it was complicated by the modest educational level of the participants. They were mostly rural and small-town men, not completely overawed by their surroundings but nevertheless coming into the experience cautiously. We knew we had to titillate their imaginations at once — or lose them irrevocably. Our touchstone here was the participation game, which we interspersed throughout the first three days of the seminar.

We decided to make even our start unconventional. The usual Indian pattern for opening a conference is a formal inauguration speech. Instead of this, we asked a well-known Indian businessman, a true entrepreneur, to reject the usual hortatory performance and instead to describe in detail just how he had accomplished the growth that led to his success. Much to the surprise and delight of the participants, our chosen entrepreneur did exactly this, telling a frank story of his life from beginnings more humble than any of them to the eminence of his present position.

A Game of Planning

This unexpected start succeeded in setting a mood of excitement, and we followed it immediately with the first interactive game, a well-known competitive group construction game called Lego Man.[7] The participants (twenty in each of two seminars) were divided into four teams and given identical sets of fifty Lego pieces of varying size, colored red and white. In the center of the room was a model of Lego Man, a figure constructed with fifty similar pieces. Each group was told that it must construct this identical man, but the process by which they did so was to be up to them. The ground rules were that only one person from each group could come to observe the Lego Man in the center at one time, that the individual pieces could not be put together until the whole group decided that it was "ready to assemble," and that an observer would time their assembly stage. With these instructions the groups were left to their own resources to accomplish the task.

Underlying this ostensibly simple game were some fundamental behavioral goals. The observers were there not only to time, but also to observe the group process of organization, planning, and execution. The groups had been told that they would be timed on their assembly, but in truth they were also being timed on their planning cycles. The observers made careful note of the interactive patterns of communication within each group and, as the group progressed, made judgments about the style and interpersonal behavior being used.

The results were productive on two fronts. The natural excitement of a carefully calibrated competitive game succeeded in bringing almost instantaneous enthusiasm from the participants. Although later in the seminar we would center on individual competitive behavior, we felt that the supportive-ness of the small group could build a competitive spirit without embarrassing anyone right at the start of the experience. Our decision proved sound. By the end of the game the natural barriers of unease and strangeness had been substantially bridged.

Equal in importance were the results of the game itself, with its stress on the planning dimensions. Here is what happened, for example, in the first seminar. Group *A* quickly announced that it was ready to assemble after a short twelve minutes of planning. This put pressure on the other three groups, who began racing back and forth to the model, trying to catch up. But Group *A* was never able to assemble the man. Groups *B* and *C* did, the former in forty-three minutes and the latter in forty-nine—with distinctly different planning-execution combinations (Group *B*, 18-25 minutes—Group *C*, 33-16). Group *D* finally assembled its model after thirty minutes of planning and an additional thirty-five minutes of assembly.

This combination of results allowed us to conduct a rich discussion of the varying strategies of the four groups. Clearly, Group *A* planned inadequately and completely botched the assembly. Groups *B* and *C* accomplished the task set forth in about the same time, but with sharply divergent planning philosophies. These differences were discussed and extrapolated to more complex planning situations, where planning-execution ratios can vary enormously, depending upon the particulars of the task. By the time the groups had been through the experience and the critique, they had learned about conscious planning, had worked together in an interpersonal relationship, had come to know themselves more thoroughly than they had before—and had enjoyed the process.

Acting Out a Story of Change

Lego, preceded by a short lecture on change, was followed with more formal articulation on basic change concepts that utilized planning as a point of departure. Now we felt that the participants were ready to begin thinking of change directly and to practice a bit of innovation. Each of the four groups was given the assignment of concocting a story of change, modeled on the one that had been told by the successful entrepreneur earlier in the day. That evening they were asked to meet privately to prepare their stories for presentation the following morning as playlets.

One might have expected these men to be timid about the acting dimensions of the assignment, but the Lego Man enthusiasm remained; four useful skits were presented the following morning. The stories were conventional in setting; generally they involved father-son relationships in a rural business setting. The changes built into the stories were also stereotyped. New businesses were opened, products were taken on. For example:

> A rich farmer and his accountant friend are talking; the friend has a son who has finished school but is lazy and has no work; he jokingly suggests to the farmer that he should marry his daughter to the accountant's son; the farmer gets angry and says that he will not marry his daughter to a loafer; the son hears about this and is ashamed; he runs away to the nearest city, starts as a cleaner of taxis, learns driving, becomes a taxi driver; he saves money, attends evening class, passes the examination for the Indian Administrative Service, becomes Collector of the District, and marries the farmer's daughter.

It mattered little to us that the stories were conventional. Rather, the structure was the key. The groups were forced to lay out a sequence of events, one following the other, and to draw the sequence to a close with a climax. Further, it required the group to articulate the stages, even to the extent of acting them out. Thus the cognitive support of change was implanted. Again, the pattern of analytical evaluation at the end, by both the faculty and the participants, reinforced the continuing intellectualization of the basic concept of change.

Brainstorming

Now we were ready to involve the groups in a more explicit exercise in combining ideas. Each of the four groups was given a bag containing fifteen items — a bar of soap, a comb, a spoon, a betel nut, a shoelace, and the like (as we explained it, "some items we collected when one of us emptied his pockets"). The assignment was to take six of the fifteen items and again create a story of change. This time the stories were to be confined to a specific set of "facts" represented by the six items. Each fact was to relate to the next in some logical order, with the last item representing the final change. Here is an example (items used — handkerchief, soap, comb, cuff link, spoon, betel nut):

> When I was thinking of starting a business, I saw a big hotel. I thought I could start a pan [bread] shop next to it. This was a small town and previously people were using the towel on their shoulders for wiping their hands. This is now becoming an outmoded practice, so I thought, "Why can't I start a business of selling small towels?" I ordered the same from a "ready-made" company. People coming from outside the town may like to have a wash with soap and for this the usual big-size soap may not be economical. If they had a smaller size it would not cost them much and the purpose would still be served. So I ordered and got some small soaps. There was a great demand and sales were increasing. As a next step I thought about selling combs. Hence I got some small combs convenient for the customers, of a size they could keep in their pocket. The combs, too, sold. Then I thought about cuff links which are required for full-sleeved shirts instead of pressed buttons, hence I also included these in my selling items and I made fairly good sales. Then I decided to move into the sale of betel nut, and this business I was doing by measuring betel nut powder with a spoon as a measure for selling to the customers. The quality I was getting was not uniform — sometimes I was giving more quantity — hence I arranged to make small packets. By this time, the quantity was uniform and I was able to save Rs. 3 per kilogram.

This story remains conventional and simplistic, but it demonstrates that an important lesson had been learned, the concept of combination. Brainstorming techniques emphasize this meshing of individual ideas to come up with a whole that is truly an innovation. To make the point in several ways, the last two of the four groups were asked not to relate their story step by step, but only to show the six items and then to tell the story that resulted from the sixth piece. The other groups were asked to attempt an inverse brainstorming — guessing the order of the five remaining items, relating them logically to the sixth, and so forth. After this, the initiating teams were asked their stories, and the differences between the two versions were discussed. In the process the underlying concept — the building of an "instinct for combination" — was hammered home.

While these stories were uncomplicated, they contained an instinctive native wisdom. The Tamil language is a rich one, and Tamil proverbs are renowned.[8] In these stories, as all through the seminars, the participants were able to illustrate complex concepts with humble everyday expressions. Here are some further examples.

On Achievement and the Use of Time

If I prepare food for a journey it won't last long. Similarly, the advice I give for your life cannot last long. It is up to you.

If it is already ten days after Christmas and you call for the Christmas Father, how foolish it will be.

The day of the new moon won't wait until the priest arrives.

If a Chettiar [caste known for attention to business] goes into the river, even if he is dying people think he does it on purpose.

On Being Realistic in Your Expectations

A man who cannot catch a cat at his native place should not try to catch an elephant elsewhere.

No matter how much a sparrow can try to fly high, it cannot become an eagle.

A man wishes to become a talukdar [a high government official] but he has got luck to grow asses only.

You cannot measure with your forearm [a common device for measurement in India, given the lack of rulers and tapes] unless you have something to measure.

On Human Nature in General

When it comes to getting others into trouble, the entire village will join together.

Can a donkey appreciate the flavor of camphor?

You have not even been invited to dinner, yet you are complaining about the plate.

A Business Game

The following day some of the more sophisticated concepts involved in achievement motivation were brought into the program. We needed a practical introduction to them and accordingly constructed our own simplified version of a business game. The faculty of the seminars wrote the game in the process of their own training, building it directly from their own experiences. This assignment to the faculty was in itself a very useful analytical experience — they were required not only to think through the best way of describing the situation but also to anticipate the range of possible answers from the seminar group. The give-and-take in this writing and role playing prior to actual use of the case was an invaluable tool for deepening the expertise of the faculty in handling case analysis.

The participants were again divided into four groups (we changed their composition at this point in order to build a wider network of relationships) and were given a simple situation:

> You are Mr. Ram Gopal, managing director of RG Products, a small company in the Guindy Industrial Estate, near Madras. You employ thirty-five men. You manufacture three simple auto parts; these are stamped and only rough-finished, so most of your employees do unskilled and semiskilled work. You have one direct competitor right in Guindy and several others in Madras. You sell to many auto supply shops, and the competition for sales is very keen. There is no union in your plant, and you have never had any serious labor trouble. Your company has been reasonably profitable in the past, but managed to just break even last year. A rather large bank loan comes due this year.

The participants were then sent to the four corners of the seminar room, and given a series of situations to analyze within their groups. They were told that they had eight minutes to come up with a solution, and that for each of the situations a different member of the group was to be Mr. Ram Gopal. At the end of the eight minutes they were to announce the group's decision and the reasoning behind it. The faculty was constituted as a "jury" and given the responsibility of assessing the quality of the decisions. A winning group would be chosen at the end.

Here are the five situations the faculty wrote:

Situation 1

> One evening you were called by telephone to send some important parts to a good customer in downtown Madras. You had a commitment at Guindy and could not leave, and your delivery truck was gone for the day. One of your skilled employees offered to drop off the parts on his way home that evening on his

motor scooter. On the way, he was very negligent and got into a serious traffic accident, where his carelessness caused another vehicle to hit a pedestrian. He was arrested and fined Rs. 75.

Should you pay all of this fine, some of this fine, or none of it? Why?

Situation 2

Several of the Guindy companies, some with unions, some without, are beginning to have labor troubles. They have formed an informal employers association and are trying to get 100 percent membership among the Guindy employers. The leaders have asked you to join and have promised that you will be made a member of the Board of Directors if you desire. Most other companies are joining, but you know several that do not intend to.

Do you join and become a member of the board, join as an active member, join but do not participate, or stay out altogether? Why?

Situation 3

A number of influential people, all members of the most important temple in the Guindy area, have formed a welfare organization to aid the residents of one of the slums nearby. They are particularly interested in improving the housing and providing a small crèche for working mothers. Only a few people from this area actually work in Guindy; none of your employees do. The organization has received much publicity and has high prestige.

The members have approached Guindy companies for contributions. If a company gives Rs. 1,000 or more, it will be listed on the new brochure as a sponsor.

Should you give more than Rs. 1,000, exactly Rs. 1,000, a token amount (Rs. 50 or Rs. 100), or nothing? Why?

Situation 4

Because of a death there is an opening on your office staff for a man whose duties are in the sales area, with responsibility primarily for the service needs of customers. You are considering these people:

Krishna, an older person already in the office, working at present on sales invoices and the like. He is loyal and trustworthy and knows the customers well (though not many of them on a personal basis). He is not very aggressive and has a meek, quiet voice.

Benjamin, one of your best semiskilled workers, ambitious, wants the job, knows the technical side of the parts very well, has little schooling, does not talk very literately, but has a pleasing way.

Shan, the young son of a close friend (one of your directors), just graduating from college with a B.Com., has worked for a few months in a similar factory, seems bright to you but a bit immature.

Which man do you choose? Why?

Situation 5

You have heard a rumor that your Guindy competitor has purchased a new machine that makes the quality of the finish on the parts that each of your companies produces noticeably better. You check with the machinery company and find such a machine has just been put on the market. If you buy it now, it will cost you Rs. 20,000. The salesman admits that probably in a year or so the price will come down to about Rs. 16,000. The machinery company has another machine, used, that will produce a finish slightly better than you now produce but not quite as good as the new machine. The used machine can be purchased for Rs. 12,000.

Should you buy the new machine now, buy it a year from now, buy the used machine, or stay with the machine you have? Why?

For the next day's experiences we planned to introduce analysis of motives, using David McClelland's categories of affiliative, power, and achievement motives. We would identify the three (using the word "social" for the affiliative motive) and briefly describe the differences among them, then center our attention primarily on practical examples of achievement motivation. In order not to have this complex set of thoughts come on our subjects too quickly, we used the five case situations in our business game not only to discuss the process of decision making itself—the major focus of the assignment—but also to note briefly the differences in the kinds of motives involved. Situations 1 and 3 primarily emphasize affiliative and social; situation 2 has its central focus on power (with some affiliative dimension too). The sequence led the teams to a primary emphasis on achievement motivation in situations 4 and 5. After the game was played, the faculty critiqued the decisions of the four groups for each of the five situations. A winner was determined, as we carefully explained, not because there was a single solution to each situation, but because the groups exhibited varying strengths in their reasoning and analytical abilities. Thus we were able to make the straightforward point that there are varying ways of looking at business motives while holding in abeyance the concepts of achievement, power, and affiliation.

A Look at Personal Motivations

After these two days of group decision making and brainstorming, the participants were directed to look carefully at their own individual motivations and drives. Initially withholding explanations of motives, we had the participants observe four standard Thematic Apperception Test (TAT) pictures, adapted to an Indian environment.[9] Each man then answered the standard questions: "What is happening here? What has led up to this situation? What is being thought by the people involved? What will happen?" Here, for example, are the reactions of three of the participants to one of the TAT pictures, a photograph of a young Indian woman sitting in the doorway of a village home with her chin resting on her hand:

Mr. *N*—Picture of a lady in sorrowful mood. Seems she is in an illusory world. She has recently lost her child. She feels that she should have taken the child to a nearby hospital, which she didn't do, when the child was suffering from illness. "Had the child been alive, it would have been a pleasant one" is her imagination. She needs consolation. She just gets up, goes inside the house and prays to God, and determines to do her other jobs, leaving her bereavements behind her.

Mr. *S*—A girl wants to continue her further studies. For that she could not get any aid from her family. She went to the house of one of her relatives expecting help and the relative was not there at that time. She is sitting remorsefully and at this point the relative comes and learns her grievance. He suggests a suitable idea to her parents and this helps.

Mr. *D*—A common farmer's family. Profession: agriculture. Due to drought there was a crop failure. He [sic—the participant identifies the woman as a man!] sits with a sorrowful face without knowing what to do further. During a drought what steps could be taken to safeguard the crop interest? Digging a deep well? Constructing small dams for storage of water? These are some of the plans he has. Nearby there is a small stream. He plans to bring water from that spring by constructing a small earthen dam across it.

We now know a bit about Messrs. *N, S,* and *D*. After their three other picture explanations, we know more. While the TATs are not to be considered definitive devices for "explaining" people, they are valuable for producing insights into the set of complex motives and values that all of us hold within ourselves. At the conclusion of the picture sequences we explained in some detail the relations between achievement motives, social (affiliative) motives, and power motives. We reminded the participants of the business game of the preceding evening, where the set of management decisions had involved these kinds of relations.

Finally, we showed the participants a simple scoring system (a condensed version of McClelland's) whereby they could take their TAT stories and analyze their own motives with regard to achievement, affiliative, and power aspects.[10] The faculty had earlier written another story, one that involved the three motives. There are a total of thirty achievement thoughts, five power thoughts, and three affiliative thoughts. The story was taped so that the participants could listen to the tape twice, first all the way through and then in segments in order to be able to mark down each time one of the three motives came up. Here is the story that the faculty wrote (A = Achievement thought; P = Power thought; S = Social, or affiliative, thought):

Today I was sitting in the shop when one of the small cultivators from the opposite side of the tank—he lives about 6 kilometers from town—came in. He asked me for three boxes of matches. Mind you, it wasn't one, but three. I got the three boxes out and told him that was "30 paise." Well, instead of paying, he moved his feet back and forth, even called me "sir" once, and started to tell me about his wife having the fever and how he thought he had planted poor seed this year. Why, he didn't want to pay anything—he wanted *three* boxes free. So I got very angry and told him, "No, I won't give you three, I won't

A   even give you one. This is a well-run shop and I deal with good

P   cultivators who pay their bills. Go away before I tell the police that there is a loiterer on my street."

I should not have gotten so mad at him, I know, but his voice reminded me so much of a boy I knew when I was young. I was preparing for an examination we were going to have in school.

A   It was a very important examination, because the person who scored the highest was going to be allowed to stand in front of the class when the school inspector came on his annual visit and describe to him what the class had been learning. I really

A   wanted to get the highest score, so that I could be the one chosen. There was this other boy in class who was quite smart too. We had often gotten the high scores in tests, and I was al-

A   ways trying to beat him. He was a rather conceited boy and thought he was better than the rest of the class—not only smarter but superior. He made me so irritated one time, when

A   he beat me in a close competition, that I got very mad after school, especially when he was bragging to a group of friends

P   about his high score, and I picked a fight with him for no reason at all, and got into all sorts of trouble with the schoolmaster. Well, when the examination I was telling you about was announced and the schoolmaster told about the winner getting to be in front of the class, I told my mother and father about it. I remember my mother's reaction very well. She said, "Oh, Ram, if you win, then you will have to be up in front of all those im-

Not S   portant people. If you stutter, or forget, all those people will
(mother says)   laugh, and all the other children will tell their parents and then the mothers will make bad remarks about you when I am a-round." I said, "Mother, you can't go through life worrying

A   about what people think of you. I do want us to have a good

S A   name here in the village. But I also want the chance to let the

S A   inspector know our family is an important one. Don't worry, mother, I'll do well in the speech."

Not A or P   My father was listening to all of this and finally he said, very

(father says)   loudly, "You must do well in the examination, Ram, or I will be very displeased. If you don't win, I will forbid you to go to the big bazaar when Pongel comes." That was the way my father

P   always was—ordering me and trying to threaten me to do things. It always made me very angry and I wanted to shout

P   back at him, but I just decided, "I'll show him that I *can* win the

A A   contest. I will try even harder."

             I thought I knew the material that was going to be on the

A A   examination quite well, but I started reviewing it again. I tested myself and kept track of how many questions I missed from the textbook by making marks in the dust. First there were about

A   ten marks. Then when I got a better score, I smoothed over that mark, and finally got it down to none. I thought to myself,

A   "This is a good way to remember—I will remember the wrong answer and the right answer." This turned out to be one of the

A   best ways I found for studying and remembering—I called it the Scratch Method.

             Well, I made a plan to myself that I would do the Scratch

A   Method every *other* night from then until the night before the

A   test itself. I decided that if I did it *every* night it would lose its effectiveness as a remembering device.

             The day of the big examination came, and I was quite ex-

A   cited, and I don't mind telling you, I was a bit nervous. But I

A   felt confident too—I knew I could score high because the Scratch Method would help me.

             My friend, the other smart boy, was there and acting very superior, like he was easily going to win. I looked at him and

A   said to myself, "I'll show you who's the best. I'll scratch you right

A   out of the competition with my Scratch Method." But seeing his

P   smug face still made me angry and I wasn't listening carefully enough when the schoolmaster was giving instructions and lost a few minutes of good time at the start because I had to reread the instructions that I hadn't listened carefully to.

             The two boys that were sitting beside me were both fun-loving types, never doing well on school work. And they weren't taking this examination very seriously either. They started fidgeting around and then started to poke each other and make a nuisance of themselves. At first they were bothering me and I was beginning to lose my concentration, but then I told myself, "I

A   know I can't make them stop it, for if I call the schoolmaster it

(no social   will make a rustle and there will be a big scene and then I will

here)   lose more time." So I pretended I was back at the house, sitting

A   outside where I studied. Soon I got my concentration back, and though they kept up their playfulness it didn't bother me at all.

A   Making myself think about studying back at the house was good, too, because it helped me bring the Scratch Method, my new learning method, back into my mind. You know, it was really remarkable. Eight of the original ten of those scratches in the dust were on that examination. Remember now, each of those eight was an important fact that I had originally made a mistake on. I had made a plan to eliminate the mistakes and

A   had eliminated *each one* of those eight scratches. Well I got *all*

A   of them right on the examination!

A   Who won the examination? Why, you know I did! Else why would I have told you the story!

The day of the school inspector's visit came, and I was the class representative up in front. I must admit that my mother's comment about making a mistake popped right into my mind just before I was to speak. I had this awful feeling, "What would

S   my friends say about me if I disgraced the class." But it all

A   worked out well. I knew what I wanted to say—I had planned it out step by step—and it went just as I had planned.

A   Afterward I told the inspector about my secret weapon, the Scratch Method. He said, "Young man, you ought to write a

A   book about that." I will, too!

We had consciously tilted all these exercises toward achievement and change; thus, in a subtle way, the participants were developing a set of cognitive supports that would allow recall at a later point of their abilities to articulate and then to act upon change when they returned to their villages. We were always building an underlying, unarticulated thread of change mentality by the persistent emphasis on the values and efficacy of change itself. Thus, in the TAT tape the participants consciously scored for all the motives, at the same time unconsciously putting primary focus on achievement values because the story emphasized achievement.

Risk

Change inevitably involves risk, so we wanted the participants to have an understanding of the relation of risk to achievement. After a short introduction of this new area, we had the participants play the well-known ring toss game.[11] Each participant was allowed four rounds of four shots each, with the goal of throwing rings onto the peg set in place on the floor. There were the usual ground rules—the participant could stand at any distance he wished (marked from 0 to 15 feet), but he had to take all four shots in a given round from the same distance. He was told that the first round was for practice and he could throw without his friends watching. The second round was "for the record" and all participants were to watch one another. In the third round the notion of varying rewards for longer-distance success was introduced; only a few points were allowed for ringers thrown from a short distance, much larger rewards for longer distances. For the fourth round the inverted scoring principle was introduced, with higher point totals given for shorter distances and vice versa. This brought typical reactions of consternation from those who already had high point totals. Some even became highly incensed: "You can't do that!" Most of the participants guessed that there was a hidden agenda involved, and the discussion that followed the fourth round clearly brought this out. The combinations of rounds 3 and 4 effectively picture the relation between the process of achievement itself and the accomplishment of a specific goal. The participants who stood very close in round 4, and therefore added significantly to their total scores, admitted they had little achievement satisfaction doing it this way. Those who continued to stand far out, often with little success in getting the ring onto the peg, found that in the process of trying to achieve for the sake of achievement alone, they were unable to reach a goal of recognized accomplishment. Thus we were able to build an understanding of medium risk. Change always involves risk; if one is unwilling to take *any* risk, one will not be a change agent. On the other hand, great risk (a gambling mentality often present in India) can also be nonproductive.

Individual Goals

In the first three days the participants had seen the groups put together ideas and treat them conceptually, to plan and then to administer. Furthermore, each man had applied these same concepts on an individual basis. By way of experiential involvement, they had worked through some sophisticated theory about how change occurs; in the process they had gained behavioral and psychological insights that came as revelations to a number of them.

Now the time was right for more explicit, practical action planning; the fourth day was devoted entirely to individual goal setting.[12] The participants had taken seriously an assignment initiated the first day, to write a newspaper story about themselves ("It is September 8, 2023. An article is being written about your life. What would you like to have it say?"), and some rather remarkable stories resulted. Here is one.

Fifty years, i.e. 18,250 days. Accordingly, one-half portion of my life. Fifty years ago when I was at the age of 30, I planned certain things to achieve certain goals.

1. I should increase my status in the Society. I should come forward in all aspects.

2. I should make others also to come forward. I should do all I can to move my country forward.

3. I should live till my 100th year.

Today I have reached my 80th year and I am very happy and proud to state that I have reached all my goals which I planned.

To increase my status in the Society and to come forward I wanted to improve my business.

Fifty years back I was doing business in groundnut and I was exporting the same from here to almost all other states. Since it was a business which was mainly based on fluctuated market I used my skill in full and I took some moderate risk also. Naturally I earned and my status raised. But I was not satisfied with this. Moreover this was a seasonal business, and hence I could do this business only for 5 months, and for the rest 7 months my manpower was idling. Therefore to work for the other 7 months also I took the fertiliser and cement agency of M/S. E. I. D. Parry Ltd. and M/S. Dalmia Cement Bharat Ltd. respectively. Since there was competition in this business, I planned certain things and I implemented those plans. If one farmer buys one bag of complex, I gave him a prize of a pencil. By selling one bag I got profit of one rupee and by giving a pencil I faced a loss of only 8 paise. Similarly if a farmer purchased 5 bags I gave him one fountain pen which costed me only 75 paise. But even then I got a profit of Rs. 4 and 75 paise out of those 5 bags. In cement business also I did the same thing. In this basis I improved my business like anything. I printed my firm's name on the pencil and fountain pen which seemed a great thing to the farmer and became a good advertisement to me. Thus I increased my status in my life and Society.

I had ancestral lands to an extent of 20 hectares. Getting loan from a bank I bought a tractor and cultivated my lands in various and new methods. I sowed high-yielding varieties. Being educated fertiliser distributor I applied required fertilisers and pesticides in time and I got good result. But I was not satisfied. I wanted others also to follow me. I called many farmers to my lands and showed them my methods and advised them to do like me. I also told them that I would assist them, and also told if they do like me, I will supply fertilisers and pesticides on loan. Certainly my advices had good effect. Many farmers followed me. I guided them properly. Even sometimes I sent my tractor to cultivate their lands. I often went and inspected their lands. Since I owned one motorcar and two motorcycles I did not find any difficulty to reach their lands. Finally all were success and got good yield. All the farmers came and praised me. I simply asked them to teach others what I taught them. To create still more interest I told the farmers that I would give a prize to that farmer who could get more yield. I selected 10 farmers, supplied fertilisers and pesticides and I taught them how to grow more. I often inspected and gave necessary advices. I created such a situation that all the 10 farmers took great interest and did their level best to get a good yield. Finally the day of harvest came. The highest quantity a farmer, Ganesh by name, got was 47 bags. I gave one clock to Ganesh and he was very much happy and pleased. Immediately he told that next time also he would try to get prize. I explained others that they too had got their prize, by means of getting more yield. Generally they got only 28 to 30 bags per hectare. But this time everybody got more than 40 bags. This is also a great prize. Everybody felt happy and decided to do again and to get prize. By this way not only the farmers got more paddy but a part of nation also. In the same manner if all farmers of our country would have done no doubt the production of our country would have been like anything. Here one thing should be noted. The clock which I presented cost me Rs. 35/. But the amount of fertilisers I supplied to the farmers was Rs. 3,500/ and the profit I received was Rs. 200/. I did not mind in losing Rs. 35/ out of my profit of Rs. 200/. I also suggested the farmers to run a poultry and to have cattles and to run a milk dairy in small if it is not possible to run in large scale.

After harvest the straw of paddy became waste, and was used only as a feeder to cattles. At the age of 35 I decided to make good use of the straw in other ways. This idea struck my mind when I saw the usage of straw as a by-product in Japan. I processed the straw and softened it and manufactured caps, mats, strawboards, and curtains. I did not stop with this. I applied for a loan in Small Industries Development Corporation and I installed an expeller to crush groundnuts. I exported the oil to foreign. By these industries I gave job to many peoples. Thus I contributed myself to some extent to moving forward my nation and the people of my nation.

Now I am 80 years old, and still it is only 20 years to live as per my goal of living. I am sure that I will certainly live for the rest 20 years. Because it is my strong confident. If a person will be confident in doing one thing definitely he will do the same. In the same manner I am confident of living for 100 year. For this myself is an example. When I was 29 year old I met with an accident when I was going in my motorcycle, and I was admitted in the hospital. Doctors told that they do not have hope. But I did not lose my hope and confident and I overcame that situation.

Since I am getting older I am not able to work briskly and hard. But I often suggest my only son and 3 brothers to do many more things and works, come still forward and be helpful to others in all aspects. I often suggest one main thing to them is "work hard and hard."

Finally and generally I want to state that while going toward progress we have to face some obstacles. It may come in any way. But we should not get ourselves disappointed or disgraced. We should find out how it came, why it came, and what is the remedy for that, how it should be removed and finally we should overcome that and proceed further.

Being a press reporter you have sacrificed your time in knowing my past and I thank you for the same. Since the time for lunch has come I request you kindly to have your lunch with me.

This story and others like it were quite evocative of overall goals and put the participants in a self-analytical frame of mind. Now the critical need was for a disciplined step-by-step framework. The faculty worked through the formal process of goal setting and establishing the sequential analysis that had the participants first stating their own general goals, listing all current problems relevant to these goals, analyzing how much control over these problems they had as individuals, then making a specific set of plans with time boundaries and risk assumptions. After getting all of this on paper, each participant discussed his plan individually with a member of the faculty. By the end of the day, most of them had at least one specific, first-step plan ready to set in motion as soon as they returned to the village.

The Demonstration Effect

The final day was devoted entirely to explanations and illustrations of new technology directly in their field of endeavor. Given our initial assumption that fertilizer distributors are potentially key change agents in the rural scene inasmuch as they sell so many of the inputs connected with the Green Revolution, the fifth day was devoted to learning more about these inputs. New pesticide-spraying machinery was demonstrated and new hand-operated cultivating machinery was demonstrated; both of these could be marketed by the distributors on a contract basis to farmers in their areas. New ideas for poultry operations and feed-store operations were suggested, which would expand the services that the fertilizer distributors might offer. The possibility of their becoming soil testers (with home-office help) was suggested. These and other ideas for service-based distributorships illustrated that the distributor really could be something different than he was before he came to the seminar — that he could have profound influence in his home area.

Were these men truly changed by the seminars? The level of enthusiasm and commitment at the conclusion was high; we can say that the seminars themselves were a "success." Still, the real payoff comes only if change actually takes place. It is perhaps presumptuous to hope to shift basic motivations and drives in five short days, no matter how intense. But one of the Government of India administrators observing the seminars commented, "If you could even change one or two of these men, and change them only in small ways, you would have accomplished an amazing thing."

We knew that only a continuing follow-up would ascertain whether significant change occurred, so a careful program was set in motion. An intrusion of events in India, though, complicated our assessment, and we need to look first at what occurred.

The Green Revolution Assailed

Indian agriculture from the vantage point of early 1972 looked rosy indeed. The key statistic of total food grain production had jumped to over 108 million metric tons in the crop season 1970-1971, and predictions were for the next season's output to exceed the last by 5 million metric tons. The euphoria of that moment is understandable; little wonder that Government of India officials were proudly announcing imminent food self-sufficiency for the country.

Unfortunately, there was a less optimistic sequel in the period 1972 to 1975. India went through agricultural difficulties in those next four years, and even though bumper crops followed in 1975-1976 and 1976-1977, most knowledgeable analysts remained cautious about the outlook for food sufficiency in India over its next few years. The effects were most clearly seen in the total food grain production; the 1971-1972 figure was down to 105 million metric tons, and the next year the total dipped below 100 (to just over 97). The next two years were little better — 104 and 101. The massive food grain imports of the mid-1960s (over 10 million metric tons in 1965-1966, 8.7 million the following year) had declined as the HYVs came into their own, and only 455,000 metric tons were imported in 1971-1972. But the following year imports jumped to 3.6 million, the next year to 4.8 million, and in 1974-1975 to almost 6.0 million.[13]

Why then had the hope of 1972 been so misplaced? The foremost reason was that the optimists had failed to reckon with India's ancient enemy, drought. Their projections had been based on the fact that in the immediately preceding two decades the monsoon had appeared to be shifting northward, bringing more abundant rainfall — and the frequency of drought had seemed to be declining to about once or twice in twenty years, whereas earlier in the twentieth century droughts had hit northern India roughly every three or four years. But the massive drought patterns that began to occur over many parts of the globe in the early 1970s disabused almost everyone of complacency. The devastating drought and famine of the Sahel in Africa, which had been worsening unnoticed for several years, burst onto the world's consciousness in 1971 and continued unabated in 1972 and 1973. Scientists soon were predicting major shifts in world climate. In the period 1972 to 1974 there were other profoundly unsettling patterns of drought — in the Soviet Union, in the western part of the United States, in parts of northern China — and in India.[14]

The monsoons were late and spotty in India in 1971-1972, and there were enough shortfalls in production around the country to bring the total crop in at a disappointing 105 million metric tons. No longer were there surpluses to share bountifully with India's neighbors. The monsoons were more erratic and the droughts worse in the following fall and winter, and by June 1973, the end of the 1972-1973 crop year, the full truth was evident — total food grains for that year were going to be well under 100 million tons.

As we carried through the Distributors for Change program that summer, there was widespread unease about the upcoming crop year. When the distributors returned to their villages at the end of the program, they were confronted with the grim fact that an unprecedented third year of tardy and inadequate monsoons was occurring. The already severe food shortage now threatened to worsen, and the ancient nemesis of famine was again all too close to reality. Some of the more pessimistic climatologists had been advancing the thesis that basic weather patterns were indeed shifting, and that many parts of the world, India included, would have to face prospects of real peril in food output. This terrifying pattern of drought seemed to threaten the very existence of the Green Revolution. But the hostile weather was not the only problem.

The Threat of the Oil Crisis

When the OPEC countries dramatically raised their prices of crude oil in late 1973, an unparalleled set of economic, political, and human reverberations was set in motion around the world. The effects were particularly traumatic on the less developed world. India, with both oil and coal reserves, had a reasonably promising long-term outlook, but the short term was another matter. The country was already low on hydroelectric power because the monsoons had left insufficient water in the rivers. Just a month before the oil crisis the president of India, V. V. Giri, had called the worsening power situation "an unprecedented national crisis." Domestic and imported oil had also been heavily utilized for power needs in industrial production and in agriculture (diesel irrigation lifts, fertilizer, powered farm equipment, and so on). Foreign currency was already painfully short; now a rapidly increasing amount would be required to finance oil imports. The anticipated shortfall in hard currency would probably force a lowering of total oil importation.[15]

Given the existing food crisis, this devastating oil situation hit directly at the heart of the Green Revolution. To achieve maximum results, the technologies of the new grains require greatly stepped-up levels of inputs—irrigation by either assured water or power-operated pumps, fertilizers, pesticides, and the agricultural equipment that makes multiple cropping possible. Now it looked as though usage levels would dwindle all across the agricultural sector.

Fertilizers made a dramatic case in point: their prices on the world market climbed steeply all through 1973 and 1974. India's domestic production of fertilizers had remained sluggish; continuing mismanagement and labor unrest in the plants was now exacerbated by power shortages from the drought. The total for all nitrogenous and phosphatic manufacturing in India was just under 1.4 million metric tons in 1972-1973, about 72 percent of capacity. For 1973-1974 it was down to about 1.38 million, only 64.7 percent of capacity. Consumption was 2.70 million metric tons in 1972-1973, about

2.78 in 1973-1974. Thus there continued to be huge imports—1.22 million metric tons in 1972-1973 and 1.24 million metric tons in 1973-1974.[16]

As the 1974-1975 season began amid continuing drought conditions over much of northern India, the world market price of inorganic fertilizers jumped sharply. Worse, the world-wide competition for purchase had made them difficult to obtain, even if India had been able to afford all of the foreign exchange required. Even before the oil crisis hit in late 1973, there was a roaring black market in fertilizers in India; urea had a legal price of about Rs. 1,000 per metric ton by mid-1973, but was selling in Tamil Nadu for more than Rs. 1,300. Individual states with better fertilizer supplies tried to embargo shipments to other states, but this only increased the temptation for questionable arrangements. One illegality spawned another, and there were widespread complaints of corrupt practices in underweighing the bags — as much as 5 to 6 kilograms for a 50-kilogram bag. Even the cooperatives, long thought by cultivators to be reasonably honest in their fertilizer marketing, more and more were being accused of being "cesspools of corruption and black marketing."[17]

The OPEC price increases in late 1973 worsened the situation considerably. The large increase in fertilizer manufacturers' cost structures because of sharply heightened oil prices combined with a worldwide scarcity situation to force prices on world markets up precipitously. The world price of urea had risen from about $50 per metric ton in 1972 and 1973 to contracts running as high as $250 per metric ton by mid-1974. India's 1.24 million metric tons of fertilizer imports in the crop season 1973-1974 had cost about $250 million. With the sharp increase in price, experts estimated that India's imports of about 1.21 million tons in 1974-1975 cost the country approximately $750 million, triple the previous year's outlay. In mid-1974, official retail prices of fertilizers were sharply increased by the Indian government, and the various state governments began to resort to rationing systems to allocate the scarce supply.

By the fall of 1974, crop shortfalls were widespread. The Indian peasant reacted in the only way he knew—he minimized the loss as best he could. With prices beyond his reach and prospects dwindling, the cultivator just ceased buying fertilizer altogether. The tremendous projected fertilizer shortage turned almost overnight into an incredible fertilizer glut.[18]

Along with this came other important developments. All through the halcyon first generation of the Green Revolution, farmers had been surprisingly quick to adopt the high-yielding varieties of seed, but had often failed to adopt all of the recommended package of inputs and practices—the combination of improved water control, increased use of farm chemicals for fertilization and plant protection, and the improved management practices of seedbed preparation, seeding rates, weed control, and timing of fertilizer ap-

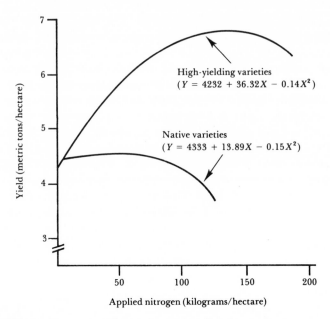

FIGURE 6A Response of rice to nitrogen applications in the dry season.

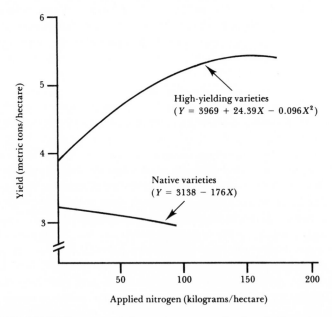

FIGURE 6B Response of rice to nitrogen applications in the wet season.

plications. One expert put the farmer's rationale well: "The search for a survival algorithm results in most participants being progressive in some aspects but not in others."[19] Fertilizer, pesticides, improved cultivation practices are all divisible inputs and can readily be shaved in the face of high costs. Dana Dalrymple, one of the most knowledgeable observers of the HYV programs, commented on this:

> Many of the same factors which retard the adoption of seeds also retard the adoption of the associated inputs . . . The main difference is that some of these other inputs have a much higher price tag to them. Fertilizer is a particularly significant cost factor. Hence many farmers have settled for a modified input package—one with a rather low investment in fertilizer. It provides some jump in yields but does not expose them to sharp risk.[20]

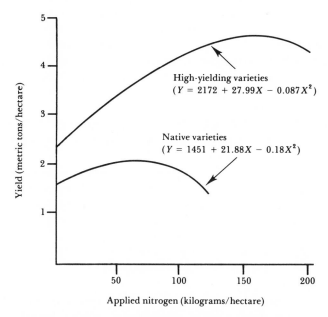

FIGURE 6C Response of wheat to nitrogen applications.

FIGURE 6 Generalized response of rice (dry and wet seasons) and wheat to nitrogen application. (Source: *High-Yielding Cereals and Fertilizer Demand,* Tennessee Valley Authority, 1970, Bulletin Y-4, pp. 6, 7, 8.)

Sometimes such a downward move will not result in a marked decrease in yield, but this depends upon where one is in the adoption process. The familiar S-shaped adoption curve describes well the effects of input on yields. Increased yields are modest at low applications, pick up heightened percentage growths as more fertilizers are applied, then begin to taper off as the familiar diminishing returns set in. The Tennessee Valley Authority studied the use of fertilizer in the HYV wheat and rice strains, and the results in Figure 6 vividly show this point of diminishing returns.

The selection by cultivators of a modified input package is important in an expanding agricultural situation; where high-yielding varieties are being widely adopted, other inputs often will show rates of adoption at varying percentages of "recommended." Some of the recommendations may not be as economic as others because of short-run price shifts. Or perhaps the particular input is simply not available in the right form at the right time.

This tendency toward inconsistent use of the package concept is even more evident in declining agricultural situations. The cultivator, faced with the need to reduce outlays, may continue the HYV seed, but cut back on fertilizer and other inputs—and not necessarily in the most effective way. There is very little in the literature to suggest a coherent input retrenchment program, so there appears to be a need for further study of this aspect of the package of practices. False starts and aborted plans are all too characteristic of the less developed world at best; it would seem wise to have better two-directional contingency planning all through LDC programs.

Some further enigmas relate to the input package itself. First, we must pay continuing attention to the HYV seed. There has been a tendency to take seed for granted, once it is released by the plant breeder. In less developed countries like India, the process of building an indigenous national seed program from an international seed source is complicated. The quality of seed stock tends to become diluted over time. Sometimes this is the fault of the seed distributor, who may pass off adulterated or defective seeds. More often, the problem lies with the farmer's lack of care in segregating seed stock from the fields (the cause of the frequently seen aberration of HYV fields with scatterings of tall traditional-variety stalks throughout).

Powered irrigation was also affected. Most of India's larger public-sector pumping stations are electrically operated; the dwindling power supply from the combination of drought and high oil prices made these irrigation systems rather undependable. Some farmers had recognized this several years back, so that many of the private power-operated irrigation systems were being run on diesel fuel (sometimes as a backup for an electrical pump, more often as an alternate choice of power source). But power supplies were painfully short by early 1974.

Some alarmist predictions had been advanced suggesting that the diminishing of inputs (for example, the decline in fertilizer application) would result in an abandonment of the high-yielding varieties. However, there appears to be no factual evidence that this occurred. To the contrary, the hectares in high-yielding varieties of wheat jumped from 7.9 million in 1971-1972 to 12.2 million in 1974-1975; HYV rice rose from 7.2 million to 11.3 million in the same period. By the 1975-1976 crop season, about one-third of India's rice area and two-thirds of its wheat area were in the HYVs, certainly a critical input to the country's record 114-million-ton food grain production in 1975-1976.[21] The high-yielding varieties are thought to do as well as or better than the traditional varieties in the absence of fertilizer. If even some fertilizer is available, the cultivator will tend to use it on the HYVs, which characteristically show higher rates of response to limited application than do the traditional varieties.

Probably a greater impact on the food supply will come if there is a shift by cultivators into more remunerative cash crops (where higher fuel costs can be more readily amortized). Groundnut and cotton prices ran high during this period in India, and the temptation to switch from food grains was ever present.[22] There are many arguments over whether less developed countries should concentrate on primary production or push toward cash crops for the world market to generate foreign exchange to purchase food needs. It is apparent that there is more than one route to self sufficiency.

A related pattern is the turn toward lower-yield crops (such as ragi or bajra), which can be grown with less danger of loss under rainfed conditions. Care must be taken not to assume that millets are always a poorer choice, for the new hybrid bajras appear to be on their way to making major contributions to food production.[23]

The Effects on Yields

As the HYV program in India gained momentum after 1967, differences between wheat and rice became evident. For wheat, there was a significant expansion of both the total area and the HYV area, with the overall expansion almost paralleling the HYV expansion. In rice, though, the total area expanded only slightly. In other words, part of the HYV expansion in wheat seemed to be carved out of other crops, while the HYV rice expansion was more nearly a substitution for traditional varieties. In the case of both wheat and rice, the general pattern was to use the better lands for the HYV expansion. Yields for HYV wheat and rice were multiples above the traditional varieties, but the latter also showed patterns of increase during the earlier years of the program—a logical expectation, since the package of practices was also applied to the fields growing traditional varieties (though at a lower rate).

The HYV yields for wheat were a higher multiple than that for rice; both rose in the 1960s and early 1970s, but then both began to fall off. For wheat, in relative terms the traditional varieties dropped more than the HYVs; for rice, the HYVs dropped more. The declining multiples looked like this:[24]

	HYV yields in India as multiples of yields of traditional varieties of —	
Crop year	Wheat	Rice
1966-67	2.87	2.58
1967-68	3.70	2.18
1968-69	3.49	2.05
1969-70	3.68	2.26
1970-71	3.44	2.27
1971-72	2.50	2.03
1972-73	2.35	1.76
1973-74	2.59	1.71

What accounted for these drops? Clearly, one prime culprit was the weather. As the HYV expansion burgeoned, a diminishing amount of irrigated land could be brought into cultivation, so that relatively poorer land was being utilized. When the drought struck, rainfed areas were severely hit. In turn, power-irrigated lands were sharply affected by the shortfalls in power (diesel fuel and/or electricity).

If we look at a standardized land base, the comparative yield levels become lower; Dalrymple estimated that the multiple on irrigated land might decrease to about 2.00 for wheat, 1.25 for rice. A study in the Philippines covering the years 1968 to 1972 alleged that when assured irrigation and equal inputs were used for both traditional and HYV, the latter's multiple was 1.14 (and only 1.03 on rainfed lowland rice). Another study of rice production in six Asian nations for the single year 1971-1972 estimated an average multiple for both wet and dry seasons at 1.32 to 1.33.[25]

The Small Farmers in the Oil Crisis

We need to consider now whether the small farmer is a special casualty in all of this. Even before the oil crisis, there had been conflicting evidence on whether the benefits of the Green Revolution accrued more heavily to certain segments of the agricultural sector.[26] Most analysts seem to agree, however, that HYV seeds can be used with uniform success regardless of the size of the farm, given three critical assumptions:

The first requirement is that the land of the smaller farmer not be seriously fragmented. In some parts of India this is a major problem, for individual holdings are as small as 25 square meters. These minuscule plots are wasteful of time and effort, and often make it extremely difficult to introduce irrigation; there also are endless squabbles over boundaries, egress, and other litigious issues.

Second, there must be a minimum feasible total holding, below which the output is too small to maintain a family at whatever is considered to be a reasonable standard of living. A. M. Khusro, a respected contemporary Indian economist, maintains that any figure less than five average (dry) acres does not fulfill the three norms of a bullock unit, a family labor-usage unit, and a family-income unit.[27] Although the exact minimum figure can be debated, Khusro's average seems a reasonable starting point.

India's rural land pattern provides a classic example of the tensions stemming from the few holding much land and the many—indeed, a great many in this case—owning very little or none. Thousands of years of rural life have formulated this pattern. Ownership of land itself is intermingled in complicated ways with other patterns of rural interpersonal relationships, especially caste and class distinctions and owner-tenant relationships. These, in turn, have been complicated by systems of dependencies from the *jajmani* system and the presence of intermediaries between owners and tenants, especially through the *zamindari* systems that originated in the early British days.

Differential treatment of large and small landholders and of tenants has persisted throughout these years and led to recurring efforts to redress the balance by spreading ownership among larger numbers of people. By the end of the 1950s almost all Indian states had ceiling legislation on their books.[28] Unfortunately, the laws were full of loopholes, with indifferent administration and consistent political sabotage. Ceilings in the early years varied enormously—Andhra Pradesh had a range of from 10 to 130 hectares (27 to 324 acres), Rajasthan (a dry state) varied from 9 to 136 hectares (22 to 336 acres), the productive Punjab and Haryana from 10 to 32 hectares (27 to 80 acres), and so on. Throughout, there were numerous exceptions. Ceilings were generally on an individual basis, not on the basis of family units, and thus gave rise to widespread evasion by families.

In 1971 major new legislation from the Central Land Reforms Committee recommended a range of 4 to 7 hectares (10 to 18 acres) for ceilings on perennially irrigated best lands and a range of 4 to 22 hectares (10 to 54 acres) for ceilings on the poorer lands. Further, they advocated that these limitations be imposed on a family basis rather than on an individual basis. Almost all the states followed these recommendations and passed legislation corresponding reasonably well to the proposals of the committee.

Implementation was halfhearted at the start, however, and evasion of the state laws common.[29] With the crash economic program coming in the wake of the government's strong measures in the spring and summer of 1975, there were renewed efforts at enforcing the statutes. Still, the number of landless people in the rural areas of India is so tremendous that even stringent laws will fall short of full-scale redistribution.

We must consider, then, whether the frontal attack on large-scale farming is an economically realistic plan for India. Experience in the Western world unquestionably indicates that larger-scale farming, with its capital-intensive base, is more productive. However, many analysts think this is not the case for India.

It is true that in the recent period of the Green Revolution, when new agricultural inputs have combined with the miracle grains to bring greatly heightened productivity, many larger farmers have been better able to take advantage of these inputs and raise their productivity more substantially than the smaller farmers. This has been particularly evidenced in the wheat belts of Punjab state. In other parts of the country the evidence is different. Probably Khusro's conclusion represents majority opinion among Indian economists: "Above the 5 acre size . . . there is nothing to choose between large farms and small farms in respect of cost efficiency and productivity; . . . Indian agriculture is typically a scene of constant return to scale . . . Ceilings are size-neutral."[30]

A third assumption is necessary about the small farmers: that they have equal access to the required modernizing inputs and the various support services. Given a certain minimum plot size, it is true that a small farmer working with the aid of his family can take full advantage of labor-intensive tasks —seedbed preparation, weeding, application of fertilizers and pesticides, cleaning and maintenance of irrigation channels, and so forth. These are all integral to HYV success. So, too, are the inputs, which vary on their divisibility. Fertilizer is highly divisible in normal times—the small farmer can buy it in India by the bag (approximately 50 kilograms) at about the same per-unit cost that the larger farmer pays (big plantations and commercial cash-crop farmers frequently obtain price concessions). However, a situation can develop in times of shortage and stringent rationing where the smallest farmers are, in fact, penalized. The shortage of urea in Tamil Nadu in mid-1974 illustrates this.

The recommended usage of nitrogen for HYV strains of rice for the state (from the Department of Agriculture) ranged from 124 to 185 kilograms per hectare, and from 46 to 69 kilograms per hectare for the traditional varieties. As we noted earlier, actual usage is usually short of recommended usage. Still, the small holders with, say, one hectare probably would be able to readily utilize a bag of urea. In the period in mid-1974 when urea was severely rationed, the amount allowed to be released per hectare dropped to 25 kilograms for the HYV and 10 for the traditional varieties.[31] Private distributors became increasingly disinclined to break a full 50-kilogram bag to serve a small farmer entitled to less, even when the manufacturers gave a small premium to the distributors to persuade them to do so.

Divisibility varies for the other inputs too. Pesticides are typically sold in small-lot quantities, with no substantial bulk discounts. An irrigation system is another matter—the cost of a tube well is substantial, a major capital expenditure. And the price of the tractor is clearly out of the ambit of a small farmer holding only one or two hectares.

The key is the role of agricultural credit. Farmers the world over depend upon credit at the start of the season, to be paid back after harvest. They also depend upon longer-term credit for the larger capital items. All the agricultural inputs, even the highly divisible ones, are typically bought on credit. The larger farmers tend even in normal times to be—or at least appear to be—better credit risks. Thus many analysts have viewed the Green Revolution as almost inherently tilting toward the larger-scale, financially stronger farmer. For example, in Keith Griffin's perceptive study, he holds that only in Taiwan is land ownership equally enough distributed in small parcels that all farmers have equal access to fertilizer, water, technical knowledge, and credit. Elsewhere, "the 'revolution' tends to occur in regions where large scale commercial agriculture already exists and, within these regions, on farms owned by large landholders . . . The technology is neutral neither as regards geographical area nor as regards social class."[32]

In times of economic distress, opportunities deteriorate for those considered to be weaker credit risks. This appears to be what happened in rural India right after the onset of the oil crisis and the inflationary thrust. In the case of fertilizer, for example, if a cultivator had already defaulted in repayment of a loan, he was not likely to get any further fertilizer in the face of combined shortage and premium price. Even if the cultivator were not a defaulter, the distributor might fear that the deteriorating economic situation would make him one (a not unfounded expectation). So the well-to-do farmer stands a much better chance of getting nutrients in difficult times than does the poorer farmer. Typically, though not always, the richer farmer is also the larger farmer. Some iniquitous practices have crept into the fertilizer picture in this recent period of distress, where some of the smaller farmers were "proxy buying" from the rationed supply—not for their own use, but to turn it over to some wealthier farmer in return for a small middleman's fee.[33] The black-market syndrome tends usually to accentuate the imbalance between rich and poor.

There are special impacts on tenants. The enormous number of landless laborers in the rural areas generally exacerbated landlord-tenant relations in the past. Infinite variations on subletting had been developed, and inasmuch as the government often tried to regulate these relationships, they were (and continue to be) shrouded in secrecy. Thus many of the tenancy arrangements are oral, most often for short time periods and with sharing arrangements that favor the owner. Fifty-fifty sharing is widespread, but there are examples extending down to recent years of sharing arrangements where up to two-thirds of the gross production is returned to the landowner. In these cases the landowner has supplied most of the inputs — perhaps even the bullocks — and thus makes his case for the higher percentage. If he pays for fertilizers and diesel fuel for irrigation, the rate perhaps might be 50:50. If the landowner supplies a larger portion, the 70:30 arrangement may be exacted; if the owner supplies *all* of the inputs the percentage may rise to 80:20.[34]

Curiously, in the recent period a leaseholder or sharecropper, if provided cash credit and loans in kind from his landlord, may be in a far stronger position than a similar tenant receiving *no* services from his landlord. Indeed, he is probably better off than the owner-operator of a similar small plot.

A complicating factor is the apparent decline of tenancy. There is substantial evidence that many landlords, seeing the higher income potentials of the HYVs, have opted to displace their tenant farmers and consolidate their holdings under one management.[35] This may fly in the face of the recent more stringent efforts by the government for land reform. In general, the necessary evidence is not yet in with regard to the long-term impacts of the Green Revolution. In the early years of the first-generation period too many sweeping claims were made about the efficacies of the new high-yielding-variety technologies. Endless golden harvests were seemingly within man's grasp. Later in this first-generation period, the complex and often conflicting effects of the new technology became increasingly apparent, and questions concerning employment effects, variable impacts on tenants and marginal farmers, and many other issues were widely debated. The recent second-generation period of fallback has accentuated these concerns. Excellent agricultural crops in India and, indeed, in most other areas in 1975-1976 immediately tended to blunt some of these worries. But the severe droughts around the world and the late monsoons in many parts of India again in the summer of 1976 should cure anyone of excessive optimism.

The Distributors for Change Seminars Revisited

When the two-score distributors from the two seminars arrived back in their villages and towns in September 1973, they faced the worsening drought situation. Then, just a month or so later, the oil crisis struck and their own situations were profoundly changed. They had increasing difficulties in supply, but what they had they could sell a dozen times over. The temptation was great to return to a sedentary peddler mentality. The problems were no longer those of persuading the cultivators to buy, but rather the delicate problem of allocating a dwindling supply, a shortfall, among an overabundance of potential buyers. At best, this would probably mean selling to the cultivators with the highest financial stability—probably the larger farmers. After all, why take any credit risk when it seems so unnecessary? Worse, there were temptations to black-market at several points during late 1973. Urea, for example, was selling at several hundred rupees above posted public prices. The package of practices concept is just as relevant in a period of falling input supply as it is in the opposite direction—proper application of the best combination of inputs, each in smaller amounts, can cut at least some of the yield loss that is inevitable with the input drop itself. The better distributors saw this and made efforts to continue a service philosophy, even as they were being pressed for allocation preferences. For most dealers, though, it was a halfhearted effort; the ridiculous ease with which products were sold in this kind of market soon bred a take-it-or-leave-it attitude. When buyer resistance finally set in, the distributor was psychologically unready to revert to a service posture. This happened in many places when the cultivators finally stopped buying fertilizer after the posted prices rose so high on June 1, 1974. Price itself, of course, was the key constraint—but the package concept of service was warped in the process.

One of the important ingredients in the strategy for the Distributors for Change seminars was to follow these forty distributors over time to see what happened to them, and at the same time to follow another group of distributors as a control. The two participating companies took responsibility for this followup. A collaborative questionnaire was designed and monthly checks made of the two separate groups of twenty; two control groups were evaluated in the same mode.

The questionnaire was divided into three basic sections: (a) outlook and attitudes (newspapers, magazines, and books read; amount of time listening to radio; meetings attended; places visited and information linkages utilized); (b) business changes (organizational changes in the company itself, policy changes, personnel changes, sales performance, new products taken up, other outside businesses instituted); (c) social and family changes (new memberships in social, political, or business groups; social obligations taken as an individual; significant events in the family during the particular month—such as marriage, births, health changes—and miscellaneous information on plans for the future within the family). We also had longitudinal data on the forty men prior to their involvement in the seminars and similar data for the thirty-six men in the control groups.

How did the test groups compare with the control groups for the twelve-month period over which this set of evaluations was conducted? The individual measures for each of the three basic sections—outlook and attitudes, business changes, and social and family changes—were summed to give three composite variables for each of the men in each of the two groups. Multiple discriminant analysis seemed best suited for comparison. The results are shown in Table 31.

The tests for discrimination for all three runs show that there is, indeed, a statistically significant difference in performance over the year between the test group and the control group for both the first company and the second company. The test group shows significantly higher indices for business changes and for social and family changes. The first company control group has a higher index on outlook and attitude; this difference was analyzed further by first company officials, who concluded, "On further examination of individual behavioral patterns, it is revealed that many in the test group were initially in a higher standard of performance than those in the control group." On the key entrepreneurial variable, the performance index for business changes, the data from both companies suggest a stronger performance by the seminar participants than by the control group. The company evaluation team concluded: "Against the environment prevailing during the observation period there is enough evidence to conclude that there has been a significant effect of the training programme on those who have participated. This is more so in comparison with the control group. It is most striking to observe that in the plans for future both under business and social classifications no member of the test group has recorded a minus point (minus indicates 'no plans') whereas under the control group a significantly large number have registered negative points."

We also wondered if we could successfully predict performance in the way that we had earlier with the Sengapalli fertilizer distributors — if we could predict these "one year later" performance variables by going back to the longitudinal data and identifying some of the key variables, such as modernization, planning, and information usage. Only four predictor variables were available: the two composite information variables, the modernization variable, and the planning variable. (The longitudinal data did not include the fifth — leadership — variable utilized in Sengapalli.) Using these four variables in canonical correlation with the three evaluation indices noted above, we were remarkably successful in predicting performance in the first company ($r^2 = .729$, significant at the .01 level). The same process for the second company was more modestly successful ($r^2 = .597$, significant at the .05 level).

The interim one year was far too disrupted for anyone to feel comfortable about drawing before-and-after comparisons; continuing evaluations will be made. Our analysis does seem to point to a preliminary judgment that the Distributors for Change seminars had a positive effect on subsequent performance. We remind ourselves that the very process of checking with these forty dealers each month about their continuing hopes, plans, and performance is itself a positive reinforcement — a "Hawthorne effect." The dealers who had

TABLE 31   Multiple discriminant analysis, Distributors for Change test group and control group.

Variable	First company		Second company		Composite	
	Test group ($n = 20$)	Control group ($n = 20$)	Test group ($n = 16$)	Control group ($n = 10$)	Test group ($n = 36$)	Control group ($n = 30$)
Outlook and attitudes						
Mean	3.1	4.7	2.56	0.6	2.86	3.33
SD	3.93	4.06	3.46	2.91	3.68	4.16
Business changes						
Mean	2.6	1.4	3.0	−0.1	2.77	0.9
SD	3.17	4.01	3.16	1.44	3.12	3.42
Social and family changes						
Mean	1.9	0.15	1.69	0.8	1.80	0.36
SD	2.13	1.59	1.66	1.31	1.90	1.52

First company:
Equality of dispersion: $F_{(6, 10462)} = 1.66$
Overall discrimination: $F_{(3, 36)} = 7.42***$

Second company:
Equality of dispersion: $F_{(6, 2389)} = 1.27$
Overall discrimination: $F_{(3, 22)} = 3.17*$

Composite:
Equality of dispersion: $F_{(6, 27087)} = 0.65$
Overall discrimination: $F_{(3, 62)} = 6.20***$

*Significant at .05 level.
***Significant at .001 level.

attended the seminars knew we would be interested in "what happened," so the higher performance by the test group is surely a composite of what happened at the seminars and what happened afterward. This composite behavioral combination of intensive seminar and explicit, self-conscious followup is really a package of training practices, which in total seems to have potential to increase innovative and change-oriented performance. We have added one further ingredient to our procedures.

Heightening Information Linkages

The pronounced associations of the composite information linkage variables with innovation and change seem to beg for additional efforts in this direction. The stories of change and brainstorming exercises in the seminars undoubtedly helped to foster this "instinct for combination." Other devices in all likelihood could be invented for use in short seminars that would aid participants' abilities to link ideas together. Still, we were left with the feeling that a more thoroughgoing effort is needed if lasting linkages are to result.

Let us return for a final visit to the fertilizer distributors. What would help them most? Primarily, they need more information. There are many lacks and discontinuities in information gathering in the less developed world, especially in rural areas. Village entrepreneurs need a larger quantum of information — from radio, from newspapers, from company suppliers back in the cities. But, as Leibenstein and others have pointed out, it is the entrepreneur who is the gap filler and input completer, who can complete the linkages, who really puts information to its most productive use. Our research suggests precisely this.

We looked, then, for ways to help the fertilizer distributor back at his own site to continue practicing the linking of information. We had earlier suggested one device — the Better Ways bulletins. The participating companies now have joined together to experiment with such an information vehicle, designed explicitly to increase the network of information flows, to share the new experiences and new-found Better Ways of the various dealers, to motivate the dealers to try new ideas, and to persuade the dealers to be *agents* of change with their constituencies, the cultivators. In content these bulletins will stress better business practices. They will not supplant the existing technical bulletins of the individual companies; rather, they will stress better methods in new ideas, to include the following: (*a*) case histories of individual distributor Better Ways, (*b*) short vignettes (including those Tamil proverbs) of ideas for change, (*c*) "stop-action" case situations that lead to question raising and renewed opportunities for testing analytical skills (in effect, the reader is asked, "What would you do?"), and (*d*) other suggestions about how new practices and new methods might be put into effect within the distribution process, and how these changes might have applicability in the realm of the cultivator as well. In all cases the various stories and situations are linked together so that the notion of information flows and linkages is introduced, and the role of key pieces of information that act as gap-filling and input-completing devices is stressed.

The first of these bulletins has now been put in the hands of all the dealers of the two organizations. The companies chose the name *Change* for the bulletin and have included a number of innovative inputs. While it is too early to assess its full impact, the bulletin does seem to be precisely the kind of instrument that might truly encourage information linkage skills.

Of necessity we leave unresolved the question of precisely how much can be accomplished by an intensive, one-week seminar of the nature of the Distributors for Change endeavor. It seems rather presumptuous to maintain that we in any way changed people's attitudes, ingrained over many years, toward their way of life within a traditional society. We do believe our research findings to be eminently valid. We believe also that the key generalizations from this research were valuable in the Distributors for Change seminars, and that they can—and will—be used in the future to hasten true innovation in rural India.

6

Fresh Thoughts about
Entrepreneurial Theory
and Practice

The question was posed at the beginning of this book, "What is a less-developed-country entrepreneur?" It was stated then that the developed countries and the LDCs differ sharply, not only in such material ways as varying gross national products, but also in value determinants, which are manifested in different ways. I have emphasized rural entrepreneurship in village India, where I isolated an innovational typology characterized by modernity, utilization of medium risk, conscious planning, and longer-run profit maximization, supported throughout by a behavioral pattern of achievement motivation. These generalizations have led me to a set of new insights about broader patterns of growth and change.

Profit Maximization and the Less Developed Countries

The research for this book has reinforced my caution in generalizing about presumed lacks of optimization or maximization attitudes in the less developed world. What to the external observer may appear to be "satisficing" behavior may in actuality be maximizing behavior. A conventional wisdom states that villagers are extremely conservative in adopting change, inasmuch as the dangers of backfire in the new idea are so severe. When risk-averse behavior is grounded in reality—as it often is—it amounts to maximizing present value. Yet the rapid adoption of the agricultural changes inherent in the Green Revolution belies simplistic characterizations. There is more change potential in the rural populace than generally expected—and some of its members are quite entrepreneurial in their outlooks. Harvey Leibenstein even conjectures that "in fact traditionalism is not the critical element but that the motivations present—e.g. the profit rates—are such that those with gap-filling capacities are willing and able to exert themselves under some motivational circumstances and reduce the degree of exertion under others."[1] The findings in this study corroborate Leibenstein's thinking. While a less-than-perfect X-efficiency may be at work, a strong thrust of straightforward profit maximization is still in evidence on the part of a small segment of village entrepreneurs.

Of the fertilizer distributors analyzed in Chapter 2, those who manifested the highest performance levels in profit maximization tended also to be the most modern and exhibited the highest incidence of the quality defined by David McClelland's concepts of achievement motivation. While the pattern exhibited considerable ebb and flow of effort, clearly an X-efficiency pattern —particularly as defined through the fabric of achievement motivation— seemed to be the dominant behavioral goal.

All the distributors in our study were from the private-enterprise sector, small firms where each of them was a "chief executive officer." Thus personal profit-seeking—private-enterprise profit maximization—characterized all of these respondents. I suggest further research to determine whether this same achievement-based pattern is also present among the individuals heading co-operatives or government fertilizer depots.

My intuitive judgment, based upon extensive association with the village entrepreneurs of Tamil Nadu, both public and private, is that with national stability, long-term planning, and a service philosophy as preconditions, private enterprise may offer greater promise to India than seemed apparent to the government in the early 1970s, a period when the "mixed economy" philosophy seemed to be tilted increasingly toward public-sector efforts.

The first precondition, the presence of a requisite degree of economic, political, and social stability, may sound almost tautological. But the entrepreneur does need to have the best possible assessment of the future in order to make a discounted risk assessment. Information alone cannot mitigate the uncertainties ahead; only wise policies, public and private, can do this. Sound information relating to these policies will allow conscious, calibrated planning, one of the abilities that enhances entrepreneurship. The less developed world tends to have serious gaps in the information-gathering process; these can be diminished, both for individuals and for the populace as a whole.

Another need in heightening stability is for a received theory of two-direction contingency planning. There is a natural tendency in planning models to accentuate new plans, new stages, new growth, all along positively sloped functions. Yet cyclicality in the world today seems especially accentuated in less developed countries, given the information gaps we have discussed and other lacks in knowledge and understanding. Carefully constructed contingency plans that account directly in the model for false starts, setbacks, and other unforeseen events seem to be particularly appropriate.

A second precondition relates to the longer-run mentality of the private-enterprise entrepreneur. The difficulties encountered by the fertilizer distributors in assessing the wide swings in fertilizer demand during the recent oil crisis is an example of the need for forward planning. The Distributors for Change seminars advocated a longer-run, service-based mentality as a powerful analytical concept with real potential for inculcating a longer-run profit-maximization focus in this industry. By their nature, modern agricultural inputs tend to buttress such a viewpoint; they require substantial capital outlays and therefore encourage a planning cycle that extends beyond one season. Yet in the seminars we did not explicitly plan for the unforeseen circumstances that arose shortly after their conclusion—an initial, accentuated short-term shortage and sharp rise in price, followed by a buyer boycott on the part of the cultivators. Black-market pricing came first, followed by distress selling—both all-too-frequent occurrences in the past. These are short-run manifestations and could have been encompassed within a longer-run point of view by adequate contingency planning. The fertilizer distributors did have significant leverage on the black-market pricing and could have foresworn the price-gouging temptation of this particular moment. If at the same time they had articulated a service mentality in the face of such temptation, they would have given strong evidence to the cultivators of their longer-run thinking.

To date, there have been profound difficulties in moving backward on the development cycle in the Green Revolution. The planning of retrenchment by the cultivator is particularly difficult, given the need to balance the total package of practices. This is precisely where the distributor can offer special help. New research has much to offer to this process of balancing the inputs for the new seeds, and these results can be made available to individuals at the end of the input pipelines—the fertilizer distributors, the village-level workers, and the agricultural implement dealers, for example.

Meaningful use of this information, however, requires an underlying mentality of service and longer-run planning and acting. David McClelland, discussing his research in India, noted this point:

> A person who cares only for achievement may be a very poor cooperator, who is relatively unconcerned about the welfare of others. It is only when achievement motivation is linked to a genuine service orientation that the nation, as a whole, develops most rapidly . . . What is unfortunately missing still in some places is the energy, devotion, and achievement enthusiasm among the leaders themselves that alone can galvanize people into the passion for progress that raises this motive in the hierarchy well above motives for personal gain, power, friendship, or loyalty. Certainly the achievement mystique cannot be developed by indirect means such as manipulation of tax laws, infusions of foreign capital, or land reform. Not even the concern for justice, important as it is, promotes automatically the concern for achievement. Justice has to do with dividing up fairly what there is to go around. Achievement has to do with creating more to divide up.[2]

This demands some operational definitions. Just how McClelland would bring about these motivational changes in a country's leadership beyond mere exhortation remains unclear. Still, one should not gainsay the values of exhortation — in the United States, we often use the term "jawboning" — in bringing about voluntary change within subsets of the total environment of a particular country. Former prime minister Indira Gandhi used such techniques extensively as part of her overall "national emergency" strategy that began in June 1975. It is still premature to assess the validity of these moves at the national level, but we can make some comments about the same efforts at the industry level. The business community in many countries is often reasonably cohesive and well organized, and while individual self-interest militates against any uniform agreement, nevertheless there are real opportunities for gaining acceptance of new principles through exhortation by industry leaders.

Is is realistic, for example, to think of fertilizer-industry top management exhorting individual distributors in the Tamil Nadu countryside to foreswear windfall profit taking in a period of shortage, under a rubric of profit-maximization concepts that would preach to them that over the longer period they would maximize their profits and provide more service by a more judicious short-term pricing strategy? We believe so, given the presence on a fairly broad scale of achievement-based mechanisms similar to the Distributors for Change seminars. The power of cognitive and group support is great and underscores the potency of a respected reference group in bringing about change in motives. In another book I have described how a service-oriented developed-world corporation was able effectively to demonstrate the validity of this long-run profit maximization rationale to a whole industry in Venezuela. (The case involved the introduction of supermarkets in retail food distribution.)[3]

A similar strong effort by senior executives and top management in the fertilizer industry might well provide the kind of impetus that would bring about the subtle shift toward a service mentality in the fertilizer industry in India. Similar situations probably obtain in other industries in India and elsewhere. What is needed is an "other directedness" that takes achievement motivation beyond the idiosyncratic personal definition to a group-based, culturally derived manifestation.

One further qualification concerning long-run profit maximization is necessary. There is an assumption in the economist's use of the term that all future contingencies affecting the income stream have been taken into account. In other words, the present value of this future stream of earnings has been maximized. With a given distribution of income, long-run profit maximization strives to ensure economically efficient allocation of resources.

This does not say, though, that maximization of long-run profits is always congruent with maximization of socially desirable change. The latter is a concept of welfare economics and takes into account parameters beyond the income stream of the individual decision-making unit. Society can, indeed, change this distribution of profits, and the new socially efficient allocation may not coincide with the previous economically efficient determination. An all-wise long-run profit maximization determination for a given firm would account precisely for such contingencies. In practice, estimates are resorted to, and there is an inevitable process of bargaining between and among interest groups in fitting themselves into national planning goals.

Innovation and Adaptation in the Less Developed World

I posited in Chapter 1 that technology *transfer* and *adaptation* carry several meanings and suggested that one make a careful distinction between the two terms. Adaptation is intrinsically different from the original innovation and the transferred variants — not just an imitation of the previous technology, but a meta-innovation.

The importance of making this careful distinction between the meta-innovation and the other essentially transferred technologies is highlighted in the recent development literature concerning questions of so-called appropriate technology. This term is now widely distinguished from earlier uses of the concept of intermediate technology. As the latter term was originally popularized by E. F. Schumacher, it was distinguished from indigenous technology (which Schumacher considered "in a condition of decay") but was also distinguished from high technology in being more labor intensive and typically on a smaller scale.[4] However, intermediate technology did not imply lesser complexity or sophistication, for its advocates envisioned a system of miniaturization of machines and adoption of micromachines that would yield production at costs not very much different from the employment of rudimentary and traditional means of production, yet provide the efficiencies of higher technologies. In effect, intermediate technology matched the sophistication of the equipment with the available levels of technological skills and the anticipated level of investment resources. In particular, the utilization of outdated, "inferior" machinery was eschewed.

More recently, the concept of "intermediate" has been reanalyzed and deepened under the rubric of "appropriate" technology. Now the focus is on developing a package of economic optimalities based upon the presence or absence of given infrastructures and inputs characteristic of the particular situation. While one can fault the word "appropriate" as being circular and self-defining, nevertheless analysts are making a useful distinction here in that for a given environment the right, or appropriate, technology could be quite congruent with a traditional village situation, yet incorporate new, innovative ideas.

Indeed, there have been recent efforts to make just this distinction. A good example is an International Labor Organization rural development effort in Tanzania that was focused on village work tools. The upgrading of these tools was fitted directly to the needs the villagers themselves regarded as important. One of the project leaders explained why:

> Previous attempts at introducing "mechanisation" had required the constant attendance of government workers such as agricultural engineers, with their relatively sophisticated management of, and accounting for, supplies of fuel and spare parts, regular maintenance, and the proper use of machinery. When the government workers were withdrawn, the machinery tended to fall into disuse . . . Innovation should start at the current level of technical competence of the village people. In most villages there are men skilled in the use of the axe, the adze, the panga, and the hoe. In many villages there are carpenters who make chairs, tables, beds, doors and houses using these implements, while in some there are smiths who forge adzes, hoes, knives and other small tools. This provides a reservoir of basic (mostly woodworking) skills which could usefully be tapped by the Project. The practical significance of such use of village skills was that it enabled the Project to go beyond the stage of intermediate technology implements to implements of even lower cash cost. Although the capital costs for intermediate technology represent a very considerable saving on those for mechanised technology, the initial cash outlays may still be beyond the reach of the village operating at or near subsistence levels . . . It therefore becomes necessary to adopt a "village technology" whereby both construction and repair can be undertaken by the villagers . . . Such beginnings provide a valuable lesson in self-reliance because implements are no longer seen as inevitably shop-bought and alien, but as self-created and capable of modification or redesign to meet special needs.[5]

One can envision other dimensions of village technology (methods, raw materials, and the like) that could readily be upgraded beyond indigenous or traditional ways.

It is for this village level that I particularly focus the definition of meta-innovation. The entrepreneurs may be "humbler," as James Berna put it in his study of South Indian rural businessmen, but the entrepreneurial or innovative act that they carry out can be very complex indeed, given the constraints and lacks we have noted. Seen in this light, the village takes on elements of excitement and promise not readily apparent before. The example of the fertilizer distributor moving from a one-man business to a two-man organization illustrates the point well. The conceptual problems in moving from one's own autonomous effort to being an executive leader of other people are quite profound in any case. In the rural areas of a less developed country, the act takes on considerably more meaning and complexity.

Sharply focused analytical work designed to identify meta-innovation and the innovators carrying it through will have high payoff in development efforts in rural areas. First, it will provide models for selection of additional innovators for training and other aid. Second, the structure of such thinking will focus on key points in infrastructure—on innovation boundaries—and will help to identify what will bring about the critical mass to allow a jump through these discontinuous barriers.

Gap Filling and Input Completing

Living in a less developed world complicates data-gathering processes. An entrepreneur in the less developed world must be fundamentally concerned with gap filling and input completing. When there are gaps, market signals for profit opportunities are blurred. Leibenstein's X-efficiencies are, if anything, more pronounced. Even in the developed world businessmen tend not to search for information as effectively as they might, and motivation in the less developed village is still less. Constantly recurring gaps in knowledge are frustrating and discourage further search.

Traditionalism in these villages exacerbates the information shortfalls. Hereditary power tends to hold sway over the powers of intellect (or, perhaps better stated, the power of ideas). Kinship and caste lines, for example, tend to fragment and erode the information process. An analyst of the caste system in South India put it succinctly:

> Among the most serious effects of these barriers were the lack of effective social communications which they engendered, and their discouraging influence on entrepreneurial morale. Where social and economic resources necessary to economic development are scattered among numerous non-competing social groups, the opportunity for change of ideas, techniques, and material resources is curtailed, reducing both the scope and incentive for development.[6]

In addition to these social rigidities and lacks in the information process are the physical constraints. Transportation and communication inadequacies have always profoundly limited rural economic development in the less developed countries. Roads are poor, mails are slow and untrustworthy, mass communications sources are available only in certain areas. All communications processes tend to be slow, and static and rumor intrude into the system.

The result adds up to uncertainty about any change. Unknown situations are risky situations, and information paucities encourage risk aversion. There are some expected effects in terms of economic development—for example, the apparent preference in the rural areas of many less developed countries for trade and other traditional activities over industrial investment. The latter is generally subject to much greater uncertainty than are investments in traditional activities. Industrial investments require judgments on more variables, projected much farther into the future, in an environment that may be offering little assurance of reasonable stability. After the villager properly discounts for the uncertainty and risk, his preference for traditional activities over industry may represent fully rational maximizing behavior.[7]

Thus skill in the treatment of information can be the crucial element in whether or not an innovation will take place in a less developed village. The innovational boundary is bridged in considerable measure when an entrepreneur amasses a minimum quantum of the information necessary to make viable a particular idea/project. Appropriate village-level technology often is far more complicated than is imagined, and the village entrepreneur in effecting innovations has probably carried through an information-gathering process of considerable complexity. The case of the one-man fertilizer distributorship is again a useful example. The information he needs in order to hire, train, and supervise a second person is far more complex than he may think. Some of the key knowledge is quite sophisticated, not readily available to him in the village. The concept of a service-based distributorship is itself a new idea, and the development by the single proprietor of a new management philosophy that incorporates a set of business goals and policies requires gaining information at this conceptual level of abstraction, bridging gaps in this information, linking ideas together, and making decisions on the basis of still-incomplete but at least minimally adequate information.

These lacks in availability and treatment of information can be ameliorated by increasing information quanta and making more effective the information diffusion process. The research in this study suggests ways of accomplishing both.

One of the most striking dimensions of the successful fertilizer distributors' pattern of operation was their treatment of information. The modern, moderate-risk-taking, short-term-planning, profit-maximizing innovators in our sample were also individuals who utilized sources of information far more meaningfully than their less innovative counterparts. An especially important factor here — with strikingly high correlations to innovative behavior — were the linkage patterns in the use of information. The distributors who utilized a wide range of sources and linked them together were those who appeared to have the most innovative thrust. No single information source stood out as having a pronounced influence on the patterns of entrepreneurial behavior. It was the moderately substantial use of a package of many information sources that seemed to produce the types of thought and idea patterns leading to innovation.

I suspect that this is a generalized phenomenon found all through rural areas of less developed countries. Rural sociologists studying the diffusion of innovation have often noted that different channels of information are associated with the various phases of the decision process in diffusion.[8] These different channels play qualitatively different roles in leading people to a decision; thus the learning effectiveness of different channels and combinations of channels depends more on how the channels are used, and for what purposes, than on the nominal efficacies of the individual channels as such. While earlier communications researchers treated the availability of multiple channels primarily as a question of picking one or another as most effective, now multiple functions are seen to be performed by given channels, with the information recipient often unable to pinpoint precisely which of several channels was most influential.

There has been great interest in these questions among rural sociologists, inasmuch as some of the best of diffusion theory has been utilized in their efforts toward agricultural innovation. Certain channels can be especially important in calling the individual's attention to the availability of a choice, while others are stronger in convincing the person of which particular choice is the correct one. Still other channels may, to use the words of communications theorist Wilbur Schramm, "trigger off the action" by giving specific instructions on how to execute the decision.[9]

Everett Rogers and Floyd Shoemaker built a set of hypotheses based upon analysis of a large number of diffusion studies; several of these reinforce our conclusions with regard to communications channels:

— Earlier knowers of an innovation have greater exposure to mass media channels of communication than later adopters (18 studies, or 62 percent, support; 11 studies do not support).

— Earlier knowers of an innovation have greater exposure to interpersonal channels of communication than later adopters (16 studies, or 89 percent, support; 2 studies do not support).

— Earlier adopters have greater exposure to mass media communication channels than later adopters (80 studies, or 69 percent, support; 36 studies do not support).

— Earlier adopters have greater exposure to interpersonal communication channels than later adopters (46 studies, or 77 percent, support; 14 studies do not support).

— Mass media channels are relatively more important at the knowledge function and interpersonal channels are relatively more important at the persuasion function in the innovation-decision process (18 studies, or 90 percent, support; 2 studies do not support).

— Cosmopolite channels are relatively more important at the knowledge function and localite channels are relatively more important at the persuasion function in the innovation-decision process (6 studies, or 86 percent, support; 1 study does not support).

— Mass media channels are relatively more important than interpersonal channels for earlier adopters than for later adopters (8 studies, or 80 percent,
support; 2 studies do not support).
— Cosmopolite channels are relatively more important than localite channels
for earlier adopters than for later adopters (9 studies, or 100 percent, support).
— The effects of mass media channels, especially among peasants in less developed countries, are greater when coupled with interpersonal channels in
media forums (3 studies, or 100 percent, support).[10]

As we talk of diffusion, we must remember we are one step removed from
the actual innovation. We have not yet answered the question of the relative
influence of these various types of channels and their sequencing on the innovator himself. Other than what we have reported, we were unable to find any
research bearing directly on this question. Note, for example, that some of
the Rogers and Shoemaker hypotheses above are at variance with our own
findings. While both early knowers and early adopters of innovations appear
to have greater exposure to both broad-based mass media channels and more
intimate interpersonal channels, Rogers and Shoemaker do premise that the
mass media channels are relatively more important in the earlier, knowledge
function. Likewise, their cosmopolite channels — those more worldly, mass-
oriented channels — are more important for earlier adopters than for later
adopters. In the research on fertilizer distributors reported in this book, there
was not only a linkage effect that put great emphasis on a *combination* of
sources, there was also a strong association between innovativeness and the
use of more personally oriented sources and interests. The person who could
link together information more directly related to his environment was the
person more likely to be the one who carried through to a full-scale idea/proj-
ect. The more typical situation in a rural area of a less developed country is
for an innovation to be a meta-innovation, where the concern is relatively less
with new scientific or technological bits of knowledge but rather with the linking together of existing knowledge within this particular environment. The
inventor in a high-technology electronics laboratory would necessarily be linking together cosmopolite information, probably stemming from mass media
sources. On the other hand, the fertilizer distributor in a rural area of Tamil
Nadu would be linking together information about various cultivators, their
fields, available inputs, and the like in making the equally innovative decision
to move from a one-man to a two-man shop.

Some cautions are now in order. There is a substantial literature in communication theory, supported by extensive research, that emphasizes that the
simple nervous system can apparently handle only a small part of the information that the sense receptors and the peripheral nervous system are capable

of receiving. The human capacity to process sensory information seems to be much less than the amount of information that would be theoretically available within a channel or set of channels. George A. P. Miller, in a provocative, seminal article, suggested that the span of immediate memory imposes severe limitations on the amount of information that people are able to receive, process, and remember.[11] Only when we are able to organize the stimulus inputs simultaneously into several dimensions and then successfully into a sequence of chunks are we able to break out of this informational bottleneck.

We need to be concerned as well for the selectivity in these sources. Y. V. Lakshmana Rao studied two South Indian villages and found that information flows seemed to be divided into these categories of recipients:

Information Indifferents
> The fatalist: the person who has no incentive whatsoever to better himself, even if he does not have enough to live on
> The passively contented: the person who has enough to live on and has no further desires
> The superior being who "knows all": the rich man who lives a closeted life and does not mix with the "stupid masses" at any level, except when approached as "the master"

Rumor Mongers
> The illiterate and ill-informed "rebels": the most dangerous element in the community, they are conscious of some change but do not understand it; they seek some personal gain (such as free land) without being willing to make any effort (receivers-senders)

Information Seekers
> Those who are expected to know: traditional village leaders, caste heads, teachers, and so on (usually receivers)
> Those who desire (or need) some material things such as land, work, tools (some receivers, some senders)
> Those who are ambitious for political power (receivers-senders), economic power (receivers), social status (receivers-senders)
> The traditional outcasts who want to belong and be accepted (receivers-senders)

Information Carriers
> Those whose status is threatened, usually older caste and village heads (receivers-senders)
> Those who have accepted change, usually the friendly elite (receivers-senders)
> The young educated villagers who identify themselves with the mass, usually those who are crusaders for equality of opportunity (receivers-senders).[12]

Rao particularly stresses the need to recognize the information carrier. It is through him that government officials and other effecters of change will be attempting to influence the cultivators. Harvey Leibenstein makes a similar point: "Various degrees of specialization may exist within these communication-decision channels so that (1) *scanners* simply transmit information to others, and these (2) *transmitters* may not be (3) *evaluators,* and, finally those who evaluate and transmit evaluations need not be the (4) *promoters* of change within the group."[13]

The carrier of information is the information broker found in the system model in the first chapter of this book. Where there is a dearth of technical know-how, potential entrepreneurs often develop a network of information brokers who can supply the bits of information that finally come together as an idea/project. On occasion, in larger towns and cities, this activity may be formalized into consulting organizations. Or an information broker may be called upon from outside the country; technical assistance may be rendered from, particularly, developed-world individuals or firms.[14]

At the village level the information broker activities will be informal. Several studies relating to diffusion in India's villages and agricultural areas all stress the importance of local sources of information — village-level workers, the agricultural extension officer, and other local government officials — together with a wide range of more personal contacts that include village and family elders and wealthier large-scale landowners. Companies with local outlets may also be influential information brokers. Marketers of tea and soap, for example, were enlisted to aid the diffusion of family planning concepts in rural India.[15] Similarly, we noted earlier the role of fertilizer manufacturers in programs of community development for the unemployed.

Recently in India bank officers have been added to this group. A number of larger banks were nationalized in 1969, and banking efforts have increased in rural and less developed areas. For this reason local representatives of the banks have now become one of the prime sources of information concerning entrepreneurship.

Further promise for heightening informational linkages in agriculture can be seen in the concept of the growth center, particularly the development within the growth center of an agro-service center. The various technical and institutional needs for agricultural inputs are brought together in a comprehensive entity that lays the basis for much more effective information interchange. Whether or not the agro-service center is a single company under a single individual or a set of related satellite organizations and individuals, recognition of the interrelatedness of the agro-service function, by its very nature, results in an increased emphasis on information linking. Again we can see the critical importance of the linking process, building on bits of information to produce the innovational spark.

In today's world certain information-processing vehicles have achieved special prominence. Plans for information transmission tend to gravitate toward these particular vehicles. For example, in the developed world electronic data processing has come to involve much more than simply a machine; it has brought about an information revolution in the underlying concepts for which the machinery and its output are only the end product. Computers and other such paraphernalia are not presently found in rural areas of less developed countries (although we should not fall into any stereotyped thinking that computers are inherently intermediate or high technology; rural India may have access to new-generation computers sooner than we expect).

Another communications device eminently adaptable to rural areas is television. The technology for rural television is already in operation in many less developed countries, and there are now major experiments utilizing it as an educational device. For example, the Indian government has been experimenting over the past half-dozen years with a Delhi-based television program, *Krishi Darshan* (Farm Forum), designed to inform farmers about new agricultural techniques. Approximately three thirty-minute programs are telecast each week to a set of villages surrounding Delhi, with community receivers in the village for viewers. With the development of the NASA satellite program, future transmission might also utilize satellite intermediaries to broadcast to an increasing number of villages. It appears that India will be giving unprecedented emphasis to television broadcasting, with plan targets that call for introduction of television coverage to 80 percent of the Indian population by about the 1990s.

Recent analyses of *Krishi Darshan* emphasize its modest, perhaps even disappointing, record. As one critic put it:

> The overwhelming impression one gets from the *Krishi Darshan* surveys is that farmers have not been receptive to the farm forum programs. First, farmers have not flocked to the sets, nor has viewing time been in demand among villagers. In most cases, less than half the members watch any given program during the first year of a teleclub's operation, and the numbers invariably dwindle thereafter. Wives and children tend to outnumber members themselves, and after the first year the set is used primarily by occasional non-club viewers . . . The real reason for the failure to attract large audiences is that programs are considered by villagers to be inappropriate. The overwhelming majority of farm viewers, when placed in interview situations, indicate that they do not understand the technical language used, cannot figure out the metric system (villagers in India use a hodgepodge of unstandardized traditional systems for counting), cannot see how the technology demonstrated on television could be meaningful to them and, in any case, could not secure the recommended inputs of seeds, fertilizer, water and so forth, even if they wanted to try *Krishi Darshan* techniques. Their most frequent recommendation for improvement of television is that the government drop its attempt to educate them and provide entertainment instead."[16]

Perhaps some of these expressed complaints stem from faulty television programming techniques. Beyond this, part of the unease probably comes from the tradition-breaking concept of beaming new ideas into a traditional environment. Even with superb programming, experience might well yield less than expectations. Such issues are beyond the scope of this study. Our point is a narrower one; concentration on single devices for disseminating information often causes overemphasis and resulting shortfalls in realizations. The use of various information sources tends to give a more balanced pattern and avoids dependence upon the success or failure of any one device. In rural areas it can be particularly important to have several alternative decision paths; if one set of data is momentarily not available, another set will suffice. Governments, private corporations, and other sources of information in the less developed world would be wise to consider diversifying their information transmission systems, even to the point of sacrificing depth for breadth of coverage.

Teaching Information Entrepreneurship

Information entrepreneurship can surely be learned. The generation, sorting, and evaluation of information in the less developed world until now has tended to be spotty, but this situation can be remedied. The computer in the developed world can be used to generate information rapidly and make it available to the rest of the world. Associated with the computer is a whole range of new quantitative techniques and information-systems concepts that have revolutionized the analytic art.

However, quantitative information alone is not enough to fill gaps and complete inputs. An entrepreneur is not created merely by supplying someone with new information and methods for treating it. One needs also to inculcate behavioral objectives that persuade toward the use of information — a "language of achievement" developed out of an achievement-oriented pattern of goal setting, encouraged by the kinds of cognitive and group supports used in such programs as the Distributors for Change seminars. Thus a whole range of qualitative information and conceptual thinking is needed to complete the entrepreneurial system.

For example, such traditional teaching techniques as the case method are startlingly new when applied to business education and executive education in the less developed world. A few years ago the Graduate School of Business of Columbia University conducted a substantial cooperative teaching program in Argentina in collaboration with the University of Buenos Aires. Several of the participating professors took with them the case-analysis and role-playing methods they had used in their classes for a number of years. According to the dean of the business school at the University of Buenos Aires, "Professors Walton and Broehl used a role-playing technique that was completely new to the faculty. This plus other innovations brought from Columbia (case studies, panel discussions, essay assignments, et cetera) generated a minor revolution in teaching methods which spread to other departments of the faculty."[17]

Leibenstein, for one, is hopeful about such efforts: "It may be difficult to train people to spot economic opportunities, but it is possible to train them to assess such opportunities once perceived. Similarly, certain managerial skills are trainable."[18] Leibenstein comes to an interesting conclusion about the supply of entrepreneurship in the less developed world, namely, that "while entrepreneurship may be scarce because of a lack of input-completing capacities, some entrepreneurial characteristics may, in fact, be in surplus supply; that is, they are unused simply because of the lack of input-completing capacity." As a consequence, even a small change in the reduction of market impediment and an increase in information may cause a more adequate supply of entrepreneurs.

One need not be as pessimistic as Leibenstein, even in the training of people to spot economic opportunities. An imaginative combination of achievement-motivation training can be put together, perhaps the case method and other devices of the business school and some of the work of the sensitivity training theorists and practitioners, to provide a form of entrepreneurial training that will inculcate an information-search concept. If Vilfredo Pareto is right that there is an inherent instinct of combination (as he puts it in his florid prose, "a hunger for combining residues"),[19] then man's eternal search for the materials of combination would seem to make training for combination possible.

Sparking Critical Mass

Linking is only a mechanistic relation until there is a confluence, a point where there are sufficient connecting ideas to produce a new idea. This is the leap across a discontinuous innovational barrier to a fruitful innovation—the process that many writers have called the "aha" stage. Analysts of innovation construct elaborate paraphernalia to bring the reader to the point of this spark, and they also follow with detailed analyses of what occurs after it. Yet this point of "aha" seems painfully unclear in most models, almost read out of the process by the simple assumption that "at this point an innovative idea occurs." The net effect is to expunge from the model the very essence of entrepreneurship, almost as if, as William Baumol put it, the Prince of Denmark had been excised from *Hamlet*.[20]

Schumpeter's theories have been enormously helpful to me, for he uses the system model as his frame and then puts special focus on the process dimensions of innovation. He calls this a "distinct phenomenon, entirely foreign to what may be observed in a circular flow or in the tendency towards equilibrium." It is a "spontaneous and continuous change," a "new combination" that intrudes into the system. It is not a gradual process in the normal changes in data, but a qualitatively new phenomenon.[21] Thus Schumpeter puts his spotlight on the synergy of bringing together new data to produce a discontinuous jump across an innovational barrier to a new idea — precisely the concept in our model. Yet Schumpeter does not tell us what made that spark, that jump, occur.

Israel Kirzner deepens Schumpeter's model by stressing the special quality of information *alertness*. We can envision an entrepreneur actively sifting and meshing information in a sedulous and self-conscious way toward that moment of coming-together when the innovation itself is born. "One can no longer interpret the decision as merely calculative — capable in principle of being yielded by mechanical manipulation of the 'data' or already *completely implied* in these data," notes Kirzner. Yet Kirzner also carries us too rapidly through this point of spark, saying only that "once we become sensitive to the decision-makers' alertness to new possibly worthwhile ends and newly available means, it may be possible to explain the pattern of change in an individual's decisions as the outcome of a learning process generated by the unfolding experience of the decisions themselves."[22] Just what this unfolding experience really is remains cloudy.

Harvey Leibenstein's theories are more satisfactory.[23] With X-efficiency knowledge and action falling short of optimization — with neither individuals nor firms taking full advantage of opportunities for gain — Leibenstein infers a range of frictional inactivity and inertia that produces two sets of bounds, or thresholds, above and below which decisions for change are made. After noting the various kinds of signals necessary to motivate the firm or the individual to act — to pass the upper bound — Leibenstein focuses again on the gap-filling and input-completing needs required for this motivation to occur. Thus in his model there is no sharp dichotomy between an existing innovational frontier and a shift in the frontier; rather, there is a series of "points." For any *given* innovational act, there is a set of necessary and sufficient pieces of information (both historical data and extrapolative assumptions) that provide the spark that brings the innovation to fruition. In Leibenstein's earlier, seminal work, *Economic Backwardness and Economic Growth,* he developed a concept of the "critical minimum effort" necessary for a given change in economic growth;[24] now he has applied this thesis directly to innovation.

What *does* make the spark occur? I have suggested that, first, there must be a process of synergy at work — a process that will produce critical mass. There is in any particular idea a set of critical minimum sufficiencies, below which no leap across the discontinuous gap will occur, above which the jump becomes possible. The more precisely we can identify these minimum or necessary sufficiencies, the more effective the innovational process will be.

The utilization of the package of practices by the Intensive Agricultural District Programme (IADP) in India illustrates these concepts well. The package approach stresses using interrelated factors—physical, social, and institutional—in strategic combinations.[25] As originally envisioned, the word "strategic" was intended only to stress the need for a balanced approach to inputs. Soon, though, these packages were expanded to include specific quantifications of inputs, and by 1963, when the Expert Committee on Assessment and Evaluation of the IADP made its first report, the word "optimum" was used as a modifier for the ingredients of the packages.[26]

Over the years, better research has made each piece of the input package more refinable; the package has begun to take on additional levels of precision that have brought heightened results for the package districts.[27] There may never be an ultimate solution that would denominate for a given hectare in a given state in India at a given season under given weather and irrigation combinations a set of exact inputs, all of which were minimum sufficiencies. The package components were always considered as "recommended," rather than as minimum or necessary, sufficiencies. Yet necessary sufficiencies are not only a theoretical potential but a practical possibility, in that present combinations of better field research and more powerful analytical tools (particularly linear programming models) allow the inclusion of theoretical ideals as practical goals.

A recent Ford Foundation report analyzing the experience of the 1960s under the IADP package program noted the "dramatic improvements in farming practices," then commented, "till now these have been, however, largely the simple package of practices—variety, fertilizer, plant protection, mechanization, etc. Now, more sophisticated demonstrations that include modern water use and management, mulitple cropping, blending of animal husbandry with crop production and complex fertilizer application—including in some cases minor elements—need to be developed. This 'new generation' of demonstrations need to have a built-in economic component that provides information as to the economic return to the farmers."[28] Care must be taken not to assume that an individual's least-cost solution in a given time period is automatically a generalized set of minimum sufficiencies; certain costs are fixed to him over the short run, but all costs are taken to be variable over the long run.

Once the minimum critical requirements are identified, any combination of quanta below these levels would fail to reach critical mass and therefore preclude the innovation. There is real need for a theory of retrenchment in the Green Revolution. Because of the world's energy shortage, certain key ingredients of the Green Revolution have been in short supply, with the expected companion effect of sharp rises in price. This has been a particular problem in the case of fertilizers for the less developed countries. Inasmuch as the recommended levels of fertilizer application were not even being met before the so-called oil crisis hit, the levels of utilization are dropping back from "recommended" at a pace that has troubled many development analysts. Yet new research evidence shows that even with lesser amounts of some of the key inputs, the new grains still can be more effective than their counterpart traditional varieties, provided there is at least some level of input.[29] Cast in the frame we have just discussed, the recommended levels were above the minimum sufficiencies; now the inputs are moving back toward the minimum level. As long as they do not reach that level, continued use of these inputs will be a productive decision at the margin. Yet we need to be quite precise about where these minima are, lest one or another of the important inputs falls below its minimum. These are practical considerations, readily susceptible to good research, and simple enough in their manifestations to be teachable to cultivators and others who might not be interested in the underlying theory but want to know what to do.

Thus the point of critical-mass synergy is important to the theory of entrepreneurship and also part of a practical set of strategies about how entrepreneurship may be heightened in its application. The Distributors for Change seminars utilized some out-of-the-ordinary training techniques (such as brainstorming and case analysis) to heighten awareness of this process of linking and the relation of the linking to critical mass.

Critical Mass in Growth Centers

If minimum sufficiencies can be ascertained at the microlevel of the individual and the firm, we can also envision them spatially at the more macrofocused growth center. Central place theory, associated with the "population threshold" concept, formed the base for our earlier analysis of growth centers. The calculation is essentially mechanical in that one or another arithmetic method is used to compute the lower bound for a given level of settlement hierarchy, beyond which any given community drops down to the next level. Thus we were able to compute for the two community development blocks in Namakkal taluk a set of what were considered to be the needed central services necessary for population centers at each level; this in turn allowed us to spell out a subset of towns at each level of hierarchy.

Earlier neoclassical versions of regional growth theory were generally not constructed to deal satisfactorily with this concept of agglomeration. More recent versions are. Gunnar Myrdal argued in one of his early books for the principle of circular and cumulative causation, with the clustering of increasing-return activities in certain areas of an economy.[30] A buildup was set in motion by increasing internal and external economies at these centers of agglomeration; the process could then become self-sustaining. Likewise, recent growth center theories have focused on the process of agglomeration consequent upon the location decisions of firms in propulsive (leading) industries along certain *poles de croissance* (the well-known Perroux terminology). This focus on growth factors indigenous to the region allows agglomeration economies and the spatial proximity of activities in certain towns or regions to induce a rate of innovation above what it might have been in the absence of this agglomeration. In turn, this intraregional spatial efficiency may have a feedback on the aggregate growth rate and can bring about what several analysts have called generative growth. There have been a number of recent efforts to quantify agglomeration economies in order to be able to subject regional growth theory to modeling techniques.[31]

Full analysis of these theories is beyond the scope of this book; focus here is on the process of innovation itself. My point is a more modest one. Practical use of hierarchical theory does not require minimum sufficiencies for each level of town. Yet there is reason to believe that there is a complex set of combinations — linkages — that come together in synergy at a particular level of town activity that can again be described precisely as critical mass. Thus it seems logical to assume that a more exact analysis of each input into a growth center in terms of its minimum sufficiencies will pay off in terms of the practical use of central place theory in regional economic development planning. For example, a certain number of village technology services are needed for a particular level of agricultural village — certain implement repair facilities, perhaps a fertilizer depot, and so forth. Each of these has its own minimum quantum of service to make it viable at this level. In this light, central place theory can move beyond the mechanistic and become normative. Thus we should be thinking of a package of inputs in terms of growth center planning also.

This same concept should be applied in regard to the agro-service centers discussed in earlier chapters. The reason stems from the argument relative to downturns in the Green Revolution. A set of hectare fields carries packages of minimum necessary inputs for given areas of agricultural application, so an agro-service center's reach is defined by a somewhat more complicated solution of the problem already solved concerning the hectare field itself. A reasonably precise solution for the individual inputs will denominate specific total levels of inputs that would be housed under one or another form of the agro-service center. Calculations would be complex, and there would be certain qualitative decisions about alternative forms of ownership and the like. Yet the process of analysis is not only methodologically possible, it also carries with it real practical advantages in centering development planning on the most parsimonious set of links to be brought together for use by given entrepreneurs.

Variations on the Growth Center Theme

The question of ownership patterns within a growth center raises some interesting strategic concerns. Should an agro-service center, for example, be housed under one umbrella organization, say under one entrepreneur, or, alternatively, should there be satellite organizations, either semiautonomous or independent? The latter model appeals to a number of analysts, who stress the stability of diversity. Albert Shapero recently described this model as the "dynamic community," where there is a set of essentially coequal organizations interacting with one another, rather than what he defines as the "in-migrant trap," where a large organization moves into an area and develops its own satellite suppliers. Shapero contends that the dependency in thinking that often seems to accompany this satellite relationship brings disincentives to the innovative process. A comparative study by Jane Jacobs of the English cities of Manchester and Birmingham, with the latter exhibiting both a higher pattern of innovativeness and a higher degree of diversity, would appear to corroborate this view.[32] (Perhaps one should define Shapero's term more precisely as "dominant-firm in-migrant trap," inasmuch as the migrant firm and/or individual coming into an area on its own is frequently the source for new ideas and innovative acts, à la Everett Hagen's deviant-culture thesis.)

Thus patterns of both horizontal and vertical integration are important in structuring a community. For example, a rural agro-service center in a village of South India needs to be organized with great care so that maximum effect is given to linking patterns leading to innovation. Shapero's warnings caution us to avert excessive dependencies. In India, for example, the venerable jajmani system has been counterproductive to innovation, and one would want to keep the functions of an agro-service center independent of rich cultivators or other dominant-firm entities. Given the power of the package concept, however, with its emphasis on building within a given organization the proper combination of critical masses necessary for innovation, one can make a strong case for putting together a set of related agricultural inputs under a single agro-service center — and this is the approach we recommend.

An interesting variation noted in recent literature might fit quite well here — the suggestion that while one might hold a set of functions within a given organizational entity, the actual founder and entrepreneur might be not one person but a set of coequal individuals that make up an entrepreneurial team.[33] The advocates of this idea posit that a careful self-assessment by the individuals involved can bring about a unique combination of specialized talent. There is also a set of potential negatives, such as conflicts in goals and values and what one writer has called the "leaderless democracy" syndrome of no one person being firmly in charge. The practicality of these new organizational models needs further study, but we can conclude that the notion of a single innovative act being accomplished by a team of individuals is not beyond the realm of possibility. Given the process envisioned in the model at the beginning of this book, and the emphasis that has been put on the linking of information, it is possible that a group of close-knit colleagues could accomplish this linking process and step across the innovation gap to a new idea as a group rather than individually. Incidentally, this is why the process of brainstorming might be relevant for carrying through team entrepreneurship, which will certainly be a subject for fruitful research in the future.

Training and Entrepreneurship

There are important implications in the concept of critical mass and in the linking of information for the selection of entrepreneurs for training programs.

I agree with Schumpeter's deduction that entrepreneurs as such do not form a social class, that their "genealogies display most varied origins — the working class, the aristocracy, the professional groups, peasants and farmers, and the artisan class."[34] Yet Schumpeter goes on to maintain that entrepreneurship is randomly distributed in the economy — his analogy to the ability to sing is a famous one. We seem to be left with only a passive role in searching out potential entrepreneurs. This is similar to the conclusion reached by many analysts of entrepreneurship, that (here using the words of W. W. Rostow in his controversial book, *The Stages of Economic Growth*) "new types of enterprising men come forward . . . A new elite must emerge . . . under some human motivation or other . . . Some group must successfully emerge."[35]

I feel that any view that holds that we must await the slow, undependable process of evolutionary change in social and psychological climates is a counsel of despair. The entrepreneur is not like other inputs, with a contribution that can be readily determined, predicted, planned for, and controlled; nevertheless, an entrepreneurial type can be identified. I suggested earlier that in rural India this would likely be a person who answered certain key questions in a "modern" way, who exhibited better than usual levels of short-term planning, who had been involved in leadership activities, who would accept medium risk, and who had an interest in and a use of information sources that emphasized the linking concept. Using these taxonomies, I suggested that a simple predictive mechanism *can* be utilized to produce a better-than-average chance of identifying entrepreneurially oriented people among a set of villagers. Further, our research points to a pattern whereby the joining together of certain critical minimum necessities in each of these predictive areas creates a package of linked strengths that is more likely to produce entrepreneurial potential.

Critical mass has an additional training parameter I wish to note. The module concept in the Distributors for Change seminars stressed the linking of disparate but theoretically related ideas that themselves could be linked by the participants at the end of the sessions. Thus the seminars took up topics related to planning, to risk taking, to brainstorming, and to problem solving, and related them all to some of the new innovations and ideas in the field involved. This quality of linking was probably enhanced by the close juxtaposition of the various topics in a concentrated five-day period. To be sure, problems are inherent in this short time span and critics might argue that one cannot bring about behavioral changes in so short a period, irrespective of what one does. For the present, although not prepared to quarrel with this judgment, I do wish to set as the penultimate words of this book my belief that the linking process and critical mass are crucial ingredients for entrepreneurship.

A final thought seems in order. The theme of this book has been that entrepreneurship is a discontinuous but identifiable act, one that can be viewed best in its system effects, and that if this view is carefully dissected, one can identify pieces of it that will allow practical training steps to be taken that will "grow" further entrepreneurship. This is indeed a noble goal, for its furtherance would be the furtherance of mankind. Innovation and change infuse the lives of every inhabitant of this globe, whether residing in a modern city of the developed world or in a traditional village of a less developed country. The person who takes these innovations and makes the idea/projects realities is a change agent, and a benefactor of moment to the world. The goal of this book has been to heighten the possibilities of identifying this person and to motivate him or her to contribute significantly to society.

Appendixes
Notes
Index

Appendix A   The Research Methodology

The two southern states of Andhra Pradesh and Tamil Nadu were chosen as the field ground for these studies. After my field trip to these two states in 1969, I chose to study fertilizer distribution on the input side and rice milling on the output side and a small number of pilot questionnaires were administered in 1970—to 47 fertilizer distributors in Chingleput district and 30 rice millers in Tanjore district, all in Tamil Nadu. The sample was balanced by picking dealers from large and small towns, from rural areas, and from a representative variety of backgrounds, but no formal randomizing was attempted. After the preliminary multivariate analysis of these pilot interviews, the questionnaire was reconstructed in its final form for application in the fieldwork of 1971.

At this point a stratified random sample was constructed, to include both assured-water and dry-farming situations, with the dealers representing large and small size and larger towns and villages. A group of fertilizer manufacturing executives and state agricultural officials was asked to help identify, through the Delphi reiterative technique, those districts and those taluks within the district that would give this requisite stratification. Five students from Madras Christian College were trained by me and my two senior Indian research associates, M. D. Gopalakrishnan and V. Ramadas, to administer the questionnaires in person (all were fluent in both English and Tamil). The districts and taluks assigned were as follows:

District: South Arcot   *Taluk:* Chidambaram
                                                   Cuddalore
                                                   Tindivanam
                                                   Kallakurichi

Tanjore   Kumbakonam
                                                   Nannilam
                                                   Aranthangi

Coimbatore   Erode
                                                   Dharapuram

187

For reasons noted in the text, only private fertilizer distributors were interviewed, with the two largest companies, E. I. D. Parry and Shaw-Wallace, chosen. Lists of all their dealers in these taluks were obtained from each of the two companies and a random sample was taken for each (the size of sample for each of the taluks having been approximated in the earlier Delphi process). The total number of dealers in the sample was 180.

This extensive sample was complemented by a separate intensive sample of fertilizer distributors in what was considered by the Delphi team to be a representative taluk (that is, having ranges of assured and rain-fed areas, of dealer size, and of village and town size). For this taluk, Namakkal in Salem district, every dealer of the two companies was included — a total of fifty-six.

The rice miller samples were more pragmatically drawn. Fifty millers were chosen, all from assured-water areas of Tanjore district. Extensive discussions with the officers of the Tanjore Rice Millers' Association produced agreement about a representative sample that included larger wholesale units and the smaller coolie mills.

The full 286 interviews were conducted over the summer of 1971 by the five-member team and my two senior associates. In addition, during that summer and again in the summer of 1973 several dozen case study interviews in considerable depth were conducted among the respondents. The typical personal interview for completion of the questionnaire took approximately 1½ hours and the case studies were generally about twice that long. Thus the total actual contact with these 236 fertilizer distributors and 50 rice millers was approximately 500 hours.

One further fertilizer distributor sample was conducted, in the state of Andhra Pradesh, with a total of 43 dealers interviewed by means of the questionnaire used in Tamil Nadu. The interviewers were research personnel from the Administrative Staff College of India at Hyderabad. In general, these interviews were briefer, although they covered the same set of questions. Only one of the two companies was involved, and the dealers came from Eluru taluk and Tanuku taluk, both in the district of West Godavari; a scattering of interviews came from several taluks in Nalgonda district. This sample gives additional perspective on the Tamil Nadu samples, for in Andhra Pradesh the typical dealership is considerably larger than in Tamil Nadu.

Three other samples were taken for comparative purposes. The first was a sample of urban and small-town small-scale manufacturers: a group of 18 engine and pump manufacturers in the town of Coimbatore and a group of 37 general manufacturers in the Guindy Industrial Estate in a suburban area near Madras. The Coimbatore group has a reputation throughout India of being extremely entrepreneurial; the Guindy manufacturers are a more representative range of talent along this line. Both samples were carefully selected on a stratified random basis; lists of the full sets of manufacturers in both locations were obtained from the two manufacturers' associations and randomly selected after having been stratified by sales size.

The second was a self-administered sample of 21 executives in large-scale textile companies in the Coimbatore area, with the administering of the questionnaires being conducted independently by the South India Textile Research Association at Coimbatore. With the individual entrepreneur filling out the questionnaire at his leisure, there was much less standardization in the responses.

A third group was a set of 25 village small-scale shopkeepers near Namakkal. Here the sampling was random — an arbitrary selection of street location was made and 25 contiguous shops were interviewed.

Thus the refined 1971 questionnaire was eventually administered to 430 people; when the 1970 pilot questionnaire responses were added to the total, something over 500 small town and village entrepreneurs had been interviewed.

The Questionnaires

The questions covered the following:

Historical and performance data on the firm:

Age of firm
New product lines
New functions
Number and description of branches
Number and description of problems at start-up
Number and description of problems at time of interview
Number and description of short-term changes planned (within six months)
Number and description of long-term changes planned (how firm will have
    changed five years later)
Sales level (recent three years)
Profit level (recent three years)
Tonnage sold (recent three years)
Number of telephone outlets in firm
Number and level of employees
Sources of financing
Most important stages of growth
Competitor evaluations.

Biodata on the respondent:

Age
Caste and subcaste
Religion and marital status
Father's occupation
Degree of urbanness in residences over lifetime
Degree of spatial movement in residences over lifetime
Number of brothers
Number of sisters
Rank among brothers
Rank among all children
Degree of spatial movement of wife
Education of respondent
Number of sons
Number of daughters
Number of years ancestors in state
Number of other firms founded by the respondent in his lifetime.

Attitudinal and behavioral data on the respondent:

A. *Leadership roles*
   Number of meetings attended/month
   Number of positions held
   Level of positions held
   Public figures most admired
B. *Communication patterns*
   Number of states visited in lifetime
   Number of other countries visited in lifetime
   Newspaper reading (minutes/day)
   Radio listening (minutes/day)
   Cinema attendance (per month)
   Number of languages (spoken, read, written)
   Furthest distance traveled in past six months (for business, for other)
   Number of business contacts/month
   Index of information sources utilized
   Index of interest in news sources
C. *Attitudes toward modernization*
   Level of education desired for son
   Number of minutes considered late
   "What is an entrepreneur?" (nine-item semantic difference test)
   Set of modernization forced-choice questions
   Attitude toward family planning
D. *Attitudes toward risk*
   Set of forced-choice "risk dilemma" questions.

The new product lines and new functions were derived from two separate questions, the first asking "What does this firm do now that it did not do at the beginning?" and the second asking a set of questions about stage of development: "What was it? Why was it done? What were the main difficulties encountered? How did you overcome them?" This also gave basic information for the number of branches. The question of other firms founded by the respondent was initially derived from this question and checked later in the questionnaire by the question, "Have you ever founded another firm or firms? (If so, please specify)." Start-up problems were also covered in this section of the questionnaire; the questions on planning—current problems, short-term changes, and long-term changes—were covered later.

The two questions relating to sales and profits are, clearly, the most sensitive on the questionnaire. In order that the respondent not feel threatened, a six-category interval scale was chosen for sales and a seven-category interval scale for profits. At each point profits were set at precisely 10 percent of sales. Of the 180 respondents in the large three-district sample, 142 answered these particular questions. Crosschecking of these data was aided by the availability of company figures on sales to the distributors. The tonnage figures were more readily obtained from the respondents; few of them made the direct association between the question about sales and the question about tonnage. In this case also the figures were corroborated against company figures. There were frequently carryovers in the individual distributor's stock, so the company's sales figures had to be cumulated on a several-year span and reconciled with the cumulative amounts taken by the dealer. Even with this refinement there were potential discrepancies. Therefore two full sets of principal-component analysis were run, one on the figures given by the dealer, another on the figures given by the companies. Multiple-discriminant analysis showed no statistically significant difference between dealer and company figures.

Biodata on the respondents were, in the main, straightforward. The attitudinal and behavioral material given by the respondents was considerably more complex, so a number of crosschecks were set up by means of paired questions. The full set of interview questions used by the Alex Inkeles team and discussed in Chapter 2 is reproduced as appendix A of Alex Inkeles and David Horton Smith, *Becoming Modern: Individual Change in Six Developing Countries* (Cambridge, Massachusetts: Harvard University Press, 1974), pp. 319-347. The "OM-12—The Short Form" is reproduced as their appendix B, pp. 348-351. The OM-12 contains fourteen questions, two of which appear on our final eight-variable scale. The coding was developed after the eight questions in the Broehl modernization index were analyzed through factor analysis. A three-vector pattern emerged, and the factor scores within these three were then combined to form a single index. The following eight questions made up the final Broehl modernization index:

(1) Two twelve-year-old boys were talking as they worked in the rice fields. They were trying to figure out a way to grow the same amount of rice with fewer hours of work. The father of one boy said: "That is a good thing to think about. Tell me your thoughts about how we should change our ways of growing rice." The father of the other boy said: "The best way to grow rice is the way we have always done it. Talk about change often wastes time and often does not help."

Which father said the wiser words?
(a) The first father
(b) The second father

(2) Some people say that a boy learns the deepest and most real truth from old people. Others say that a boy learns the deepest and most real truth from books and in school.

What is your opinion?
(a) Most truth from old people
(b) About equal truth from both
(c) Most truth from books and school

(3) Today in India one often hears people say the old ways are slipping away and many things are changing.

How do *you* feel about this? Are these changes in India:
(a) Too fast?
(b) Too slow?
(c) Just right?

(4) There were two sons of an old and noble family, both of whom wanted to help their country. One set out to be a holy man. He gave up all his worldly possessions in order to go about the country showing the path to the good and religious life. The other son set out to establish a great textile mill. His factory gave work to hundreds of his countrymen (all of whom he treated fairly) and also produced inexpensive goods that many people needed.

Which of these two men do you personally admire more?
(a) Holy man
(b) Factory owner
(c) Both, equally

(5) At a certain foundry the boss does not have a man do several different jobs, but instead asks him to do one simple job over and over again. Is it because:
(a) The man can be made more efficient that way?
(b) That is all rural Indian workers can be trained to do?
(c) Management runs the factory and has the right to arrange the work?

(6) In your line of work would you say that when difficulties come up in the way of the work:
(a) Almost all get solved?
(b) Most get solved?
(c) Many do not get solved?
(d) Most do not get solved?

(7) To be successful in life, do you feel that it is more important to have good luck or to make good plans?
(a) Much more important to have good luck

(b) A little more important to have good luck
(c) A little more important to make plans
(d) Much more important to make plans

(8) In some jobs there are opportunities to get ahead and improve your situation, while in others there are no such opportunities. In your work what opportunities do you have to get ahead and improve your situation?

(a) No opportunities
(b) Little opportunity
(c) Some opportunity
(d) Much opportunity

Three of the "risk-dilemma" questions were adapted from the well-known study by Nathan Kogan and M. A. Wallach, *Risk Taking: A Study in Cognition and Personality* (New York: Holt, 1964), and the following question was also developed to emphasize business risk:

Suppose you see an opportunity to increase the business your company does. There are several ways this can be done, and the choice is up to you. Which way would you be inclined to take?

(a) A way involving considerable risk of losing your investment, but with a quite high possible return
(b) A way involving some risk, with a medium return
(c) A way involving very little risk, but with a small return
(d) Stay out altogether, unless there was a low risk and considerable possible return

Several indices of risk were developed from these four questions. First, the four questions were coded from high to low, cumulated and defined as "high risk." A good case can be made, however, that the individual who makes a single high-risk choice is often not a risk taker but has the mentality of a gambler, and that therefore the outlier does not measure risk taking but quite the opposite. Therefore a coding was generated whereby the next-highest choice was given the highest rank and the high choice was given equal weighting with the no-risk choice. This index was called "medium risk." A similar dichotomy was developed on the single question dealing with business risk. Two variations of the medium risk concept were also measured, by use of a quadratic equation containing the values of the answers above or below the mean.

We were interested to see how the rural businessmen would define "entrepreneur." There is no exact Tamil equivalent of this word. We were looking for a way of describing the entrepreneur in the Schumpeterian sense — as the man who changes production functions. The closest we could come was a set of Tamil descriptors of "the businessman who accomplishes important things." The research team agreed on a common way of articulating this and memorized the agreed set of sentences for the interviews. The device used was a semantic difference test, where the respondents were queried, "What is an entrepreneur?" and asked to choose from these nine pairs in the three categories of evaluation, potency, and activity:

Evaluation
   Relaxed-tense
   Dishonest-honest
   Thrifty-generous
Potency
   Powerful-weak
   Rural-urban

Activity
   Young-old
   Defensive-aggressive
   Cooperative-competitive
   Organized-unorganized

Our definitions of these three categories are congruent with those of Charles E. Osgood, George J. Suci, and Percy H. Tannenbaum in *The Measurement of Meaning* (Urbana: University of Illinois Press, 1971). We tested our results in applying them to the fertilizer distributors by factor analysis and found that the three categories were, indeed, adequate descriptors. The first and third pairs in the "evaluation" dimension were closely linked in their own vector. The pair "powerful-weak" appeared to be more strongly linked to "young-old" than to "rural-urban" (the latter did not weight heavily in any of the vectors). The pair "dishonest-honest" appeared to load its own vector. The last three of the four pairs in the "activity" categories always loaded heavily together. We gave the same set of choices to a group of American graduate students and faculty and asked them to define a United States entrepreneur. Here are the tabulations from the Indian and American groups:

	Definition of entrepreneur	
Word pairs	Indian ($n = 142$)	American ($n = 54$)
Relaxed-tense	Both	Tense
Young-old	Both	Young
Rural-urban	Both	Urban
Dishonest-honest	Honest	Honest
Thrifty-generous	Generous	Thrifty
Cooperative-competitive	Cooperative	Competitive
Organized-unorganized	Organized	Organized
Defensive-aggressive	Defensive	Aggressive
Powerful-weak	Powerful	Powerful

We then made up two indices, one based on the Indian definition of entrepreneurship, the other on the American, and determined correlations with our other data on these distributors. Only a few statistically significant results emerged. Those Indians who answered close to the American definition tended to be those who were more planning oriented and more risk accepting. On the other hand, there were no important relationships to the actual performance variables, nor to other variables such as modernization.

The Multivariate Analysis

The questionnaire had a total of 210 separately coded variables. Some were cumulated to become composite variables—for example, travel to the several states became a "travel index." Another considerable segment of the 210 items comprised nominal data—for example, caste and community differences. There were also many interval measures, such as tonnage figures per year and age of respondents. Others were ordinal by nature, but with certain assumptions about the relations of the choices within the questions, one could treat them as metric surrogates and use correlation and regression analysis as well as factor analysis.

Principal-component analysis is an excellent device for analyzing data of this nature, as it requires no pre-existing theory of functional relationships, can handle masses of diverse data that involve large numbers of social and economic characteristics, and is not sensitive to the scales chosen for the

TABLE A-1   Eigen roots for 42 original variables of a sample group of 142 South Indian fertilizer distributors.

Root	Size	% trace	Cumulative %
1	5.45	12.98	12.98
2	3.36	8.01	20.98
3	2.95	7.03	28.01
4	2.53	6.02	34.03
5	2.20	5.23	39.26
6	1.96	4.67	43.93
7	1.79	4.26	48.19
8	1.64	3.90	52.09
9	1.50	3.57	55.66
10	1.41	3.36	59.01
11	1.28	3.05	62.06
12	1.22	2.89	64.96
13	1.10	2.63	67.58
14	1.04	2.48	70.07
15	1.02	2.43	72.49

quantification of given variables. A group of 42 variables appeared to be the most useful starting point for multivariate analysis.

Rotated factor patterns (using varimax) were employed, based on analyses of correlation matrices. Here the eigen root pattern gives strong clues to the number of factors that can be drawn upon to explain important percentages of variance. Table A-1 gives the eigen root patterns for the 42 variables; there are 15 roots above the arbitrary figure of 1.0. An eight-vector solution is shown in Table A-2. The number of variables was eventually reduced to 18, several of them composites of those in the original 42; a hierarchical clustering program was particularly helpful here. The following are the 18 key variables:

(1) Respondent age
(2) Respondent education
(3) Respondent spatial living pattern
(4) Age of firm
(5) Index of information sources used
(6) Index of information interest patterns
(7) Leadership index
(8) Broehl modernization index
(9) High-risk index
(10) Medium-risk index
(11) Number of short-term plans
(12) Number of long-term plans
(13) Number of same endeavors
(14) Number of new functions
(15) Number of other firms founded
(16) Sales level
(17) Growth pattern (generated from tonnage sold)
(18) Profitability

TABLE A-2   Factor patterns (after varimax rotation) showing correlations among 42 original variables of a group of 142 fertilizer distributors and eight new composite factors.

Variable	1	2	3	4	5	6	7	8	Row SS
1. Age of firm	−0.28	0.52	0.08	0.20	0.09	0.17	0.08	−0.34	0.55
2. Number of problems	0.11	0.15	0.07	−0.11	−0.07	−0.03	0.04	−0.55	0.36
3. Age of respondent	−0.19	−0.01	0.03	−0.03	0.10	0.65	−0.05	0.06	0.47
4. Urban index	0.01	−0.13	−0.63	0.03	−0.02	−0.19	−0.08	0.03	0.46
5. Spatial index	−0.02	0.05	−0.49	−0.06	−0.46	0.16	−0.19	−0.11	0.54
6. Education	0.15	−0.15	−0.43	0.29	0.04	−0.44	0.04	0.23	0.57
7. Travel	0.04	0.01	−0.68	0.03	0.21	0.28	−0.02	0.00	0.59
8. Other information index	0.30	−0.11	−0.06	0.31	0.33	0.25	0.14	−0.49	0.62
9. Newspaper	0.15	−0.05	−0.25	0.14	0.19	0.00	0.60	0.00	0.50
10. Radio	0.12	0.19	0.03	0.02	−0.04	−0.16	0.50	−0.08	0.34
11. Cinema	0.11	0.05	0.06	−0.05	−0.06	−0.51	0.39	−0.01	0.44
12. Language	0.23	−0.10	−0.73	0.22	0.01	−0.07	0.00	−0.05	0.65
13. News interest	0.74	0.14	−0.15	0.14	0.22	0.02	0.17	−0.23	0.75
14. Distance traveled	0.04	0.01	−0.37	0.04	0.52	−0.06	0.13	0.18	0.47
15. Meetings	−0.02	−0.02	−0.11	0.57	−0.02	−0.07	0.15	−0.05	0.39
16. Leadership position	0.04	−0.06	−0.06	0.90	0.04	0.06	−0.02	−0.04	0.82
17. Leadership index	0.10	−0.02	−0.06	0.89	0.07	0.03	−0.09	−0.06	0.83
18. Problems mentioned	−0.15	−0.04	0.13	0.09	0.06	0.09	0.36	−0.61	0.56
19. Short-term changes	0.18	0.02	0.03	−0.02	0.30	−0.32	−0.19	−0.47	0.49
20. Long-term changes	0.39	−0.20	0.08	0.09	−0.24	−0.02	0.03	−0.53	0.54
21. Optimism index	0.36	−0.14	0.07	−0.21	0.01	0.01	−0.21	−0.41	0.41
22. High risk	−0.28	−0.32	−0.50	0.01	0.33	−0.17	−0.04	0.05	0.57
23. Medium risk	0.45	−0.12	−0.27	−0.29	−0.01	−0.01	0.18	0.03	0.41
24. "U.S. entrepreneur"	−0.19	0.06	−0.08	−0.06	0.11	−0.56	−0.12	0.02	0.40
25. "Indian entrepreneur"	0.47	0.12	−0.08	−0.03	−0.05	0.39	−0.01	0.09	0.41
26. New modernization	0.61	−0.24	0.21	0.02	0.25	−0.25	0.06	−0.01	0.59
27. Inkeles index	0.02	0.06	−0.26	−0.02	−0.01	−0.03	−0.52	0.06	0.35
28. Broehl index	0.57	−0.26	0.05	0.06	0.15	−0.24	−0.23	0.03	0.53
29. Political news	0.75	0.11	−0.22	0.15	0.10	0.01	0.23	−0.24	0.77
30. Cultural news	−0.14	−0.13	−0.26	0.06	−0.56	−0.04	0.25	−0.07	0.49
31. People source	0.34	−0.09	−0.01	0.29	0.08	0.23	0.05	−0.55	0.57
32. Organizational source	0.01	−0.04	−0.12	0.07	0.66	0.03	0.17	0.00	0.48
33. Same endeavors	−0.01	−0.24	−0.14	0.06	0.38	−0.20	−0.15	−0.33	0.40
34. Different endeavors	−0.07	−0.12	−0.13	0.06	−0.11	−0.11	0.01	−0.58	0.39
35. Branches	−0.14	−0.40	−0.11	−0.01	−0.13	−0.01	−0.06	−0.37	0.35
36. Other firms	0.24	−0.06	−0.05	0.00	−0.54	0.07	−0.10	−0.03	0.37
37. Sales	0.10	−0.59	−0.37	0.02	−0.06	0.01	−0.11	−0.32	0.61
38. Profit level	0.12	−0.90	−0.12	0.00	−0.10	−0.07	−0.02	−0.05	0.85
39. Tonnage	0.08	−0.69	−0.22	−0.10	−0.12	−0.03	−0.12	0.02	0.57
40. Growth	0.01	−0.02	−0.12	0.29	0.18	−0.29	−0.45	−0.08	0.42
41. Employees	0.01	−0.56	−0.03	0.16	0.00	0.25	0.09	−0.18	0.45
42. Profitability	0.08	−0.68	0.18	−0.02	0.08	−0.10	0.07	0.22	0.57
Column SS	3.29	3.41	3.00	2.66	2.41	2.17	1.92	3.01	21.68

Appendix B   A schematic outline of the Distributors for Change program

Day 1

Introduction to the course by the instructors: A clear initial structure is presented that describes very frankly the objectives of the program. Participants are told that they will learn something about the most recent research on change and how this change is linked directly to an individual's executive performance, productivity, and profitability—and ultimately to national economic growth. The program is intended to increase their own strengths in recognizing change possibilities and raising their level of "change abilities." Participants are also told that no indirect or hidden methods will be employed; they alone can make the commitment to become change agents.

Detailed presentations about the nature of change: After brief descriptions of the characteristics of men with strong change motivation and the relation of this change motivation to outstanding entrepreneurial behavior, a distinguished visitor—a well-known and outstanding South Indian entrepreneur—describes his business life, with emphasis on his innovative behavior.

Self-presentations in small groups: Each person describes who he is to the members of his small group (five people). Each person then states what he hopes to get out of the course—his expectations. (Thus each person participates and begins to develop group trust and provide feedback on his own interests, thereby making each aware of the feelings and needs of the others in the group.)

Games to develop group feeling and self-awareness: A simple game is introduced (the Lego Man competitive construction game) that allows interpersonal involvement. Some stress is placed on emerging group awareness and the group supportive role; the primary focus will be on the substantive issues of planning.

Success stories from the group: After each member of the group discusses examples of change in his own business life, the group works together to make up a hypothetical "story of change" (the composite story of a successful dealer), to be presented by the group to the other three groups the following morning.

Personal goal setting—first iteration: At the end of the afternoon sessions each participant is asked to write down his own broad view of his goals in life, using a mockup of the front page of the Tamil daily newspaper. ("This is a newspaper story about you and your accomplishments, written some year in the future. Please write what you feel would be the ideal description of you and your accomplishments, if you were able to reach all your goals in life.")

Day 2

Brief critique of previous day: The instructors review the material covered, manner of presentation, relevance, and so forth.

Presentation of each group's hypothetical story: Each group presents its case in the manner it chooses (each is encouraged to role-play its own case). After each case and again at the end of the four, the instructors draw the change concepts from the case, to lead to the "change theories" that follow.

Presentation of change-theories concepts: Key concepts of innovation theory are presented, using specific illustrations from the four hypothetical stories and from other similar materials. Certain correlations are drawn with achievement-motivation theories—achievement and innovation are linked and distinguished from the affiliative and power motives of achievement-motivation training. Ways are demonstrated for objectively measuring change potential.

Brainstorming games: The concept of brainstorming is introduced and is both described and acted out by the instructors themselves (the instructors having previously developed a role-play brainstorming example). The group is then asked to try two simple brainstorming exercises:

(a) Bags containing fifteen identical unrelated small items, such as a pencil and a lock washer, are given to the groups. Each is asked to develop a story with a "change and innovation" central focus; six of the fifteen items are to be worked in as part of the story.

(b) Two of the four groups are asked to present their story, together with their final conclusions about change. After this, the other two groups are asked to present only their change conclusion, and then the other two groups are asked to try to guess how the individual items in the bag are related to this change conclusion.

Introduction of the basic theme of the conference and subsequent bulletin series: At this point the brainstorming concepts are summarized and the theme "There is always a better way" is introduced. At the same time mention is made of potential future uses of the Better Ways bulletins.

Evening session: Simple business game—individual groups in a stop-action tactics exercise. (The four groups constitute themselves as small companies and make a series of executive decisions. The staff introduces certain changes, and each group reacts. The final decisions of each group are made public in a joint session, and the winners are determined.)

Day 3

Brainstorming from pictures: A variation of the TAT (Thematic Apperception Test) is introduced by the use of the TAT picture sequence. The participants are asked to make their own notes (not to be handed in, inasmuch as some of the respondents may not be fully literate) in answer to the following questions:

(a) What is happening here? Who are the people?
(b) What has led up to this situation? What has happened in the past?
(c) What is being sought? What is wanted? By whom?
(d) What will happen? What will be done?

The simple scoring method for change potential, introduced the previous day as a variation on the achievement-motivation scoring, is reviewed again. A two-step procedure for analyzing the TAT picture is then used:

(a) Each individual is asked to score his own story privately.
(b) A tape recording of a successful, and if possible well-known, Indian entrepreneur in the fertilizer business or a related one (not the same person as the distinguished visitor) is played to the group—first straight through, then with breaks in the presentation so that the participants can attempt to score the change potential of the entrepreneur.

Reintroduction of the relation between achievement and innovation: The other elements of the achievement action syndrome—moderate risk taking, attention to feedback, assumption of personal responsibility—are related again to the elements of innovation and initiative.

The ring-toss game is played to illustrate the relationships among these various elements. Each participant is given the opportunity to play, and a throughgoing critique follows.

Evening session: Informal (but planned) group social evening (motion pictures and refreshments).

Day 4

Introduction of individual goal setting: Personal goals and goal setting are discussed. Attention is given to such conflicts as those between family life and career. A detailed examination follows of possible causes of failure and how they can be avoided. Personal blocks to success are discussed. A cartoon is given to each participant, which shows a person being held back by several personal blocks, and the participants are asked to put names on each block. Then follows a discussion of world blocks and the writing of each participant's list of external blocks to success. This is followed by an examination of certain Indian cultural norms, for example, the emphasis on criticism (rather than praise) and its relation to fear of failure, the relation of an authoritative father figure to a son who is low in achievement motivation, the contradiction between the emphasis on achievement and those basic values which stress nonattachment and lack of concern for outcome of actions.

Personal goal setting: Each participant is asked to develop in an organized way (using a career planning guide) a set of concrete goals for his business, with the time spans spelled out in detail. Emphasis is on short-term versus long-term goals, related back to the specific blocks the participant had noted in the previous exercise. Each participant is asked to elaborate in specific detail *one* short-term goal he will strive for immediately.

Small-group discussion and evaluation of goal-setting exercises: The small groups of the first day are reconstituted and individual goal setting and removal of blocks to these goals are discussed. The group is asked to concentrate on not only the larger, "innovative" ideas that a man might have, but also the smaller, "There is always a better way" dimensions.

Individual counseling with instructors: At the end of the group session the instructor makes appointments with each of the members of his group for twenty-minute private sessions.

Evening session: Short presentations are given by the two honorary cochairmen, followed by a major address by the distinguished visitor and an extensive question-answer session with all participants.

Day 5

Application of innovative concepts specifically to fertilizer distribution: The full group having been reconstituted, attention is focused specifically on company-dealer and dealer-industry relations. A "large-frame" brainstorming session is held, with all the participants, all the instructors, and all the fertilizer executives acting as one large brainstorming group. The concept of a package of practices is stressed, as is the role of the fertilizer dealer as not just a retail seller but a change agent. Emphasis is placed on specific, practical new ideas for the fertilizer business at the level of the dealer, at the level of the company, and at the level of the industry; these in every case are related back to specific planning steps that are necessary on the part of both the individual dealers and the companies themselves. Each of these ideas, and their specifics in regard to planning, are entered on large chart boards at the front of the room. Finally, the entire group adjourns to the grounds of the hotel to see new, innovative agricultural equipment demonstrated.

Reintroduction of the Better Ways bulletins: After reconvening in the seminar room, the participants discuss the need for a longer-term vehicle for keeping ideas moving into the hands of fertilizer distributors. The chart board illustrations are shown to be the first stage of what can readily be a whole series of new ideas that could be put in the hands of individual dealers. The development of a specific series to accomplish this — the Better Ways bulletins — is introduced by means of innovative visuals and then discussed. The key responsibility of individual dealers to send their ideas forward for incorporation in the bulletins is elaborated in detail. Tentative commitments are made for such a flow.

Establishment of ongoing dealer enclaves: Stress is again laid on encouraging the full group to organize itself for continued association beyond the initial seminar. Key potential leaders, previously identified by the instructors, are asked to commit themselves to such leadership roles, and the group then makes specific plans about a further meeting. Each of these specific planning steps is to be followed up by company officials, both with the individual distributors and with the overall group.

Course-end evaluations by participants and by staff, and presentation of diplomas.

Awards and final testimonials.

Notes

Chapter 1   An Entrepreneurial System Model

1. Two excellent annotated bibliographies on entrepreneurship have recently been published: James W. Schreier and John L. Komives, *The Entrepreneur and New Enterprise Formation* (Milwaukee, Wisconsin: Center for Venture Management, 1973); and "Provisional Annotated Bibliography on Entrepreneurship and Small Enterprise Development" and supplement no. 1, prepared for the Research Planning Workshop on Ways of Developing Entrepreneurial Initiative in Rural Centers and Low-Income Urban Communities, Technology and Development Institute, East-West Center, Honolulu, May 19-June 6, 1975.

2. The seminal book here is Bronislaw Malinowski, *Argonauts of the Western Pacific* (London: Routledge, 1922). See also the works of Karl Polanyi, especially *The Great Transformation* (New York: Holt, Rinehart & Winston, 1944) and his book with Conrad W. Arensberg and H. W. Pearson, *Trade and Market in the Early Empires* (New York: Free Press, 1957); see also George Dalton, ed., *Primitive, Archaic and Modern Economies: Essays of Karl Polanyi* (Garden City, New York: Anchor Books, 1968). Simon Rottenberg discusses the barter syndrome in his review of *Trade and Market in the Early Empires* in *American Economic Review* 48 (1958):675-678. I was particularly aided also by an unpublished paper by Steven Hymer and Steven Resnick, "Responsiveness of Agrarian Economies and the Importance of Z Goods," Center Discussion Paper no. 25 (revised), Economic Growth Center, Yale University, October 1967.

3. "Cultural Values in India's Economic Development," *Annals of the American Academy of Political and Social Science* 305 (1956):81-91.

4. "Introduction: Peasant Character and Personality," in Jack M. Potter, ed., *Peasant Society: A Reader* (Boston: Little, Brown, 1967), pp. 304-305, 311.

5. Cambridge, Massachusetts: Harvard University Press, 1964.

6. Here I draw particularly on Everett E. Hagen's work, especially "The Entrepreneur as Rebel against Traditional Society," *Human Organization* (1960-1961): 185-186 and *On the Theory of Social Change* (Homewood, Illinois: Dorsey Press, 1962). See also Erich Fromm, *Social Character in a Mexican Village: A Socio-psychoanalytic Study* (Englewood Cliffs, New Jersey: Prentice-Hall, 1970), and the Oscar Lewis typologies of poverty: *Life in a Mexican Village: Tepoztlan Restudied* (Urbana:

University of Illinois Press, 1951); *The Children of Sanchez* (New York: Random House, 1963); *Pedro Martinez* (New York: Random House, 1964); *La Vida* (New York: Random House, 1966). Lewis' work also includes the classic study of an Indian village, *Village Life in Northern India* (Urbana: University of Illinois Press, 1958).

7. Paul Hiebert, *Konduru: Structure and Integration in a South Indian Village* (Minneapolis: University of Minnesota Press, 1971), p. 72.

8. "Some Themes in the Culture of India," unpublished manuscript, Cambridge, Massachusetts, p.15. A later version of this paper is included as chapter 4, "The Power of Giving: Traditional India," in McClelland's most recent book, *Power: The Inner Experience* (New York: Irvington Publishers, 1975). Throughout this study I have drawn substantially on McClelland's theories; the clearest exposition of these is in *The Achieving Society* (New York: D. Van Nostrand Company, 1961). Other writings by McClelland that were particularly helpful are the following: "Business Drive and National Achievement," *Harvard Business Review,* July-August 1962; "Changing Values for Progress," mimeographed typescript, SIET Institute, Hyderabad, India, October 8, 1963; "Toward a Theory of Motive Acquisition," *American Psychologist* 20 (1965): 321-333; *Assessing Human Motivation* (New York: General Learning Corporation, 1971); *Motivational Trends in Society* (New York: General Learning Corporation, 1971). See also McClelland and David G. Winter, *Motivating Economic Achievement* (New York: Free Press, 1969). Also of particular interest to me were field research and field training on achievement motivation: for example, see P. S. Hundal, "A Study of Entrepreneurial Motivation: Comparison of Fast- and Slow-progressing Small-scale Industrial Entrepreneurs in Punjab, India," *Journal of Applied Psychology* 55 (1971): 317-323; Joel Aronoff and George H. Litwin, "Achievement Motivation Training and Executive Advancement," *Journal of Applied Behavioral Science* 7 (1971):215-229; Denton E. Morrison, "Achievement Motivation of Farm Operators: A Measurement Study," *Rural Sociology* 29 (1964):367-384. An interesting effort to apply achievement motivation concepts widely among American industry has been made by McBer and Company of Boston; see their Business Leadership Training Program series of manuals, published in 1974. See also David C. McClelland and Robert S. Steele, *Motivation Workshop* (Morristown, New Jersey: General Learning Press, 1972). David G. Winter contrasts the achievement motive with power concepts in *The Power Motive* (New York: Free Press, 1973). Bernard Weiner reviews the literature on achievement motivation in *Theories of Motivation: From Mechanism to Cognition* (Chicago: Markham Publishing Company, 1972), pt. 4. Another useful set of readings is in David C. McClelland and Robert S. Steele, *Human Motivation: A Book of Readings* (Morristown, New Jersey: General Learning Press, 1973. The reference to semen is in G. Morris Carstairs, *The Twice-Born* (Bloomington: Indiana University Press, 1958), p. 84.

9. Arnold M. Rose, "Sociological Factors Affecting Economic Development in India," *Studies in Comparative International Development* 3 (1967-1968), Rutgers University, New Brunswick, New Jersey, p. 258.

10. For excellent discussions of caste as a concept see Andre Beteille, *Castes: Old and New* (Bombay: Asia Publishing House, 1969); J. H. Hutton, *Castes in India* (London: Oxford University Press, 1969); and Milton Singer, *When a Great Tradition*

Modernizes (New York: Praeger, 1972). An interesting distinction between traditional caste forms and more modern caste associations is given in Richard G. Fox, "Resiliency and Change in the Indian Caste System: the Umar of U.P.," *Journal of Asian Studies* 27 (1967):575-587.

11. William H. Wiser, *The Hindu Jajmani System* (Lucknow: Lucknow Publishing House, 1936); William H. Wiser and Charlotte Wiser, *Behind Mud Walls* (New York: Richard R. Smith, 1930); reprinted with addenda by Charlotte Wiser in 1964 and again in 1970. See also Oscar Lewis' description of the jajmani system in his *Village Life in Northern India* (Urbana: University of Illinois Press, 1958), pp. 55-84.

12. "Toward a Model of the Hindu Jajmani System," *Human Organization* 12 (1963):11-31.

13. *Village Life in South India* (Chicago: Aldine Publishing Company, 1974), pp. 57-58.

14. See particularly *The Theory of Economic Development: An Inquiry into Profits, Capital, Credit, Interest, and the Business Cycle,* trans. Redvers Opie (Cambridge, Massachusetts: Harvard University Press, 1934), and *Business Cycles* (New York: McGraw-Hill, 1939), esp. pp. 87-192.

15. The Berna book is *Industrial Entrepreneurship in Madras State* (Bombay: Asia Publishing House, 1960). For technology transfer, see particularly B. N. Bhattasali, *Transfer of Technology among the Developing Countries* (Tokyo: Asian Productivity Organization, 1972) and UN Industrial Development Organization, *Guidelines for the Acquisition of Foreign Technology in Developing Countries* (New York: United Nations, 1973). The distinctions between original, transferred, and adaptive innovation are discussed in Thorkil Kristensen, *Development in Rich and Poor Countries: A General Theory with Statistical Analyses* (New York: Praeger, 1974), pp. 14-17. Also helpful are Daniel L. Spencer and Alexander Woroniak, *The Transfer of Technology to Developing Countries* (New York: Praeger, 1967); Jack Baranson, *Industrial Technologies for Developing Economies* (New York: Praeger, 1969); Robert E. Driscoll and Harvey W. Wallender, *Technology Transfer and Development: An Historical and Geographic Perspective* (New York: Fund for Multinational Management Education, Council of the Americas, 1974). There are two excellent recent books relating to technology transfer to India: V. N. Balasubramanyam, *International Transfer of Technology to India* (New York: Praeger, 1973) and Bepin Behari, *Economic Growth and Technological Change in India* (New Delhi: Vikas Publishing House, 1974).

16. In the excellent review article on innovation by Morton I. Kamien and Nancy L. Schwartz, "Market Structure and Innovation: A Survey," *Journal of Economic Literature* 13 (1975):1-37, a number of the references cite this process of imitation. See also their article, "Timing of Innovations under Rivalry," *Econometrica* 40 (1972): 43-60, and W. L. Baldwin and G. L. Childs, "The Fast Second and Rivalry in Research and Development," *Southern Economic Journal* 36 (1969):18-24. Concerns about mimicry are scattered throughout the literature on "appropriate technology." Some recent examples of more factious arguments are found in Ernest Feder, "Six Plausible Theses about the Peasant's Perspectives in the Developing World," *Development and Change* 5 (1973-1974):1-24; "Vendetta against Indigenous Technology," *Economic and Political Weekly* (Bombay), April 5, 1975.

17. Dennis P. Slevin, "The Innovation Boundary: A Specific Model and Empirical Results," *Administrative Science Quarterly* 16 (1971):515-531, and Erik Dahmén, *Entrepreneurial Activity and the Development of Swedish Industry, 1919-1939,* trans. Axel Leijonhufvud (Homewood, Illinois: Richard D. Irwin, 1970). Dahmén's work has been particularly highlighted by Alexander Gerschenkron in his appendix chapter, "A Schumpeterian Analysis of Economic Development," in *Continuity and Other Essays in History* (Cambridge, Massachusetts: Harvard University Press, 1968).

18. Harry W. Richardson, *Regional Growth Theory* (New York: John Wiley, 1973), p. 127.

19. "Entrepreneurship and Development," *American Economic Review Papers and Proceedings* 58 (1968):77, 79.

20. Leibenstein's first major statement of the X-efficiency concept came in "Allocative Efficiency versus 'X-efficiency,' " *American Economic Review* 56 (1966):392-415. This was considerably expanded in his article, "Organizational or Frictional Equilibria, X-efficiency, and the Rate of Innovation," *Quarterly Journal of Economics* 83 (1969):600-623, and consolidated in his most recent book, *Beyond Economic Man: A New Foundation for Microeconomics* (Cambridge, Massachusetts: Harvard University Press, 1976). See also his articles, "Comment on the Nature of X-efficiency," *Quarterly Journal of Economics* 86 (1972):327-331, and "Competition and X-efficiency: Reply," *Journal of Political Economy* 81 (1973):765-777. An interesting study of the X-efficiency concept as applied to India is that of Ken Jameson, "Comment on the Theory and Measurement of Dynamic X-efficiency," *Quarterly Journal of Economics* 86 (1972):313-326. The quotation in the text is from "Notes on X-efficiency and Technical Progress," in Eliezer B. Ayal, *Micro Aspects of Development* (New York: Praeger, 1973), p. 21.

21. *Competition and Entrepreneurship* (Chicago: University of Chicago Press, 1973), p. 68.

22. *Economic Backwardness and Economic Growth* (New York: John Wiley & Sons, 1957), chap. 8.

23. See Pareto in S. E. Finer, ed., *Sociological Writings* (New York: Praeger, 1966), particularly propositions 966 and 970. See also Pareto's *The Mind and Society* (New York: Harcourt, Brace, 1935), p. 590.

24. Kirzner, *Competition and Entrepreneurship,* p. 152, quoting George J. Stigler, "Imperfections in the Capital Market," *Journal of Political Economy* 75 (1967):291.

Chapter 2   India's Agriculture and Agro-Industries

1. See Office of the Agricultural Attaché, American Embassy, New Delhi, *Brief on Indian Agriculture,* 1973; K. C. Ghosh, *Famines in Bengal, 1770-1943* (Calcutta: Indian Associated Publishing Company, 1944); and J. J. Singh, *Famine in India* (New York: India League of America, 1945). The lower figure for the 1943 famine is the official total by the Government of India's Famine Inquiry Commission. The report from the commission is given in *Census of India, 1951* (New Delhi: Government of India Press, 1955), vol. 1, pt. 1B. However, other authorities consider the higher figure to be realistic. The reasons for this very large figure (whichever total is correct) lie in special features attendant to the presence of World War II. A great natural calam-

ity, the Midnapore cyclone, had laid waste considerable portions of West Bengal in October 1942, with resultant crop losses. Rice imports had been cut off from Burma after the Japanese conquest in the spring of 1942, and there was even a threatened invasion of Bengal during this period. These probably contributed measurably to the lack of effective countermeasures, despite apparent past efficacy of the famine code (see *Collier's Encyclopedia,* 1969, vol. 9, p. 552).

2. United States Department of Agriculture, Economic Research Service, "India — Briefing Paper," FDCD/ERS August 21, 1975; Population Reference Bureau, *World Population Data Sheet,* April 1976. For an interesting view of the 1971 Indian census, see Robert Cassen, "Welfare and Population: Notes on Rural India since 1960," *Population and Development Review* 1 (1975):33-70.

3. Perhaps the best single source today concerning the population issue in India is David G. Mandelbaum, *Human Fertility in India* (Berkeley: University of California Press, 1974). Another useful reference is the series of *American Universities Field Staff Reports* by Marcus F. Franda (all in the AUFS South Asia series): "Mass Vasectomy Camps and Incentives in Indian Family Planning," vol. 16, no. 7, 1972; "Marketing Condoms in India: The Nirodh Program," vol. 16, no. 8, 1972; "Militant Hindu Opposition to Family Planning in India," vol. 16, no. 11, 1972; "Population Variables in India's Fifth Five-Year Plan," vol. 18, no. 4, 1974; "Shifts in Emphasis in India's Population Policy," vol. 18, no. 7, 1974; "Societal Responses to Population Change in India: The Wingspread Conference," vol. 19, no. 2, 1975.

4. See, for example, R. O. Whyte, *Land, Livestock and Human Nutrition in India* (New York: Praeger, 1968), pp. 28-30.

5. Census of India, 1951, vol. 1, "General Report," pp. 141, 164-166.

6. *Prospects for Indian Development* (London: Allen & Unwin, 1962), p. 125. Malenbaum draws on data from V. G. Pansi's classic study, "Trends in Areas and Yields of Principal Crops in India," Ministry of Food and Agriculture, Government of India, *Studies in Agricultural Economics,* vol. 1 (Delhi, 1954).

7. Ministry of Information and Broadcasting, Government of India, *India: A Reference Annual* (New Delhi, 1965), pp. 166-167.

8. Ford Foundation, Agricultural Production Team, *Report on India's Food Crisis and Steps to Meet It* (Ministry of Food and Agriculture, Ministry of Community Development and Cooperation, Government of India, April 1959); Sudhir Sen, *A Richer Harvest* (New York: Orbis Books, 1974), p. 143.

9. For a general discussion of the agricultural strategy recommended by the Ford Foundation group and the subsequent administrative developments see Dorris D. Brown, *Agricultural Development in India's Districts* (Cambridge, Massachusetts: Harvard University Press, 1971).

10. Ibid., pp. 8-12.

11. There is an extensive literature on the Community Development Programme. I found the discussion by John Mellor, Thomas F. Weaver, Uma J. Lele, and Sheldon R. Simon in *Developing Rural India* (Ithaca, New York: Cornell University Press, 1968), chap. 2, to be particularly helpful on the inception and early thinking. V. P. Pande's book, *Village Community Projects in India* (Bombay: Asia Publishing House, 1967), has an excellent discussion of the pre-republic community development programs, including an analysis of the early Christian missions. A comprehensive book is S. C. Jain,

Community Development and Panchayati Raj in India (Bombay: Allied Publishers, 1967). Douglas Ensminger, for many years the Ford Foundation's representative in India, later summarized his thoughts on community development and related topics in his book, *Rural India in Transition* (New Delhi: All India Panchayat Parishad, 1972). His earlier book, with several colleagues, also covers community development well: *India's Roots of Democracy* (Bombay: Orient Longman, 1967). See also B. Mukerji, *Community Development in India* (Bombay: Orient Longman, 1962); Council for Social Development, *Action for Rural Change: Readings in Indian Community Development* (New Delhi: Munshirim Manoharlal, 1970); Henry Maddick, *Panchayati Raj* (London: Longman, 1970). For an interesting international comparison of the program in India to that in the Philippines, see E. H. Valsan, *Community Development Programs and Rural Local Government* (New York: Praeger, 1970).

12. Ministry of Information and Broadcasting, Government of India, *India: A Reference Annual* (New Delhi, 1974), p. 194.

13. An excellent source for understanding the VLW concept is Victor S. Doherty, *Adapting Extension Programs in Rural India* (New Delhi: Ford Foundation, 1971). See also Mellor et al., *Developing Rural India,* pp. 34-41. On training of the VLW see Richard L. Shortlidge, Jr., "University Training for *Gramsevaks* in India: An Example of Recurrent Education in a Low-Income Country," *Economic Development and Cultural Change* 24 (1975):139-154.

14. F. C. Fliegel, P. Roy, L. K. Sen, and J. E. Kivlin, *Agricultural Innovations in Indian Villages* (Hyderabad: National Institute of Community Development, 1968).

15. Ibid., p. 103, for the quotation. The second study is P. Roy, F. C. Fliegel, J. E. Kivlin, and L. K. Sen, *Agricultural Innovation among Indian Farmers,* (Hyderabad: National Institute of Community Development, 1968). See also Kivlin and his three colleagues, *Innovation in Rural India* (Bowling Green, Ohio: Bowling Green State University Press, 1971).

16. Gilbert Etienne, *Studies in Indian Agriculture: The Art of the Possible* (Berkeley: University of California Press, 1968), pp. 19-21.

17. The various research institutes connected with the Green Revolution are discussed in a report by the Consultative Group on International Agricultural Research, *International Research in Agriculture* (New York, 1974). The best single source on world diffusion of the new varieties is Dana G. Dalrymple, *Development and Spread of High-Yielding Varieties of Wheat and Rice in the Less Developed Nations* (U.S. Department of Agriculture, Foreign Agricultural Economic Report no. 95, July 1974). The dimension of the new varieties in India is usefully treated in M. S. Randhawa, *Green Revolution* (New Delhi: Vikas Publishing House, 1974). See also Marcus F. Franda, "Food Research in India," *American Universities Field Staff Reports,* South Asia series, vol. 18, no. 9, 1974.

18. See especially Louis Dupree, "Bangladesh," *American Universities Field Staff Reports,* South Asia series, vol. 16, no. 6, 1972.

19. Fertiliser Association of India, *Fertiliser Statistics, 1972-73* (New Delhi: December 1973), p. II-34.

20. Ford Foundation, *Report on India's Food Crisis,* pp. 54-55; H. R. Arakeri, G. V. Chalam, P. Satyanarayana, and Roy L. Donahue, *Soil Management in India*

(Bombay: Asia Publishing, 1962), p. 78; Mellor et al., *Developing Rural India*, p. 100.

21. Ford Foundation, *Report on India's Food Crisis*, pp. 54, 180-185.

22. Ibid., p. 171. The most prominent of these early proposals, by the Bechtel Corporation, is discussed in Ashok Kapoor, *International Business Negotiations: A Study in India* (New York: New York University Press, 1970).

23. Howard R. Erdman, *Politics and Economic Development in India: The Gujarat State Fertilizers Company as a Joint Sector Enterprise* (Delhi: D. K. Publishing House, 1973); W. D. Posgate, "Fertilizers for India's Green Revolution: The Shaping of Government Policy," *Asian Survey* 14 (1974):744-745.

24. All 1971 census figures are from *India: A Reference Annual*, 1974.

25. The Sivaraman Committee report in 1965 recommended that each depot serve a target population of 5,000 to 10,000; this would probably result in a slightly larger cultivator population per depot. See the *Report of the Committee on Fertilisers* (Ministry of Food and Agriculture, Government of India, 1965), p. 55.

26. Ibid., p. 48.

27. Ibid., pp. 49-50.

28. For an excellent description of the efforts of the cooperatives to market fertilizer, see C. V. Raghavulu, "Fertiliser Distribution through Cooperatives," *Economic and Political Weekly* (Bombay), October 4, 1969.

29. *Report of the Committee on Fertilisers*, p. 51.

30. David C. Warner, "Building Market Institutions for Development: The Case of Fertilizer in India," Ph.D. dissertation, Syracuse University, 1969.

31. The various statistics are from *Tamil Nadu: An Economic Appraisal* (Madras: Finance Department, Government of Tamil Nadu, 1972), vols. 1 and 2.

32. There are many excellent resource materials on agriculture in Tamil Nadu. In addition to the yearly *Tamil Nadu: An Economic Appraisal*, the following are especially helpful: P. K. Venkateswaran, *Agriculture in South India* (New Delhi: Ministry of Food and Agriculture, 1961); M. S. Randhawa, M. S. Sivaraman, I. J. Naidu, and Suresh Vaidya, *Farmers of India* (New Delhi: Indian Council of Agricultural Research, 1961), vol. 2, sec. 1; M. S. Randhawa, *Agriculture and Animal Husbandry in India* (New Delhi: Indian Council of Agricultural Research, 1962); Government of Madras, *Report of the Committee on Agricultural Production* (Madras, April 1966); Etienne, *Studies in Indian Agriculture;* Fertiliser Association of India, *Seminars on Agricultural Production in the Southern Region* (Madras, March 9, 1969); and Francine R. Frankel, *India's Green Revolution: Economic Gains and Political Costs* (Princeton, New Jersey: Princeton University Press, 1971).

33. The statistics are from *Tamil Nadu: An Economic Appraisal; The New Year Book*, 1971 (Calcutta: S. C. Sarkar, 1971); and United Nations, *Statistical Yearbook* (New York: United Nations, 1972).

34. Fertiliser Association of India, *Fertiliser Statistics, 1972-73*, p. III-15.

35. United Nations, *Production Yearbook* (Rome: Food and Agricultural Organization of the United Nations, 1971). Quotation from Commissioner of Fertiliser in *Economic Times* (Bombay), April 12, 1973.

36. UN, *Production Yearbook*, 1971, and United States Department of Agriculture, *Foreign Agriculture*, March 25, 1974.

Chapter 3   The Fertilizer Distributor as Change Agent

1. The special dimensions of South Indian caste are described in Dagfinn Sivertsen, *When Caste Barriers Fall* (New York: Humanities Press, 1963); Dharma Kumar, *Land and Caste in South India* (Cambridge: Cambridge University Press, 1965); and Andre Beteille, *Caste, Class and Power* (Berkeley: University of California Press, 1965).

2. National Council of Applied Economic Research, *Demand for Fertilisers in the Southern Region in 1975-1976*, July 1970, and Brindavan C. Moses, "Demand for Fertilisers in Chingleput District: A Report of the Research Program by the Department of Economics of the Madras Christian College on behalf of AMOCO, India, Ltd.," December 1970.

3. We particularly wish to thank Professors R. Subramanian, M. Palanisami, and E. Disengu Setty, who aided us in classifying and categorizing South Indian castes. See their study, "Caste in a Cluster of South Indian Villages — A Study in Social Relationship," *Indian Journal of Social Work* 33 (1973):293-296.

4. Perhaps the most sophisticated way to have analyzed these patterns of irrigation would have been to define a radius around each dealer and then assess the amount of land in this area having assured irrigation. Our statistics were not refined enough to be able to do this, so we adopted a more "rough-and-ready" methodology. Our large sample of 180 distributors was a stratified random sample from eleven separate taluks in three districts. Four of these taluks, Chidambaram and Cuddalore in South Arcot district and Kumbakonam and Nannilam in Tanjore district, were areas where there was a considerable amount of irrigated land. Tindivanan and Kallakkurichi in South Arcot and Arantangi and Pattukkotti in Tanjore were areas of predominantly rainfed irrigation. Two taluks, Erode and Dharapuram in Coimbatore district, were in between. We therefore used the tripartite classification "dry," "assured," and "middle."

5. The prices of tractors were scaled upward in June 1974. The new schedule contained only three price differentials, the result of grouping together tractors with little difference in horsepower and fixing a single price for them. Thus the 25 hp and 26.5 hp tractors cost the same, Rs. 30,410; the 35 hp sold at Rs. 31,710; and the 44 hp, 46 hp, and 50 hp tractors were grouped together with a uniform price of Rs. 40,670. See *Economic Times* (Bombay), June 12, 1974.

6. Ford Foundation, Agricultural Production Team, *Report on India's Food Crisis and Steps to Meet It* (Ministry of Food and Agriculture, Ministry of Community Development and Cooperation, Government of India, April 1959), pp. 41-45, 248-254.

7. Many of the concepts of the "demonstration effect" are detailed in my study of Latin America, *International Basic Economy Corporation* (Washington, D.C.: National Planning Association, 1968).

8. Alex Inkeles and David Horton Smith, *Becoming Modern: Individual Change in Six Developing Countries* (Cambridge, Massachusetts: Harvard University Press, 1974), p. 15. For critiques of the modernization concept see Albert O. Hirshman, "Obstacles to Development: A Classification and a Quasi-Vanishing Act," *Economic Development and Cultural Change* 13 (1965):385-393; John H. Kunkel, "Values and Behavior in Economic Development," *Economic Development and Cultural Change* 13 (1965):257-277; Irving L. Horowitz, "Personality and Structural Dimensions in

Comparative International Development," *Southwestern Social Science Quarterly* 51 (1970):494-513; R. Kenneth Godwin, "Two Thorny Theoretical Tangles: The Relationships between Personality Variables and Modernization," *Journal of Developing Areas* 8 (1974):181-198; and Godwin's "The Relationship between Scores on Individual Modernity Scales and Societal Modernization," *Journal of Developing Areas* 9 (1975): 415-431. The analysts of Indian modernization include: L. Rudolph and S. Rudolph, *The Modernity of Tradition* (Chicago: University of Chicago Press, 1967); Morris David Morris, "Trends and Tendencies in South Indian Economic History," *Indian Economic and Social History Review* 5 (1968):319-388; T. Scarlett Epstein, *South India: Yesterday, Today and Tomorrow* (New York: Holmes & Meier, 1973). The Singer quotation is from *When a Great Tradition Modernizes* (New York: Praeger, 1972), p. 272.

9. Here I have drawn heavily on a similar schema in Godwin, "Two Thorny Tangles," and Inkeles and Smith, *Becoming Modern,* pp. 11-12.

10. Inkeles and Smith, *Becoming Modern,* p. 12.

11. See the two Godwin pieces (note 8).

12. A. Inkeles, "The Modernization of Man," in M. Weiner, *Modernization* (New York: Basic Books, 1966); D. Smith and A. Inkeles, "The OM Scale: A Comparative Socio-Psychological Measure of Individual Modernity," *Sociometry* 29 (1966):353-377.

13. "The Multidimensional Scaling of Elastic Distances," *British Journal of Marketing and Statistical Psychology* 19 (1966):181-196.

14. Private report, A. V. Mehta, AMOCO India, Ltd., New Delhi, August 8, 1970.

15. *Green Revolution: A Case Study of Punjab* (Delhi: Vikas Publishing House, 1974).

16. Nicholas Wade, "Green Revolution (II): Problems of Adapting a Western Technology," *Science* 186 (1974):1189-1190.

17. *From Zamindar to Ballot Box* (Ithaca, New York: Cornell University Press, 1969), p. 145.

Chapter 4   Village Entrepreneurs in Action

1. The Pilot Research Project in Growth Centres, sponsored by the central government, was begun as part of the Fourth Plan. Its aim has been to evolve a broad research methodology for identification of potential growth centers, based on a carefully prepared inventory of local needs and future strengths, and then to provide social and economic inputs to these newly designated growth centers. The program was assigned to the Department of Community Development of the Ministry of Food, Agriculture, Community Development, and Cooperation, with the Ford Foundation and the Council for Social Development the implementing agencies. Progress reports and a set of related technical studies are available through the New Delhi office of the Ford Foundation; perhaps the best single summary is that of Douglas Ensminger, "Growth Centres and Viable Rural-Urban Communities," an address given at the Delhi Management Association, April 16, 1969.

2. An excellent set of reports is available on the Mohanur-Namakkal Growth Centre Project; they are summarized in *Integrated Area Development*: *Mohanur and*

Namakkal Blocks, Pilot Research Project in Growth Centres, Salem (Tamil Nadu), October 1973.

3. Fertiliser Association of India, *Fertiliser Statistics, 1972-73* (New Delhi: December 1973), p. I-183.

4. "Regional Plan for Tiruchirapalli-Tanjavur Region," Directorate of Town Planning, Government of Tamil Nadu, January 1973, and R. P. Misra, K. V. Sundaram, and V. L. S. Prakash Rao, *Regional Development Planning in India* (Delhi: Vikas Publishing House, 1974).

5. There is an extensive literature on the application of central place theory to growth centers. The studies relative to India include E. A. J. Johnson, *The Organization of Space in Developing Countries* (Cambridge, Massachusetts: Harvard University Press, 1970), which devotes a substantial amount of its analysis to India. Johnson also made a direct central place application to India in his *Market Towns and Spatial Development in India* (New Delhi: National Council of Applied Economic Research, 1965). Other more recent studies include Lalit K. Sen, Sudhir Wanmali, Saradindu Bose, Girish K. Misra, and K. S. Ramesh, *Planning Rural Growth Centers for Integrated Area Development* (Hyderabad: National Institute of Community Development, 1970); and Lalit K. Sen, *Readings on Micro-Level Planning and Rural Growth Centres* (Hyderabad: National Institute of Community Development, 1972). Related works on regional development in India are Brian J. L. Berry, *Essays on Commodity Flows and Spatial Structure of the Indian Economy* (Chicago: University of Chicago Press, 1966); T. B. Lahiri, *Balanced Regional Development* (Calcutta: Oxford and I. B. H. Publishing Company, 1970); and Misra, Sundaram, and Prakash Rao, *Regional Development Planning*.

6. An example of the almost-alarmist writings on this issue can be seen in Nicholas Wade, "Green Revolution (II): Problems of Adapting a Western Technology," *Science* 186 (1974):1186-1187.

7. The two information linkage variables, those we called other information and news interest, appear to have statistically significant correlation with performance variables across a number of studies we have done: among all the fertilizer and rice miller samples we conducted in India, among our samples of various other small businessmen in that country, and in two samples we conducted among small-town businessmen in New Hampshire.

8. The r^2 for this root is .227.

9. None of the discriminant analysis runs produced statistically significant differences at the .05 level or lower; the runs did satisfy the equality of variance hypothesis.

10. See particularly Indian Institute of Management (Ahmedabad), *Modernization in Rice Industry*, 1969; J. P. Norman Efferson and Klaus Senglemann, *An Appraisal of Rice Drying, Storage, Processing and Marketing in the Philippines* (Manila: Ford Foundation, October 1969); "Modernisation of the Rice Milling Industry," *Economic and Political Weekly* (Bombay), July 11, 1970; Uma J. Lele, *Food Grain Marketing in India* (Ithaca, New York: Cornell University Press, 1971); United Nations Industrial Development Organization, "Report of the Interregional Seminar on the Industrial Processing of Rice," Madras, November 19, 1971; C. Peter Timmer, "Employment Aspects of Investment in Rice Marketing in Indonesia," Stanford Food Re-

search Institute *Bulletin*, April 1972, and "Choice of Technique in Rice Milling on Java," *Indonesian Economics Study* 9 (1973).

11. Food and Agriculture Organization of the United Nations, "Rice Milling in Developing Countries," *Commodity Bulletin Series* 45 (1969):2; Lele, *Food Grain Marketing in India*, p. 180.

12. "A Survey of the Food Processing Industry in Tamil Nadu," *Tamil Nadu Nutrition Study*, vol. 2 (Haverford, Pennsylvania: Sidney M. Cantor Associates, 1973); and Barbara Harriss, "Milling Technologies: A 'Which' Guide to Appropriate Rice Processing Technologies in South Asia," *Project on Agrarian Change in Rice-Growing Areas of Tamil Nadu and Sri Lanka*, Seminar at St. John's College, Cambridge, December 9-16, 1974, p. 8.

13. The concept of the fully integrated rice mill has existed for a number of years; the term "modern rice mill," particularly as it has been applied in India, dates from the late 1960s.

14. See especially the two Timmer articles cited in note 10 and Lele, *Food Grain Marketing in India*, p. 180.

15. James E. Wimberly, *Evaluation of Modern Rice Milling Program in India* (New Delhi: Ford Foundation, October 1969).

16. This first piece by Timmer ("Employment Aspects") was based on research done in 1971; the technical information on various rice milling facilities was based upon an engineering report (noted on p. 68 of the article) that did not include the newer technology.

17. Timmer, "Employment Aspects," p. 85.

18. Timmer, "Choice of Technique," p. 9.

19. See, for example, Yasumasa Koga, "Recent Development of Compact Rice Milling Unit," *Farming Japan*, Satake Engineering Company, Tokyo.

20. Timmer does make the assumption that "all these together are taken as the class 'rice mills'; they do not have mechanical drying equipment but rely solely on sun drying. Consequently, the SRM [small rice mills] are assumed to suffer high physical (and monetary) losses during processing, not so much in the milling *per se* but lack of control in the drying" ("Choice of Technique," p. 5).

21. There is a sharp difference between coolie and wholesale mills both in volume of paddy processed and in number of employees.

22. Haim Halperin, *Agrindus: Integration of Agriculture and Industries* (New York: Praeger, 1963); D. Weintraub, M. Lissak, and Y. Azmon, *Moshava, Kibbutz and Moshav: Patterns of Jewish Rural Settlement and Development in Palestine* (Ithaca, New York: Cornell University Press, 1969), and *Immigration and Social Change: Agricultural Settlement of New Immigrants in Israel* (Jerusalem: Israel University Press, 1971); Joseph Klatzmann, Benjamin Y. Illan, and Yair Levi, *The Role of Group Action in the Industrialization of Rural Areas* (New York: Praeger, 1971), pp. 83-90.

23. *Economic and Political Weekly* (Bombay), April 20, 1968.

24. The classic study is Alfred Weber's *Theory of the Location of Industries,* trans. C. J. Frederick (Chicago: University of Chicago Press, 1929).

25. *Market Towns in India,* p. 128. See also Harold R. Wilson, *Rural Wheat Storage in Ludhiana District, Punjab* (New Delhi: Ford Foundation, 1970); John R. Moore,

S. S. Johl, and A. M. Khusro, *Indian Foodgrain Marketing* (New Delhi: Prentice-Hall of India, 1973).

26. See the discussion of this problem in a Brazilian context in my book *International Basic Economy Corporation* (Washington, D.C.: National Planning Association, 1968), pp. 65-74.

27. See, for example, P. Haggett and K. A. Gunawardena, "Determination of Population Thresholds for Settlement Functions by the Reed-Muench Method," *Professional Geographer,* 16, no. 4 (1964), 6-9; D. B. W. M. Van Dusseldorp, *Planning of Service Centres in Rural Areas of Developing Countries* (Wageningen, Netherlands: International Institute for Land Reclamation and Improvement, 1971).

28. I found this to be true in my earlier study of this type of mechanized service company in Brazil (*IBEC*).

29. Sen et al., *Planning Rural Growth Centres,* pp. 149, 158.

30. Ministry of Information and Broadcasting, Government of India, *India: A Reference Annual,* 1974, pp. 195-195B.

31. There is a burgeoning literature on questions of mechanization and the levels of "appropriate technology." Desmond L. W. Anker reviews recent studies in "Rural Development Programs and Strategies," *International Labour Review* 108 (1973):461-484. The International Labor Organization has recently compiled a number of these studies in *Mechanisation and Employment in Agriculture* (Geneva, 1973). The Ford Foundation held a major Seminar on Technology and Employment in New Delhi, March 21-24, 1973; a number of position papers were reprinted by the foundation.

Interest in questions of labor-surplus economies has heightened also since the seminal pieces in the early 1950s by Ragnar Nurkse, *Problems of Capital Formation in Underdeveloped Countries* (Oxford: Blackwell, 1953), and W. Arthur Lewis, "Economic Development with Unlimited Supplies of Labour," *Manchester School of Economic and Social Studies* 22 (1954):139-191. Three excellent articles are J. N. Sinha, "Agrarian Reforms and Employment in Densely Populated Agrarian Economies: A Dissenting View," *International Labour Review* 108 (1973):395-419; Eric S. Clayton, "A Note on Farm Mechanisation and Employment in Developing Countries," *International Labour Review* 110 (1974):57-62; and Roy E. Harrington, "Agricultural Engineering and Productivity," *Annual Proceedings,* American Association for the Advancement of Science, January 30, 1975. The Ford Foundation sponsored two major conferences on employment in the less developed world: the Seminar on the Employment Process, Bogotá, Colombia, February 21-23, 1973, and Rural Development and Employment, Ibadan, Nigeria, April 9-12, 1973. A number of papers have been published from the two sets of proceedings.

The Luddite history in agriculture is analyzed in E. J. Hobsbawm and George Rude, *Captain Swing* (London: Lawrence and Wishart, 1969). The recent Indian experience is noted in the *Indian Express* (Madras), July 25, 1969, and *The Hindu* (Madras), August 6, 1971.

32. See the various references in note 31; a particularly good summary is that of Eugene Staley, "What Can be Done to Promote Adoption and Use of Appropriate Technology?" in the Ford Foundation Seminar on Technology and Employment, New Delhi, March 21, 1975.

33. The quotation is from Clayton, "A Note on Farm Mechanisation," p. 61. See also his book, *Economic Planning in Peasant Agriculture: A Study of the Optimal Use of Agricultural Resources by Peasant Farmers in Kenya* (Ashford, Kent: Wye College, 1963) and his "Mechanisation and Employment in East African Agriculture," *International Labour Review* 105 (1972):309-334. The case studies are in I. Inukai, "Farm Mechanisation, Output and Labour Input: A Case Study in Thailand," *International Labour Review* 101 (1970):453-473, and Carl H. Gotsch, "Tractor Mechanisation and Rural Development in Pakistan," *International Labour Review* 107 (1973):133-166.

34. *Indian and Foreign Review,* September 15, 1971.

35. *The Hindu* (Madras), July 29, 1971.

36. The conference, a National Seminar on Agro-Services, was sponsored by the Ministry of Agriculture, Government of India, and the National Alliance of Young Entrepreneurs, New Delhi, July 3-4, 1971.

37. Official figures on college-graduate unemployment vary widely according to the source; the total figure used in the press includes agricultural engineering graduates. See, for example, *The Hindu* (Madras), August 11, 1974.

38. *The Hindu* (Madras), July 30, 1971.

39. *Economic and Political Weekly* (Bombay), "Review of Agriculture," September 1971, esp. pp. A 148-A 151.

40. The company involved is Shaw-Wallace, Ltd., Madras. A position paper with this title is available from the firm.

41. See "Introducing ASO," *Green Revolution Series No. 1,* Agricultural Services Organisation, Bombay, n.d.

42. H.P. Nanda, "Young Entrepreneurs and Agro-Service Centres," *Report of 2nd National Seminar on Agro-Services* (Ministry of Agriculture, Government of India, May 1973), p. 28.

43. C. V. Baxi, "Backward Area Development: Expanding Institutional Set-Up," *Economic and Political Weekly* (Bombay), June 12, 1974.

Chapter 5   The Nurturing of Change Agents

1. The seminars were conducted in Madras over the period August 27 to September 6, 1973, with participation from E. I. D. Parry, Ltd., Shaw-Wallace, Ltd., and Madras Fertiliser, Ltd. Funding was provided by the Ford Foundation, New Delhi.

2. *Motivating Economic Achievement* (New York: Free Press, 1969).

3. Eugene Staley and Richard Morse, *Modern Small Scale Industry for Developing Countries* (New York: McGraw-Hill Book Company, 1965).

4. Government of Maharashtra, "Maharashtra Action Research Project in Occupational Education and Training," report and papers of a workshop held at Poona, September 21-27, 1969 (State Institute of Education, 1970); Eugene Staley, *Work-Oriented General Education* (Bombay: Popular Prakashan, 1973); and Pratima Kale, "Evaluative Research Project in Occupational Education and Training, Maharashtra," Maharashtra Action Research Project in Occupational Education and Training, Ford Foundation (New Delhi), April 1973.

5. V. G. Patel, "Report on the Third Entrepreneurship Development Pro-

gramme," Gujarat State Financial Corporation and Gujarat Industrial Development Corporation (Ahmedabad, n.d.), and his "Entrepreneurship," Entrepreneurship Development Project of GIIC, GIDC, GSFC (Ahmedabad, n.d.).

6. Fundacion Venezolana para el Desarrollo de Actividades Socioeconomicas, "Aims, Content and Organization of the Motivation Training Courses," Caracas, n.d.

7. W. B. Brendon Reddy and Otto Kroeger, "Intergroup Model-Building: The Lego Man," 1972 *Annual Handbook for Group Facilitations* (Iowa City: University Associates, 1972), pp. 36-39.

8. For an excellent set of Tamil proverbs that apply to agriculture, see M. S. Randhawa, M. S. Sivaraman, I. J. Naidu, and Suresh Vaidya, *Farmers of India* (New Delhi: Indian Council of Agricultural Research, 1971), vol. 2, pp. 395-396.

9. The four Thematic Apperception Test pictures were adapted for a West African Peace Corps Program by Development Research Associates, Cambridge, Massachusetts, and modified by us to fit the Indian context. We were guided by Henry A. Murray's manual, "Thematic Apperception Test," Harvard Psychological Clinic, 1943.

10. McClelland's scoring systems have gone through a number of iterations; we began with the system used in David C. McClelland and Robert S. Steele, *Motivation Workshops* (Morristown, New Jersey: General Learning Press, 1972), pp. 33-51. We used a single dimension for both the power and the affiliative motives (the latter we called "social"); for the achievement motive we asked the participants to score a point each time they saw one of the following achievements: competing with others, competing with yourself, doing something special — a change, thinking about plans in the future, thinking about personal blocks, and thinking about world blocks.

11. Of the several versions of ring toss we used the one in McClelland and Steele, *Motivation Workshops,* pp. 85-89.

12. We drew on a number of goal-setting exercises we had used in the past. Of particular help were David A. Kolb, "Achievement Motivation Development Course: Future Planning Manual," Development Research Associates, Cambridge, Massachusetts, n.d.; and George A. Ford and Gordon L. Lippitt, "A Life Planning Workbook," NTL Learning Resources Corporation, Fairfax, Virginia, 1972.

13. Gilbert Etienne, *Studies in Indian Agriculture: The Art of the Possible* (Berkeley: University of California Press, 1968), pp. 19-20; V. S. Vyas and S. C. Bandyopadhyay, "National Food Policy in the Framework of a National Food Budget," *Economic and Political Weekly* (Bombay), *Annual,* March 1975.

14. The concern for basic shifts in climate has been analyzed in many conferences and publications. For an excellent review see T. Alexander, "Ominous Changes in the World's Weather," *Fortune,* February 1974. The literature of the Sahelian drought is extensive; see V. DuBois, "The Drought in West Africa," *American Universities Field Staff Reports,* Africa series, vol. 15, nos. 1, 2, 3 (1971); Claire Sterling, "The Making of the Sub-Saharan Wasteland," *Atlantic Monthly,* May 1974.

15. Marcus S. Franda, "India: 'An Unprecedented National Crisis,' " *Common Ground* 1 (1975):69-70. See also Franda's "India and the Energy Crunch," *AUFS Bulletin,* Asia, 18 (1974), no. 1; Laura Henze, "Agriculture in India: The Withering of a Revolution," *Environmental Action,* May 11, 1974; and John B. Parker, "India: Sum-

mary," Economic Research Service, United States Department of Agriculture, August 21, 1975.

16. A complication for those concerned with planning was caused by varying predictions of fertilizer consumption. As the *New York Times* put it in its issue of April 4, 1974, fertilizer imports for India for the year 1973-1974 were from 1.3 million to 1.5 million metric tons, "depending on the source." The *Economic Times* (Bombay) estimated on May 5, 1974, that fertilizer consumption in the crop year 1973-1974 would be 3.4 million metric tons; just a few months later, on September 3, 1974, it estimated the figure at 2.78 million.

17. *Economic Times* (Bombay), March 15, April 25, July 15, and September 6, 1973, and August 16, 1974. The quotation is from the April 25 issue. See also *The Hindu* (Madras), August 22, 1973.

18. See, for example, *Economic Times* (Bombay), October 24 and November 25, 1974.

19. Barbara Harriss, "Innovation Adoption in Indian Agriculture—The High Yielding Varieties Programme," *Modern Asian Studies* 6, pt. 1 (1972):97.

20. Dana G. Dalrymple, "The Green Revolution: Past and Prospects," draft manuscript, July 22, 1974, Foreign Development Division, Economic Research Service, United States Department of Agriculture, p. 14.

21. The allegation of acreage drops is discussed in Nicholas Wade, "Green Revolution (II): Problems of Adapting a Western Technology," *Science* 186 (1974):1186-1192. The HYV hectare and production statistics are from John Parker, "India's 1975/76 Food Grain Production," July 23, 1976, Economic Research Service, United States Department of Agriculture, and "The Agricultural Situation in the Far East and Oceania," Foreign Agricultural Economic Report no. 121, June 1976.

22. *Economic Times* (Bombay), July 4, 1974.

23. William J. Staub and Melvin G. Blase, "Induced Technological Change in Developing Agricultures: Implications for Income Distribution in Agricultural Development," *Journal of Developing Areas* 8 (1974):587.

24. Dana G. Dalrymple, "Measuring the Green Revolution: The Impact of Research on Wheat and Rice Production," Foreign Development Division, United States Department of Agriculture, Foreign Agricultural Economic Report no. 106, July 1975, p. 25.

25. L. J. Atkinson and David Kunkel, "HYV in the Philippines: Progress of the Seed-Fertilizer Revolution," unpublished manuscript, December 10, 1974, Economic Research Service, United States Department of Agriculture; and Teresa Auden and Randolph Barker, "Changes in Rice Farming in Selected Areas of Asia," *Bulletin*, International Rice Research Institute, December 1, 1973, table 8.

26. See especially Francine R. Frankel, *India's Green Revolution: Economic Gains and Political Costs* (Princeton, New Jersey: Princeton University Press, 1971); Guy Hunter and Anthony F. Bottrall, eds., *Serving the Small Farmer: Policy Choices in Indian Agriculture* (London: Overseas Development Institute, 1974); and Keith Griffin, *The Political Economy of Agrarian Change: An Essay on the Green Revolution* (Cambridge, Massachusetts: Harvard University Press, 1974).

27. *Economics of Land Reform and Farm Size in India* (Madras: Macmillan India,

1973), p. xix. See also Joan P. Mencher, "Conflicts and Contradictions in the "Green Revolution,' " *Economic and Political Weekly* (Bombay), *Annual,* February 1974, p. 313.

28. Khusro, *Economics of Land Reform,* pp. xiii-xvii. For two excellent studies of programs in individual states see Baljit Singh and Shridhar Misra, *A Study of Land Reform in Uttar Pradesh* (Honolulu: East-West Center Press, 1964) and K. S. Sonachalam, *Land Reforms in Tamil Nadu* (New Delhi: Oxford and I. B. H. Publishing Co., 1970).

29. See, for example, Wolf Ladejinsky, "Land Ceilings and Land Reform," *Economic and Political Weekly* (Bombay), *Annual,* February 1972; N. L. Singh, "Ceiling on Land Holdings," *Eastern Economist,* May 19, 1972; Utsa Patnaik, "Economics of Farm Size and Farm Scale," *Economic and Political Weekly* (Bombay), *Annual,* August 1972; T. K. Lakshman, "Land Ceilings in Karnataka," *Economic and Political Weekly* (Bombay), September 29, 1973; Ruddar Datt, "Land Reform Programme," *Economic Times* (Bombay), November 27 and 28, 1973; and D. K. Marothia, "Land Ceilings Won't Benefit Tarai," *Economic Times* (Bombay), May 22, 1975.

30. Khusro, *Economics of Land Reform,* p. xii.

31. Barbara Harriss, "Marketing Scarce Fertilisers: India," *Project on Agrarian Change in Rice-Growing Areas of Tamil Nadu and Sri Lanka,* Centre of South Asian Studies, University of Cambridge, December 9-16, 1974.

32. Griffin, *The Political Economy of Agrarian Change,* pp. 52, 209.

33. *Economic Times* (Bombay), April 25 and June 28, 1974.

34. Inasmuch as tenancy arrangements are often under the table, precise statistics are difficult to find. Some good sources for this analysis are Wolf Ladejinsky, "A Study on Tenurial Conditions in Package Districts," Planning Commission, Government of India, New Delhi, 1965, and his "Land Ceilings and Land Reform," *Economic and Political Weekly* (Bombay), *Annual,* February 1972; Frankel, *India's Green Revolution;* and Manilal B. Nanavati and J. J. Anjaria, *The Indian Rural Problem* (Bombay: Indian Society of Agricultural Economics, 1970).

35. Griffin, *The Political Economy of Agrarian Change,* passim; and Frankel, *India's Green Revolution,* pp. 34-35, 69, 167-169.

Chapter 6   Fresh Thoughts about Entrepreneurial Theory and Practice

1. "Entrepreneurship and Development," *American Economic Review Papers and Proceedings* 58 (1968):81.

2. "Changing Values for Progress," unpublished manuscript, SIET Institute, Hyderabad, India, October 1963, pp. 11, 19-20.

3. Wayne G. Broehl, Jr., *International Basic Economy Corporation* (Washington, D.C.: National Planning Association, 1968), pp. 87-94, 296-299.

4. E. F. Schumacher, *Small is Beautiful* (New York: Harper & Row, 1973).

5. George MacPherson and Dudley Jackson, "Village Technology for Rural Development," *International Labour Review* 111 (1975):103-104.

6. T. W. Shea, "Barriers to Economic Development in Traditional Societies: Malabar, A Case Study," *Journal of Economic History* 19 (1959):509.

7. Alex Alexander, "The Supply of Industrial Entrepreneurship," *Explorations in Entrepreneurial History,* New Series, 4 (1967):139-140.

8. There is a succinct discussion of multiple channels of communication in Paul F. Lazarsfeld and Herbert Menzel, "Mass Media and Personal Influence," in Wilbur Schramm, ed., *The Science of Human Communication* (New York: Basic Books, 1963), pp. 105-107. Schramm discusses the general issue of communications channels in "Channels and Audiences" in Ithiel de Sola Pool, Frederick W. Frey, Wilbur Schramm, Nathan Maccoby, and Edwin B. Parker, *Handbook of Communication* (Chicago: Rand McNally College Publishing Company, 1973), pp. 116-140, which includes an excellent bibliography.

9. *The Science of Human Communication,* pp. 122-123.

10. Everett M. Rogers and F. Floyd Shoemaker, *Communication of Innovations* (New York: Free Press, 1971), pp. 348-349, 372-374, 383.

11. George A. P. Miller, "The Magical Number Seven, Plus or Minus Two: Some Limits on our Capacity for Processing Information," *Psychological Review* 63 (1966): 81-97. See also Schramm's references in "Channels and Audiences," pp. 122-123.

12. Y. V. Lakshmana Rao, *Communication and Development: A Study of Two Indian Villages* (Minneapolis: University of Minnesota Press, 1966), pp. 93-94.

13. "Organizational or Frictional Equilibria, X-efficiency, and the Rate of Innovation," *Quarterly Journal of Economics* 83 (1969):619.

14. For a general discussion of the problems of firms as sellers of information, see Armen A. Alchian and Harold Demsetz, "Production, Information Costs, and Economic Organizations," *American Economic Review* 62 (1972):777-795.

15. Marcus F. Franda, "Marketing Condoms in India: The Nirodh Program," *American Universities Field Staff Report,* South Asia series, vol. 16, no. 8, 1972.

16. Marcus F. Franda, "Television in India," *American Universities Field Staff Report,* South Asia series, vol. 19, no. 4, 1975, pp. 11-12. For earlier views on *Krishi Darshan,* see B. P. Sinha and Prayag Mehta, "Farmers' Need for Achievement and Change-Proneness in Acquisition of Information from a Farm-Telecast," *Rural Sociology* 37 (1972):417-427. The overall policy of the Government of India concerning educational television is discussed in Lakshmi Prasid Vepa, *Satellite Educational Television for India: An Examination of Economic and Policy Aspects* (Cambridge, Massachusetts: MIT, Center for International Studies Monograph, 1969).

17. William Lesley Chapman, "Experiment in Argentina: The Bitter and the Sweet," *Columbia Journal of World Business* 1 (1966):55.

18. "Entrepreneurship and Development," pp. 82-83.

19. See Pareto in S. E. Finer, ed., *Sociological Writings* (New York: Praeger, 1966). See also Pareto's *The Mind and Society* (New York: Harcourt, Brace, 1935), p. 590.

20. "Entrepreneurship in Economic Theory," *American Economic Review Papers and Proceedings* 58 (1968):66.

21. Joseph A. Schumpeter, *The Theory of Economic Development: An Inquiry into Profits, Capital, Credit, Interest, and the Business Cycle* (Cambridge, Massachusetts: Harvard University Press, 1934), pp. 62, 64, 65. For a useful analogy from the biological sciences see Stephen Toulmin, "Innovation and the Problem of Utilization," in William H. Gruber and Donald G. Marquis, eds., *Factors in the Transfer of Technology* (Cambridge, Massachusetts: MIT Press, 1969), pp. 24-38.

22. *Competition and Entrepreneurship* (Chicago: University of Chicago Press, 1973), pp. 35-36.

23. See especially Leibenstein's article, "Organizational or Frictional Equilibria."

24. *Economic Backwardness and Economic Growth* (New York: John Wiley & Sons, 1957), chap. 8.

25. M. S. Randhawa, *Intensive Agricultural District Programme,* Ministry of Food and Agriculture, Government of India, August 1965, p. 9.

26. Expert Committee on Assessment and Evaluation, Intensive Agricultural District Programme, *Report* (1961-1963), Ministry of Food and Agriculture, Government of India, 1963.

27. Two excellent evaluations of the IADP Programme are D. K. Desai, "Intensive Agricultural District Programme: Analysis of Results," *Economic and Political Weekly* (Bombay), *Annual,* June 1969; and Dorris D. Brown, *Agricultural Development in India's Districts* (Cambridge, Massachusetts: Harvard University Press, 1971).

28. A. A. Johnson, "Indian Agriculture into the 1970's—Components of Modernization," Ford Foundation (New Delhi), June 1970, p. 106. Harry W. Richardson gives an excellent summary of this neoclassical theory in *Regional Growth Theory* (New York: John Wiley, 1973), chap. 2.

29. See Dana G. Dalrymple, "Measuring the Green Revolution: The Impact of Research on Wheat and Rice Production," Foreign Development Division, United States Department of Agriculture, Foreign Agricultural Economic Report no. 106, July 1975.

30. *Economic Theory and Underdeveloped Regions* (London: G. Duckworth, 1957).

31. The growth-pole literature is summarized in several articles in Niles M. Hansen, *Growth Centers and Regional Economic Development* (New York: Free Press, 1972). See also Richardson, *Regional Growth Theory,* chaps. 7 and 8.

32. Albert Shapero, "Entrepreneurship and Regional Development," Proceedings of the International Symposium on Entrepreneurship and Enterprise Development, Cincinnati, Ohio, June 16, 1975; and Jane Jacobs, *The Economy of Cities* (New York: Random House, 1969).

33. The Institute for New Enterprise Development (INED) in Belmont, Massachusetts, has been active in studying this phenomenon. See, for example, several writings of Jeffrey A. Timmons: "Entrepreneurial Behavior," Proceedings, First International Conference on Entrepreneurship, Center for Entrepreneurial Studies, Toronto, November 1973; *The Entrepreneurial Team: Formation and Development* (Boston: Northeastern University, 1973); and "The Entrepreneurial Team: An American Dream or Nightmare?" unpublished manuscript, Northeastern University, January 1975.

34. *Business Cycles* (New York: McGraw-Hill Book Company, 1939), vol. 1, p. 104.

35. *The Stages of Economic Growth* (Cambridge: Cambridge University Press, 1960), pp. 6, 26, 50, 51.

Index

F

M